Doing Economics

Doing Economics

What You Should Have Learned
in Grad School—But Didn't

Marc F. Bellemare

The MIT Press
Cambridge, Massachusetts
London, England

The MIT Press would like to thank the anonymous peer reviewers who provided comments on drafts of this book. The generous work of academic experts is essential for establishing the authority and quality of our publications. We acknowledge with gratitude the contributions of these otherwise uncredited readers.

This book was set in Sabon LT Std by New Best-set Typesetters Ltd. Printed and bound in the United States of America.

Library of Congress Cataloging-in-Publication Data

Names: Bellemare, Marc F., author.
Title: Doing economics : what you should have learned in grad school—but didn't /
    Marc F. Bellemare.
Description: Cambridge, Massachusetts : The MIT Press, 2022. | Includes bibliographical
    references and index.
Identifiers: LCCN 2021038731 | ISBN 9780262543552 (paperback)
Subjects: LCSH: Economics—Study and teaching (Higher) | Economists. | Proposal writing
    for grants. | Mentoring. | Life skills.
Classification: LCC HB74.5 .B49 2022 | DDC 330.071—dc23
LC record available at https://lccn.loc.gov/2021038731

10   9   8   7   6   5

For Sophia, who I hope will more easily figure out the rules of whatever game she chooses to play.

And for Janet, whose love of her fellow creatures inspires me daily to become a better version of myself.

Contents

Preface   ix
Acknowledgments   xi

1   Introduction   1

2   Writing Papers   5

3   Giving Talks   39

4   Navigating Peer Review   61

5   Finding Funding   101

6   Doing Service   121

7   Advising Students   151

8   Conclusion   167

References   171
Index   177

Preface

"It's strange, isn't it?" the woman said in a pensive voice. "Everything is blowing up around us, but there are still those who care about a broken lock, and others who are dutiful enough to try to fix it . . . But maybe that's the way it should be. Maybe working on the little things as dutifully and honestly as we can is how we stay sane when the world is falling apart."
—Haruki Murakami, *Men without Women*

This book came into being because of the pandemic.

In 2018, well before the words "COVID-19" and "coronavirus," or even the word "pandemic" became part of our everyday language, I went to Rome for an event at the Food and Agriculture Organization of the United Nations. One evening over drinks, my colleague Sara Savastano suggested I should assemble some of the material I had written on my blog since 2010 into a manual for her staff. As the new director of the International Fund for Agricultural Development's (IFAD) Research and Impact Assessment (RIA) division, Sara oversaw the work of a team of economists whose job it was to evaluate the impact of IFAD's projects. When she started in that position, she had found the quality of the papers produced by the RIA staff to fall short of what it could have been, and so she had made it one of her goals to improve the papers written by the economists in her shop. Following that conversation, IFAD hired me as a consultant to write a document on how to write impact evaluation papers. I delivered that how-to manual to them in early 2020.

Although I had always planned to turn that manual into a working paper, little did I know at the time that it would turn into what would ultimately get me through *annus horribilis* 2020. Indeed, in the early days of the COVID-19 lockdowns, I realized that if I was going to maintain my sanity, I would need to work on something that was different from my usual responsibilities—and different from my new "job" as half-time homeschooling teacher.

It was then that I realized that the how-to I had written for IFAD could work nicely as a book chapter, and that I had similar thoughts to share on other aspects of doing economics. In April 2020, I pitched the idea of this book to a number of presses. By the end of June, most of them had responded favorably and invited me to submit a formal proposal. At the end of August, I signed a contract with MIT Press.

As I write these lines in late fall 2020, we are headed into what looks like a difficult winter of lockdowns due to rising COVID-19 infection rates. But if I have learned one thing over the last year, it is that the obstacle is the way, as Ryan Holiday put it (Holiday 2014), and that "working on the little things as dutifully and honestly as we can is how we stay sane when the world is falling apart."

Acknowledgments

It takes a village to raise a child, according to an alleged African proverb. Similarly, it would have been impossible for me to write this book without the support of several people, to whom I would like to express my gratitude.

Un grande ringraziamento to Sara Savastano, who provided the impetus for this project.

I am grateful to Chris Barrett, whose influence on my life cannot be overstated. Not only was Chris directly responsible for my meeting my wife, but as my advisor at Cornell, he taught me a lot of the unwritten rules of the economics profession. When I started working on the proposal for this book, his comments on my draft proposal were invaluable.

I am equally grateful to Tim Beatty, thanks to whom I started co-teaching our department's second-year paper seminar as soon as I joined the University of Minnesota in 2013. Though he dislikes the label because it makes him feel old, Tim has been a wonderful mentor, with whom I have had many fruitful conversations about the profession over the years, and there is more than a little of those conversations in this book.

I did not know how to navigate the process of publishing a book, but thanks to an early conversation with Kim Yi Dionne, I went in knowing how to go about it and what to look out for. I also learned the true meaning of *haba na haba hujaza kibaba*—little by little fills the measure, Kim's favorite Swahili proverb—by working on this book.

I have benefited from comments by Jeff Bloem, John Cranfield, Liz Davis, Paul Glewwe, Eva-Marie Meemken, Jeff Reimer, and Joe Ritter, who read early versions of chapter 2. Similarly, Jenn Cissé, Brady Horn, Robbin Shoemaker, and Dawn Thilmany McFadden provided excellent comments on chapter 5, while Mike Shor pointed me to the data on indirect cost recovery rates I discuss in that chapter. My coauthor Seth Gitter sat down for a conversation about advising undergraduates, which informed a lot of the content of chapter 7. Teevrat Garg read through drafts of chapters 2, 3, and 4, and provided excellent insights about writing papers for and publishing in general science journals. Finally, I am grateful to Amy Damon, Christine Moser, and Aine Seitz McCarthy, all of whom offered their much-needed perspectives on finding funding (chapter 5) and advising students (chapter 7). This latter chapter also benefited from Lindsey Novak's insights.

I wish to thank Emily Taber, my editor at MIT Press, for making the process of writing my first book easy, and the two anonymous reviewers she chose to review the proposal for this book as well as the first full draft for their constructive comments and sharp insights about how to make the book appealing to a broader audience. I am also very grateful to Chad Zimmerman at a competing press, who came up with the title for this book, and who graciously let me use it.

Finally, I am grateful to my wife Janet and my daughter Sophia, who put up with my having to miss many daycare drop-offs and weekend activities because I was working on this book. I love you both (and the dogs) more than words can express.

Sub umbra alarum tuarum, יהוה

1

Introduction

I believe that what we become depends on what our fathers teach us at odd moments, when they aren't trying to teach us. We are formed by little scraps of wisdom.
—Umberto Eco, *Foucault's Pendulum*

When I started graduate school in 2001, someone—I wish I could remember who, after 20 years—suggested I buy a copy of William Thomson's *A Guide for the Young Economist*. Considering when and where I earned my PhD, this was an excellent recommendation: at the turn of the century, economics had not quite yet taken an empirical turn and, consistent with Leijonhufvud's (1973) tongue-in-cheek ethnography of the profession three decades prior, theory still had pride of place in economics. This was especially true at Cornell, where the Department of Economics' leading faculty members at the time were theorists, from whom even Applied Economics graduate students like me had to take their first-year courses. For me and many of my classmates, Thomson's book was a treasure trove of advice on how to write, present, and review theoretical papers in economics.

Twenty years later, economics has become resolutely more empirical as a result of increasing data availability and the decreasing costs of computational power (Backhouse and Cherrier 2017a, 2017b). Nowadays, an overwhelming majority of young economists are drawn to applied fields when the time comes to specialize. Indeed, seven of the last ten recipients of the John Bates Clark Medal, awarded to the US-based economist under the age of 40 who has made the most significant contribution to economic thought or knowledge, have been applied economists. Similarly, about half of the ten most recent Nobel Prizes in Economic Sciences have been awarded to economists whose work is mainly empirical. Economics-adjacent disciplines (e.g., business, public policy) and other social-science disciplines (e.g., political science, sociology) have followed suit, and have likewise become much more empirical. Yet there is no guide available to applied economists that does what Thomson's book did for budding economic theorists.

In a 1999 interview on NPR, science fiction author William Gibson said that "the future is already here, it's just not evenly distributed." Likewise with a lot of the information contained in this book: it is already here, it is just not evenly distributed. This is especially so given that many graduate programs in economics, applied economics, business, or public policy—programs that purport to train people in the art of doing research, writing about it, presenting it, and so on—do not systematically train students in what it means to work as a research economist. Even when one manages to glean some of that knowledge from one's advisors and other mentors, it usually comes in bits and pieces, when those advisors and other mentors are trying to teach one something else altogether.

I would go further: I believe that with respect to technical skills, most PhD programs train their students in ways that are roughly comparable. Where the quality of training differs between "good" and "bad" PhD programs is in whether students are taught the kind of interstitial knowledge presented in this book. In other words, there is a substantial hidden curriculum when it comes to doing economics.

My objective in writing this book is to help equip anyone who has the time to read it with some of the tools necessary to apprehend life as a research economist.

Before I address what this book will be discussing, I should address what it will not be discussing, and why.

There are library stacks full of books dedicated to teaching, and I have never felt particularly effective in the classroom, so I will not be discussing teaching. I will also not be covering the job market for PhD economists, as there are a myriad of resources dedicated to that topic (see for instance Cawley 2018). Moreover, in the case of both teaching and the job market, things are changing so rapidly (e.g., the widespread adoption of videotelephony that was forced on almost all of us in early 2020) that discussing those topics would render this book dated before it reaches its readers' hands.

Graduate programs aim to train researchers, and the primary means by which a researcher communicates her findings is by writing them up in the form of papers. I thus start in chapter 2 with how to write papers. This chapter is the result of seeing students struggle with the same things over and over during the course of teaching our department's second-year paper seminar for six years. In fact, it is my hope that this chapter will provide a convenient syllabus outline for anyone teaching a one- or two-semester qualifying research paper seminar.

Having written a paper, a researcher will often seek to improve it by incorporating other researchers' comments on her work. The easiest way to solicit other researchers' comments on one's work is by presenting it to them in the context of seminars, conferences, and workshops. Chapter 3 thus discusses how to give talks.

Once she has incorporated those comments by other researchers that ultimately allowed her to improve her work, a researcher will seek to submit that work to a peer-reviewed journal. Most first-time submitters to peer-reviewed journals, however, have little to no idea what to expect from the process. Chapter 4 thus offer a discussion of how to navigate the peer-review process.

There was a time when a social scientist could spend her whole career without having to get grants to fund her work. But with ever-declining numbers of economists doing theory, and with many of the publicly available data sets having been picked clean a long time ago, a social scientist who wishes to sustain her research agenda will more often than not have to find funding to assemble, collect, clean, and analyze data, and in some departments, one only gets to work with graduate students by funding them through grants. Chapter 5 thus discusses the various aspects of funding one's research program through grants.

In most professions, opportunities arise for professional service, but perhaps nowhere more so than when working as a researcher. Universities are governed by faculty; professional associations, though they sometimes hire professional administrative staff, are nevertheless run by people from the profession they represent; institutions rely on peers to evaluate their own for tenure or promotion; and most peer-reviewed journals worth publishing in rely on reviewers and editors who are researchers themselves. Moreover, in the last ten years or so, many of the conversations between colleagues that used to take place over coffee or lunch have gone public. They are now taking place on social media, and have *de facto* become public goods—and thus a form of professional service. But if she were to try to figure out how much and what kind of service to do, or how to get to do a specific kind of service, the average early-career researcher in economics would be at a loss. Chapter 6 thus offers an in-depth discussion of doing professional service.

Sooner or later, social scientists in academia have to advise students. Yet beyond one's own relationships with one's advisors, there is little guidance about how to advise graduate students. There is even less guidance about how to advise undergraduates. Chapter 7 thus offers some thoughts about advising graduate students (both master's and PhD students) and undergraduate students, and it differentiates those thoughts by type of institution.

I conclude in chapter 8 by offering personal thoughts about the economics profession as a whole, and about the many ways one can be successful.

2

Writing Papers

A good film makes you forget that you are watching a film. Similarly, a good research paper makes you forget that you are reading a research paper. The authors tell you a story. They take you on a tour of what they have done: what they have asked themselves, how they have answered it, how they have made sure their answer was robust, and what, if anything, we can learn from their results for policy or for business.

But just as a good film immerses you in the world it creates and makes you forget the various tropes and techniques used in the making of it, a good research paper is one that makes you forget to notice its overall structure as well as the various rhetorical devices employed by the authors.

How do you write a good research paper? In my experience, most research economists have spent too little time thinking about that question, and even the most successful economists would have a hard time articulating a clear answer to the same question.

This state of affairs is due both to *what* economists read, and to *how* they read it.

Regarding what economists read, the syllabus for most graduate field courses usually consists of a "best of" for each topic covered—those papers that have shaped how people working in the field think and what they know about that topic. For instance, the syllabus for a graduate development economics course will almost surely include Foster and Rosenzweig (1995) and Suri (2011) in its reading list under the topic of technology adoption. In that literature, those two articles are widely understood to be among the most important.

This applies mainly to more junior readers—the more senior one gets, the more one has been exposed to bad papers by virtue of having reviewed more papers—but reading only the best papers is a double-edged sword. To be sure, those are the papers we learn the most from when it comes to how our peers think about a given topic. At the same time, those papers tend to be the most polished ones—those nearest to perfection—on a given topic. But it is difficult for one to learn what makes a paper good if all one ever reads is perfect papers. To carry the film analogy further, if all you ever watch are those films on the British Film Institute's list of the 50 greatest films of all time, and you never watch any bad (or even average) movies, it will be difficult for you to discover what actually makes those top-50 films any good.

Regarding how economists read, the syllabi of most graduate field courses often lists so many articles as to cause graduate students to quickly develop a skill Mortimer Adler referred to in his classic *How to Read a Book* as inspectional reading (Adler and Van Doren 2014). When reading academic papers, inspectional reading involves reading the introduction, looking at the methods and results, and (maybe) reading the conclusion before moving on to the next item on one's reading list. Reading papers that way is a good way to develop one's knowledge of the literature on a given topic, but it is hardly a recipe for learning how to write good papers.[1]

The goal of this chapter is thus to help readers write applied papers for eventual submission and publication in peer-reviewed journals. To do so, the various components of a research paper are discussed in as much detail as possible, roughly in the order in which they are tackled in the context of a research project.

---

1. Knowing is half the battle, so knowing that many readers will read your paper inspectionally can make you a more effective writer because it forces you to put more thought into writing your introduction, your methods and results sections, and your conclusion. If you know that many of your readers are unlikely to bother with reading, say, your background section, you should state the most important facts of that section in your introduction. The greatest sin an academic writer can commit is the sin of omission, which consists in leaving important information out of a paper. The second greatest sin an academic writer can commit is one of commission, and it consists in forcing the reader to rifle through the paper hunting for a specific bit of information. The opportunity cost of a reader's time is high, so the average reader is more likely to give up on reading a paper than to hunt for information. This is especially true when a relatively junior writer (e.g., a PhD student or an assistant professor) is writing to impress more senior readers (e.g., a faculty advisor, a journal editor, or journal reviewers).

2.1 Structure

Before producing any kind of work, it helps to know what the typical structure of such work looks like, and to write down a rough sketch of that structure. In its most abstract sense, the structure of the typical economics paper—applied or otherwise—is as follows:

1. Title
2. Abstract
3. Introduction
4. ...
5. Summary and Concluding Remarks
6. References

Depending on the type of paper one writes, the fourth item will change. Since this chapter is geared toward writing applied papers, the structure above will typically be modified as follows:

1. Title
2. Abstract
3. Introduction
4. Theoretical Framework
5. Data and Descriptive Statistics
6. Empirical Framework
7. Results and Discussion
8. Summary and Concluding Remarks
9. References
10. Appendix

This structure is not set in stone. A frequent departure from the sequence above is when items 5 and 6 are switched around so that the Empirical Framework section comes before the Data and Descriptive Statistics section—something that is often a matter of taste, if not of expositional clarity. Similarly, a paper investigating a question that has often been asked (e.g., the effect of adopting a minimum-wage policy on unemployment) might not require a Theoretical Framework section at all because the theory behind that question is well known and is the stuff of textbooks. Or there might be a Background section after the Introduction, where important contextual details are given that fit neither in the Introduction nor in the Descriptive Statistics section. Some papers might require a major overhaul of that structure. Even in such cases, it helps to be familiar with the usual structure. A good analogy in this case is this: before jazz legend John Coltrane ever thought of recording avant-garde albums like *A Love Supreme* (1965), he first learned how to operate within the (much more regimented) structure of bebop on albums like *Blue Train* (1957), and before that as a sideman on albums by Miles Davis.

What does this mean for an economist? It means that before you break the rules, you have to learn them. So before thinking of writing a paper whose structure is barely recognizable to the average reader, an economist should make sure to have written enough papers that follow the usual structure laid out above. In other words, freedom from structure tends to be a privilege granted to more experienced researchers, who have accumulated enough good will from their readers that they are allowed to bend the rules a little bit.

The remainder of this chapter will not follow the structure just given. Though it would certainly be easier for me to write a chapter whose subsequent headings follow that exact structure in order, it turns out that the structure in which we present our work in a research paper tends to be very different from the structure in which we actually do the work.

2.2   Theoretical Framework

Since the goal of empirical economics is generally to answer questions of the form "Does x cause y?" or "If x increases by one unit, how many units does y change by?," most applied work in economics begins with a theoretical hypothesis about the relationship between x and y.

The best research articles tend to focus on a single question (e.g., "What is the impact of having a land title on agricultural productivity?") or on the mechanisms behind a given question (e.g., "If land titles improve agricultural productivity, do they do so because land titles allow landowners to use their land as collateral?") Thus, a first decision has to be made about what empirical relationship of interest a given article will focus on. In other words, the best empirical articles tend to be rather narrowly focused on a single question, and so you will almost inevitably have to leave some material on the cutting room floor.[2]

---

2. This is not to say that there are no good papers looking at several research questions at once. But at this point in time, what tends to be rewarded by the economics profession is answering a single, relatively narrow research question well.

The question, then, is how to take your hypothesis and convert it into a proper theoretical framework for an empirical economics article. Here, there are two possible scenarios: (i) you are investigating a question which has already been studied by theorists, or (ii) you are investigating a question which has not already been studied by theorists.

In the first scenario, there are two options. The first option is to include a theoretical framework in the article by incorporating or adapting somebody else's theoretical framework lock, stock, and barrel. Though it often feels like a research paper has to innovate on all fronts, that is not the case. For applied papers in particular, what matters is that the research question, the empirical strategy, or both be novel. In most cases, it is fine to use someone else's theoretical framework—provided that you clearly state that you are doing so and cite the source of your theoretical framework.

A closely related option is to adapt somebody else's theoretical framework to suit your needs—say, by incorporating an additional variable, or by relaxing or making additional assumptions to suit the needs of your application. In the second scenario, when you are investigating a question for which the theory of change has not already been studied by theorists, you have to clearly state the theoretical reasons behind your hypothesis. In some cases, this may require a formal theoretical model. In other cases, it is enough to merely present a verbal conceptual framework.[3] In all cases, your theoretical framework—be it mathematical or verbal—should start from the primitives and make the necessary assumptions to generate the result "x causes y through mechanism m"; no more and no less.

Generally when writing papers that combine theory and empirics, you should make sure that your empirics actually test the testable predictions of your theory. A prediction that is not tested empirically should not be included in your theoretical framework, and your hypothesis tests should be grounded in your theoretical framework. In other words, avoid any disconnect between your theory and your empirics.

One could write an entire book on how to write economic theory (and some have; see Thomson 2011), so nothing more will be said on this topic save for the following: writing theoretical models in economics is an art form, and if you have not learned how to do it in graduate school,

---

3. One possibility is to make a theoretical argument without math, in words, and to leave the math to an appendix. See, for instance, Sánchez de la Sierra (2020).

it is perhaps best to work with someone who has as a coauthor. When it comes to publishing an applied economics article, better an informal, chatty conceptual framework than a bad formal theoretical model.

That said, even if your working paper includes an elegant theoretical model, it will sometimes happen that you will be asked by reviewers or by an editor to get rid of your theoretical model before your paper can be published, or to put said theoretical model in an appendix. If that happens, know that this is not uncommon. In that sense, having a theoretical framework in your paper often only serves as a signal that you know what you are doing. This is especially true for job-market papers, which are used to show the breadth of their author's skills in addition to making a contribution to research.

2.3   Data and Descriptive Statistics

After developing your theory of change, you have presumably gone in search of data to test the predictions of that theory. As with writing formal theoretical models, entire books have been written about the dos and don'ts of data collection (see Deaton 1997 or Glewwe and Grosh 2000 for survey data, and Gerber and Green 2012 or Glennerster and Takavarasha 2013 for randomized controlled trials), so this section will not discuss where the data come from, and assume that you already have them. Rather, this section will focus on how to present your data in the context of an economics article.

The best Data and Descriptive Statistics sections answer all of the reader's questions about the data. Specifically, a good Data and Descriptive Statistics section first discusses where the data come from, when they were collected, by whom, how the observations that compose the sample were chosen for inclusion (i.e., the survey methodology, or how regions, communities, firms, households, individuals, etc. were all chosen), what population the sample is representative of, what the target sample size was and how that sample size was determined (e.g., via power calculations), what the actual sample size is, what the nonresponse rate was, what the attrition rate is if the data are longitudinal, and how missing data were dealt with (e.g., whether observations were simply dropped, or whether some values were imputed and, if so, how the imputation was done). Broadly speaking, the information presented here allows the reader to judge the external validity of the results contained in a paper (and sometimes their internal validity, as is the case when the data suffer from attrition), or how those results might be used for out-of-sample predictions.

After presenting those basics, a good Data and Descriptive Statistics section introduces all the variables used in the paper (and no variable not used in the paper) by precisely and concisely explaining what they measure, and how they do so. For instance, people often derive their income from many difference sources. So if an "income" variable is included in the analysis, the reader needs to be told what the various income sources are. This may seem tedious—and if it seems tedious to you as writer, imagine what it is like to the reader—but it can nevertheless contain crucial information.

The good news is that it is relatively easy to present that information when one has access to the survey questionnaires that were used to collect the data, which is almost always the case. Moreover, one way of presenting that information optimally is by creating a table of variable descriptions, where each line is a specific variable retained for analysis, where the first column gives the name of that variable (and the unit of measurement in parentheses), and where the second column gives precise measurements. Figure 2.1 shows one such table. This allows presentation of a lot of required but tedious information in a compact manner, which minimizes reader discontent: those who want to know all there is to know about the data can read the table, and those who do not can just skip it to focus instead on variable names.

At this point, it is time to present and discuss descriptive statistics. Here, whereas it used to be sufficient to simply present a table of means and standard deviations, it has become practically necessary in cases where the variable of interest (i.e., the treatment variable) is composed of a small number of categories to show the results of balance tests, namely tables where each line is a variable retained for analysis, where means and standard errors are shown conditional on treatment status, and wherein one assesses whether the mean of each variable systematically differs across treatment statuses by reporting p-values for a test of difference in means. Though the textbook example involves only treatment and control, it is increasingly common for studies to include more than two treatment arms, and so any meaningful balance test must be reported for each pairwise comparison of means. With two treatment arms, this means (i) treatment 1 versus control, (ii) treatment 2 versus control, and (iii) treatment 1 versus treatment 2.

With experimental data, the idea behind such balance tests is to show the reader that randomization was done properly. With observational data, where we would not expect the data to be balanced, the idea behind such balance tests is to assess how unbalanced the data are—an idea

Data Description for Selected Variables

Variable	Description
Dependency Ratio	Percentage of individuals under 15 and over 64 within the household.
Assets (100,000 Ariary)	Sum of the values of the household's assets (i.e., animals, house, television, radio, car, and bank account balance) and agricultural equipment (i.e., hoe, harrow, cart, plow, tractor, and small tractor).
Income (100,000 Ariary)	Sum of the proceeds from animal sales, agricultural and non-agricultural wages, and proceeds from leases of cattle and equipment.
Liquidity Constraint Dummy	Dummy for whether the household is liquidity constrained.
Plot Size	Area covered by the plot in ares (1 are = 0.01 hectare = 100 square meters.)
Plot Value (100,000 Ariary)	Price expected by the landowner if she were to sell her plot.
Formal Title Dummy	Dummy for the presence of a formal title.
Relationship Length	Number of years the landlord and tenant have been contracting with one another.
Kin Dummy	Dummy for a contract signed between kin.
Tenant Introduced by Kin	Dummy for a contract signed with a tenant whom the landlord met through a member of her extended family.
Introduced by Other than Kin	Dummy for a contract signed with a tenant whom the landlord met through someone who is not a member of her extended family.
Tenant is Friend	Dummy for a contract signed with a tenant who is a friend of the landlord.
Tenant Chosen for His Wealth	Dummy for whether this particular tenant was chosen because of his wealth.
Tenant Chosen for His Honesty	Dummy for whether this particular tenant was chosen because of his honesty.
Tenant Chosen for His Ability to Bear Risk	Dummy for whether this particular tenant was chosen because of his ability to bear risk.
Tenant Chosen to Return a Favor	Dummy for whether this particular tenant was chosen because the landlord wanted to return a favor.
Time Spent Looking for a Tenant	Number of days spent looking for a potential tenant.
Other Potential Tenants Considered	Number of other potential tenants considered when looking for a tenant.

Figure 2.1
Example table of variable descriptions from Bellemare (2012).

which comes from the matching literature (Morgan and Winship 2015). With perfect random assignment across treatment and control groups, there should be fewer than 1 in 10 pairwise comparisons differing at less than the 10 percent level of statistical significance, fewer than 1 in 20 pairwise comparisons differing at less than the 5 percent level of statistical significance, and fewer than 1 in 100 pairwise comparisons different at less than the 1 percent level of statistical significance. In cases where pairwise comparisons return too many systematic differences, one should ideally control for the relevant covariates in a regression or matching context when estimating treatment effects.[4]

Beyond the usual table of means and standard deviations and one or more tables showing the results of balance tests, a good Data and Descriptive Statistics section can also be used to explore the data nonparametrically by showing kernel density estimates of the relevant variables (i.e., outcome and treatment variables at a minimum, but also controls suspected to be the source of treatment heterogeneity) when they are continuous, histograms of the relevant variables when they are categorical, or cross-tabulations (i.e., two-by-two tables) in cases where both the treatment and the outcome are binary.

When writing a Data and Descriptive Statistics section, there are a few mistakes you should avoid making. The first is for the writeup to present a boring enumeration of means. If a gender variable is merely used as a control in the analysis, there is little use to stating in the text that "37.4 percent of respondents are female" when the reader can look that up for herself; the only variables that typically deserve discussion here are the outcome and treatment variables, any variable that is used for identification (e.g., an instrumental or forcing variable), or anything that really stands out. Generally, a good rule of thumb is to keep the discussion of the descriptive statistics to a few sentences.

The second such mistake is the use of the past tense in discussing the data and descriptive statistics. The example above stated how "37.4 percent of respondents are female," and not how "37.4 percent of

---

4. Comparing means across treatment and control groups is the strict minimum when it comes to testing for balance. A more restrictive approach consists in running a joint test (i.e., F-test) of whether all means are simultaneously the same across groups. Another, more restrictive approach consists in conducting tests of equality of distributions for pairwise comparison using a Kolmogorov-Smirnov test or using Bera et al.'s (2013) smooth test for equality of distributions.

respondents were female." Scientific communication in English is more effective when using the present tense to discuss your data or results, and just as you should avoid the passive voice, you should also avoid the past tense in research papers, except when summarizing and concluding. Indeed, the past tense should be largely kept for when you discuss what other researchers have done before you, and the future tense for what you are planning on doing or what others should be doing in the future. The present tense is ideal because it refers to that which occupies the reader right now, which is your paper.[5]

Finally, another mistake is to present numbers that either have too many decimal places because they are too small (usually, three decimal places is more than enough, and at any rate it is always possible to rescale a variable to make its magnitude fit with that of the other variables) or to present numbers that are difficult to interpret in tables, such as $1.37e + 8$, or anything other than units readers are used to dealing with (for instance, it is always possible to express a dollar amount in thousands or hundreds of thousands if need be). In other words, even if the empirical work regresses the logarithm of income on the treatment variable, the table of descriptive statistics should report the mean of the income level, not the mean of the logarithm of income. Ultimately, although a lot of what goes into a Data and Descriptive Statistics section might seem like useless posturing, as stated before, a good Data and Descriptive Statistics section should allow the reader to form reasonable expectations about the sign and the magnitude of the estimates of interest, and to get an idea of how those estimates are likely to vary across a given conditioning domain.

2.4   Empirical Framework

After discussing the data and presenting descriptive statistics, you normally turn to discussing your empirical framework, that is, the research design you use to empirically answer your research question.

An empirical framework consists of two related components: (i) an estimation strategy (i.e., what is estimated, how it is estimated, and how statistical inference is conducted), and (ii) an identification strategy (i.e.,

---

5. In his classic *On Writing Well*, Zinsser (2006) writes: "[T]he whole purpose of tenses is to enable a writer to deal with time in its various gradations, from the past to the hypothetical future." My editor at MIT Press also tells me that analysis of literature and film also uses the present tense when describing a book or a film.

what feature of the data allows making a causal statement or, if that is not possible, how we know we are getting close to making such a statement).

2.4.1 Estimation Strategy

An estimation strategy typically consists of the equations to be estimated in an effort to answer a research question. Though it may be possible for a savvy reader to recover the estimated equations in a paper by looking at the tables therein, that is not always possible. At any rate, the amount of work a reader should have to do should be kept to a minimum, so presenting the equations to be estimated is very much the norm.

Ideally, those equations will be as parsimonious as possible. Although a regression might include 10 to 15 control variables, it is best to put all of those into a vector x of control variables. What deserves its own variable in an equation to be shown in an estimation framework? For starters, the dependent variable (labeled y) should be included along with the treatment variable (labeled either D or T), the (vector of) controls (labeled x), an intercept term (labeled α), and the error term (labeled ϵ).

Here are, in no particular order, a few other norms that are best followed:

- All variables should have the proper subscripts, usually labeled i, j, k, l, and so forth, from the smallest (e.g., individual) to the largest level (e.g., region).
- Latin letters should denote variables. Greek letters should denote coefficients.
- If the estimation strategy subsection features several different specifications of the same equation, coefficients should also have subscripts. In other words, one should not reuse estimand notation. If β is used to denote the coefficient of interest in a regression of y on D, it should not be reused to denote the coefficient of interest in a regression of y on D and x as well—the two estimands being different, the notation used to denote them should also be different. This is best done by adding numerical subscripts to each coefficient, so that in the former specification, the coefficient on D would be denoted β_0 and in the latter, β_1. Or it can be done by adding letter subscripts to each coefficient, so that for example β_r and β_s can respectively refer to reduced-form and structural estimates of the same coefficient.
- The estimation strategy subsection should also specify what estimation method is used to estimate each estimable equation. We are generally

interested in $E(y|x)$, but $E(y|x)$ could be estimated in a number of different ways parametrically, semiparametrically, or nonparametrically. With a binary outcome variable, the reader needs to know whether a linear probability model, a probit, or a logit is estimated. In cases where it is ambiguous, the estimator (e.g., least squares, maximum likelihood, or generalized method of moments) also needs to be specified.

• After presenting the estimable equations, it is a good idea to discuss the relevant hypothesis tests. In a regression of the form

$$y = \alpha + \gamma D + \beta x + \epsilon, \tag{2.1}$$

for instance, the relevant hypothesis test would be of the form $H_0 : \gamma = 0$ versus $H_A : \gamma \neq 0$. Here, note that a hypothesis test always tests for an equality sign. So while a paper might test the (theoretical) hypothesis that changing D from 0 to 1 causes an increase in y (and further assesses by how much y increases in response to the change in D), statistically speaking, the same paper tests the (null) hypothesis that the association between D and y is not statistically significantly different from zero.

• The estimation strategy subsection also needs to discuss inference, meaning whether and how the standard errors are robust (and if so, robust to what; it is not enough to say that the standard errors are robust if the Huber-Sandwich-White correction is used, but it is warranted to say that they are robust to heteroskedasticity), whether and how they are clustered (and if so, at what level and why; see Abadie et al. 2017 for a primer), and whether sampling weights were used to bring the sample closer to the population of interest (and if so, how they were constructed; see Solon et al. 2015 for a primer).

2.4.2   Identification Strategy

After showing and discussing what equations are estimated, there needs to be a discussion of how the coefficient pertaining to the causal relationship of interest is identified.

The term "identification" has gone through several meanings over time (Lewbel 2019). For better or for worse, the term more often than not refers to *causal* identification nowadays in applied papers. What is causal identification? Briefly, it refers to situations where a coefficient is more than just a (partial) correlation between the dependent variable y and some variable of interest D, and where the estimated coefficient instead reflects a relationship from cause D to effect y.

Although an unbiased coefficient estimate implies an identified—that is, causally identified—coefficient estimate, the converse is not true. There are situations where one knows a coefficient to be biased, but where a statistically significant coefficient estimate can still be used to denote a causal relationship.

If you are fortunate enough (i) to have experimental variation in your treatment variable, and (ii) balance tests suggest the experimental assignment of observations to treatment and control groups was truly random, your identification strategy section can be kept short, as your results are causally identified by virtue of experimental assignment. In other words, you can estimate what Pearl (2009) denotes $E(y|do(x))$; that is, the (causal) effect of treatment x on outcome y.

If you have (i) experimental variation in your treatment variable but (ii) balance tests suggest the experimental assignment of observations to treatment and control groups was not truly random, your identification strategy section can also be short, as you only need to explain how you will add in control x on the right-hand side of your equation of interest to help rectify the situation, but only somewhat, as unobservables are also likely to be unbalanced when the observables are unbalanced.

If you do not have experimental variation in your treatment variable, there is yet more work to be done. This chapter cannot dive into causal identification with observational data, but there are nevertheless certain things that can be discussed as being necessary in any good identification strategy section:

• Explain intuitively why your results have a shot at causal identification. Practically speaking, this means that you have to tell your reader why your results bring us closer than ever before to making a causal statement about the relationship of interest. In the best-case scenario, this will be because you have a research design (e.g., a strictly exogenous instrumental variable such as a lottery) which clearly allows thinking of treatment as if it were randomly assigned. In less-than-ideal scenarios (e.g., an instrumental variable that is only plausibly exogenous; cf. Conley et al. 2012), you need to explain why, even though your research design does not yield clean and clear causal identification, your results are the best in the literature.[6]

---

6. This presumes that your research design *is* the best thing out there. In cases where your research design is second- (or third-, or n^{th}-) best, unless you significantly improve on external validity, you will need to adjust your set of target journals downward.

• Discuss in turn the three following sources of statistical endogeneity:[7] (i) reverse causality, (ii) unobserved heterogeneity, and (iii) measurement error, explaining whether each of those sources of statistical endogeneity is a concern in your application, and how it is dealt with in your application. Here, if there are issues, admit to them, and explain how they might bias your estimate of the coefficient of interest. Be honest about what your paper can and cannot do.

• Once that is done, there is one more threat to internal validity to be considered, namely violations of the stable unit treatment value assumption (SUTVA). What SUTVA means is specific to each application, but in short, if you observe the effect of a treatment D_{it} on outcome y_{it}, where i denotes an individual unit of observation and t denotes a time period, it has to be the case that the value of D_{it} does not affect the value y_{-it}, $y_{i,-t}$, or $y_{-i,-t}$. In other words, there cannot be any spillovers from one unit being treated to another unit's outcome, and there cannot be any spillovers from one unit being treated at a given point in time to that same unit's outcome in the future, nor can there be any spillovers from one unit being treated at a given point in time to other unit's outcome in the present or in the future. The SUTVA can be extremely difficult to satisfy. That said, one can often test for SUTVA violations; see Burke et al. (2019) for an example of a paper where the authors deal with SUTVA violations very well.

• Again, because this is important: if your results are not causally identified, *be honest* about what they can and cannot do. And generally, do not make claims that are not backed up by your research designs of your results, no matter how much you wish those claims to be true. Editors and reviewers would much rather deal with manuscripts wherein the author candidly admits to the limitations of their findings than with manuscripts wherein the author tries to deceive the reader. In plain English: the former

---

7. I talk explicitly of statistical endogeneity—what makes $Cov(D, \epsilon|x) \neq 0$—because many research economists still confuse theoretical and statistical exogeneity. Theoretical exogeneity is when a given variable is determined outside of a given theoretical framework (e.g., prices and income in the typical utility-maximization problem). Statistical exogeneity is when $Cov(D, \epsilon|x) = 0$ in the regression framework we have been considering. Though the two share the same "exogeneity" and "endogeneity" terminology, there is little overlap in their respective meanings. It is a poor empirical economist who says his results are causally identified because his treatment variable is theoretically exogenous.

kind of manuscript has a much better chance of not being rejected than the latter.

2.5   Results and Discussion

The section of an applied economics article that discusses the paper's findings is obviously the most important section of the paper. Somewhat paradoxically, it is perhaps also the least-read section of a paper: after a reader has read the title, the abstract, the introduction, looked at a few tables, and maybe looked at the Empirical Framework section to answer any lingering questions, your reader knows whether she can trust you and your findings, and she is often only interested in your core finding. Only reviewers and critical readers (e.g., graduate students reading your paper for a class, should your article end up on someone's syllabus, or for their dissertation) will read the entirety of the results section. Nevertheless, results sections have their own structure, which is discussed below.

2.5.1   Order of Results

There is a certain logical order in which results should be presented. Typically, results progress from most parsimonious (e.g., a simple, bivariate regression of y on D) to least parsimonious (i.e., a regression of y on D and a full set of control variables x). With experimental variation in D, this is not as useful as with observational variation in D. In the former case, adding controls on the right-hand side of the equation of interest will in principle not change the sign and the magnitude of the estimated treatment effect. Rather, it will only make the estimate of the treatment effect more precise (i.e., it will reduce the standard error around it).[8]

In the latter case, where one cannot assume that $E(y|x) = E(y|do(x))$, the most-to-least-parsimonious approach is one first step toward assessing the robustness of one's results: if the sign and the magnitude do not change much or at all as one adds in control variables on the right-hand side, this suggests that one's results are already somewhat robust. This is in the spirit of Altonji et al.'s (2005) approach to robustness (although Oster 2019 critiques Altonji et al. 2005 and suggests a new method

---

8. A colleague who has run numerous RCT notes that in his experience, adding controls tends to have almost no effect on the standard errors, with the only exception being when the baseline value of the outcome is added as a control variable in an ANCOVA (analysis of covariance) setup (McKenzie 2012).

aimed at assessing how important unobserved heterogeneity is in a given application).

2.5.2 Robustness Checks

After presenting the core results in a paper, it is time to turn to robustness checks. There was a time when it was sufficient to present one or two tables of empirical results to convince the reader that there was a "there" there; times have changed, and as a consequence of the Credibility Revolution (Angrist and Pischke 2010), which has led to greater emphasis being placed on causal identification and inference, standards of evidence are considerably higher than they were in the early to mid-2000s. Authors now have to work hard to convince readers that their results were not cherry-picked, which means that establishing the robustness of a finding involves its own set of complications.

In many cases, the outcome we are interested in has more than one measurement. "Welfare," for instance, can be measured in a number of ways: household income, household income per capita, household income per adult equivalent, household consumption expenditures, household consumption expenditures per capita, household consumption expenditures per adult equivalent, subjective well-being of the respondent, and so forth. If you have access to all seven of those measures of "welfare," one first step toward establishing that your result is robust might be simply to re-estimate your core equation for each of those measures, showing that the result holds across all of them.

Similarly, you may have different measures of the treatment variable. In most randomized controlled trials (RCTs), there is one (and only one) treatment variable (unless there are several treatment arms, and unless those treatment arms are interacted). But with observational data, it might be possible to look at different measures of the treatment variable. In the contract farming literature, for example, one can look at whether a household participates in contract farming (i.e., contract farming at the extensive margin), but one could also look at the proportion of one's crop acreage that is under contract (i.e., contract farming at the intensive margin).

Now imagine that you have those two measures for the treatment variable, and the aforementioned seven measures for the outcome variable. This allows estimating 14 different specifications of the core equation of interest. If the finding holds for each one of those specifications, that goes a long way toward establishing that the finding is robust.

One can also check for robustness by conducting placebo and falsification tests. In the former case, a "fake" treatment (i.e., a variable that is correlated with the treatment, but which presumably does not cause the outcome) is used in lieu of the actual treatment. In the latter case, a "fake" outcome (i.e., a variable that is correlated with the outcome, but which presumably is not caused by the treatment) is used in lieu of the actual outcome. In both cases, robustness comes from the lack of a statistically significant finding, since a statistically significant finding hints at the fact that the core results might be spurious. In difference-in-differences studies—a methodology where the frontier has been evolving rapidly over the past few years—one should analyze trends.

Yet another kind of robustness check comes in the form of looking at different estimators. Most empirical economics articles, for instance, rely on some linear, fully parametric regression. If the treatment is continuous, it might be useful to estimate specifications that allow for a more flexible functional form (e.g., a restricted cubic spline), which would allow one to determine whether the relationship between y and D is generally monotonic. Very often, robustness checks of this kind are where modest methodological contributions—a paper's third contribution, as listed in the introduction—come from.

2.5.3   Treatment Heterogeneity

It is rare that the treatment effect we are interested in estimating is homogeneous across the population of interest. After assessing the robustness of your results, you may be interested in looking at whether the treatment varies for various subgroups (e.g., men vs. women, rural vs. urban, black vs. white, by income quintile, etc.) This section is where this is assessed. Keeping with the contract farming example, suppose you were interested in whether the impacts of contract farming differ between male and female respondents. This alone would bring the number of estimated specifications up to 28 (i.e., seven measures of welfare, two treatment measures, and male vs. female respondents). From this, it is rather it easy to see why the average applied paper is now typically 50 pages—if not longer.

One good thing about exploring treatment heterogeneity is this: doing so can salvage a null finding (i.e., an effect that is statistically insignificant) because average effects can mask a tremendous amount of heterogeneity. So before calling it quits, saying that an intervention or treatment has had "no effect" and abandoning an entire research project, it is well worth thinking about whether the treatment effect might be heterogeneous, and whether said heterogeneity is of interest for policy or business.

When I write that exploring treatment heterogeneity can salvage a null finding, you should not conclude from that statement that when you have a null finding, you should explore treatment heterogeneity. If you wish to explore treatment heterogeneity, you need to have a good reason (usually stemming from your theoretical framework) for doing so. Anything else will reek of p-hacking (i.e., the phenomenon whereby researchers slice their data until they find something significant to report in their paper), which leads to plain bad science.

2.5.4   Mechanisms

As a result of the Credibility Revolution (Angrist and Pischke 2010), applied microeconomists have been answering questions of the form "Does D cause y?" or "What is the effect of D on y?" first and foremost.

In recent years, however, much has been written in the quantitative social science literature about how to test for whether a given variable m is a mechanism whereby some other variable D causes some outcome y—what is called mediation analysis—and this remains a very active area of research.[9] A good section on mechanisms does its best to investigate potential mechanisms. In the best-case scenario, this involves a proper mediation analysis. In many cases, this means doing what one can do with the data at hand, such as presenting descriptive (i.e., not causally identified) regressions or correlations. In other cases, this means simply admitting that there are some mechanisms one cannot test for, not even with imperfect proxies. When anything but the ideal is feasible, you should clearly explain why you cannot test for specific mechanisms to leave no doubt in your readers' minds that you have thought about the question "How does D cause y?"

2.5.5   Limitations

A good Empirical Results section should be honest about what it can and cannot do. Though this is often discussed quickly in the Conclusion, it should be discussed more fully in a separate subsection of the estimation results section.

What limits one's results? Typically, limitations come in three varieties. First and foremost, internal validity may be limited. In other words, one might not be able to make a causal statement but instead only get close

---

9. This section's placement in this chapter in no way indicates that you should think about mechanisms *ex post*. It merely indicates that the section in which you empirically test for mechanisms should come after your main results. Ideally, the presumed mechanisms whereby your treatment variable affects your outcome of interest should be discussed as part of your theoretical framework.

to doing so relative to the literature. For instance, your instrumental variable might only be plausibly exogenous, but not strictly so. This would be a good time to remind the reader that this is so.

Second, external validity may be limited as well. This is often the case with lab or a lab-in-the-field experiments,[10] or with RCTs. Or you may have a strictly exogenous instrumental variable, but it is not entirely clear who the compliers and defiers are, and so who the local average treatment effect applies to is a nebulous subset of the sample.

Finally, the variables you use as your treatment or your outcome variable might only be proxies for what you are truly interested in. For instance, though you may be interested in looking at whether economic shocks push people to commit suicide, data on suicides may not be available (or suicides may be significantly under-reported), and so you might have to resort to using mortality rates instead.

2.5.6   Tables

Before closing out this section, I would like to discuss some miscellaneous pieces of advice regarding tables of empirical results. In no particular order:

- The titles of your tables should be self-explanatory: "OLS Results for the Effect of Participation in Contract Farming on Household Income," or "OLS Results for the Effect of Years of Education on Wage by Gender." The titles should thus tell us what is being estimated (e.g., OLS), what the relationship of interest is (i.e., the effect of participation in education on wage), and what subset of your sample, if any, it applies to (i.e., male and female respondents separately).
- Coefficient estimates and standard errors should be reported with the same number of decimal places throughout your tables—usually two or three.
- Some people like to omit control variables, preferring instead to include a line that says "Controls? Yes" in the second (i.e., bottom) half of the table. Though this is fine to save space in a published article, a working paper should show everything to the readers (especially the reviewers and the editor). The obvious exception is for individual, household, or community fixed effects, of which there are usually too many to list. If you

---

10. Lab-in-the-field experiments are lab experiments that are conducted with "real" subjects (e.g., firm managers) in the field, outside of the experimental lab.

must include a line at the bottom that says "Controls? Yes," make sure the notes to the table (i.e., right under the table) include a detailed list of which controls are included—a careful reader will want to know whether you condition on colliders or include as control a variable that lies on the causal path between the treatment and outcome variables.[11]

• The last lines of the table should list the number of observations, the R^2 (I prefer the usual R^2 to the adjusted one, because this tells me how much of the variation in y is explained by the variables on the right-hand side, without any arbitrary correction for the number of observations and parameters), maybe the results of a test of joint significance of the variables on the right-hand side, and various lines indicating which controls are included (e.g., state fixed effects, a linear time trend, year fixed effects, state-specific linear trends, state-specific quadratic trends, region–year fixed effects, and so on).

• Finally, the notes to the table should present all symbols for statistical significance (typically, * for statistical significance at less than the 10 percent level, ** at less than the 5 percent level, and *** at less than the 1 percent level; for completeness and transparency, none should be omitted), and additional symbols if necessary.[12] For instance, you may have adjusted your p-values for multiple comparisons, bootstrapped your standard errors, or done some randomization inference, all of which would lead to different inferences and critical levels of statistical significance, in which case you might use the symbols †, ††, and ††† to denote significance at less than the 10, 5, and 1 percent level for this additional version of the standard errors.

• Present estimation results for the same estimation sample. That is, as the number of control variables increases, the sample size is nonincreasing due to missing variables. If the sample size decreases as you throw

---

11. A collider is a variable caused by two separate, possibly unrelated variables. Conditioning on a collider or on a variable that lies on the causal path between the treatment and outcome variables is problematic because it introduces bias (Morgan and Winship 2015).

12. That being said, at the time of writing, the AEA journals have moved away from relying on asterisks (i.e., "stars") or other typographical symbols to denote statistical significance. It remains to be seen, however, how many other journals will follow suit. Here, the best thing to do is to read a journal's formatting guidelines before submitting.

controls on the right-hand side, this involves an apples-to-oranges comparison (different estimation samples are representative of different populations). Instead, take your smallest sample size (as dictated by missing observations) and use that sample for all specifications.

• For variable names, use plain English words like "Years of education," "Age squared," and "Female" and not Stata or R codenames like "Edu," "AGE_2," or "SEX."

• Ultimately, it always helps to put yourself in your reader's shoes, and the right question to ask yourself (or a friend who owes you a favor) is this: When given only the tables, can one write down the exact regression that was estimated? Or is one left with more questions than one has answered after looking at the tables?

2.6 Summary and Concluding Remarks

Many economics papers title their conclusion "Summary and Concluding Remarks," which is a pretty good indication of how a conclusion should proceed. What I learned in high school was that a good conclusion should have two main parts: (i) a summary of what you have spent the several pages before the conclusion doing, and (ii) the way forward.

The following guidelines should help cut down on the transaction costs one faces when writing a conclusion by providing a roadmap. Strictly speaking, a conclusion should be structured as follows:

• *Summary*. You have surely heard that when writing a research paper, "tell 'em what you're going to tell 'em, tell 'em what you want to tell 'em, and tell 'em what you just told 'em." Writing this part of a conclusion is tedious—you have just spent 40 or more pages telling them—but it needs to be there, and it needs to be different enough from the abstract and the introduction. This does not mean this part must say something new; it just needs to be different enough. If possible, tell a story—a story about the paper's contribution, and the gap it fills.

• *Limitations*. Some people like to have a "Limitations" section at the end of their results section; I like to have that myself, as discussed above. But even then, the conclusion should (re-)emphasize the limitations of your approach.

• *Real-World Implications*. Presumably, your work has some sort of implication for policy, business strategy, or something else in the real world. This will not always be the case—some papers make a purely technical point, or a point that is only ancillary when it comes to making other policy-related points. Discuss what those implications are. Do not make claims that are not supported by your results. Try to assess the cost of what you propose in comparison to its benefits. You can do so somewhat imperfectly (this is probably where the phrase "back-of-the-envelope calculation" most often comes up in economics papers), since the point of your work was presumably about only one side of that equation— usually the benefits of something, sometimes its costs, but rarely both. In two or three sentences, identify the clear winners and losers of what your results suggest. Also discuss how easy or hard it would be to implement.

• *Implications for Future Research.* No work is perfect. Your theoretical contribution could be generalized or broadened by relaxing certain assumptions. Your empirical contribution could probably benefit from better causal identification for better internal validity. Even with an RCT with perfect compliance and a perfect average treatment effect estimate, you are likely to have some treatment heterogeneity that is not accounted for, or you might want to run the same RCT in additional locations for external validity. If you are writing a follow-up paper, this is a good place to set the stage for it.

2.7 Title, Abstract, and Introduction

The title, abstract, and introduction of a paper are, in order, the three most important marketing tools for any paper. This probably is doubly true for empirical papers, wherein authors rarely advance the frontier of knowledge theoretically or methodologically. Indeed, readers are probably more likely to put up with a bad title, a poorly written abstract, a meandering introduction—or all three—if they know that a paper will change their understanding of how the world works, or if they know that it will give them new tools they can use in their own research. Those same readers are unlikely to have that kind of patience for empirical papers, which are about the sign and magnitude of an empirical relationship, and how the authors estimated that relationship. Consequently, the following subsections focus on these components of an applied economics paper.

2.7.1 Title
It is difficult to pinpoint exactly what makes a good title. Much like US Supreme Court Justice Potter Stewart famously said of hard-core pornography in *Jacobellis v. Ohio*, when it comes to a good title, "I know it

when I see it." Colleagues who tend to publish in general-science journals like *Science*, or *Proceedings of the National Academy of Sciences* (*PNAS*) often insist that we should state our results in our titles. While that may be true for the papers we submit to those general-science journals, titles conform to a certain norm in economics which is best followed if you want your papers to look like they fit in.

To that end, it is perhaps easier to define what makes for a bad title. For starters, any title which emphasizes the technique you are using is sure to turn off most readers, unless you develop said technique. Spare your would-be readers titles—especially subtitles—of the form "A Semiparametric Investigation" or "Nonparametric Evidence from [Your Context]." Long titles also tend to make readers not want to read your paper. That is probably why there is an inverse relationship between the length of a paper's title and the number of times that paper gets cited (Letchford et al., 2015).

For an empirical economics paper—that is, a paper that asks an empirical question of the form "What is the effect of D on y?"—it is safe to go with a title of the form "The Impacts of D on y: Evidence from [the Context You Are Studying]." A variant on this theme is a title of the form "D and y," with or without the subtitle after the semicolon.

There is also the question of whether you should be cute or funny—for lack of a better term, let's refer to either as "clever"—in your title. If you are going to have a clever title, make sure it appeals to as many people as possible, and make sure it actually makes sense. What often works here is common sayings, adages, dicta, proverbs, short biblical passages, or titles of famous films, books, or TV shows. Ultimately, if you are going to take the clever route, make sure the cleverness is warranted, and that the clever part of your title perfectly fits your paper.

2.7.2   Introduction

I list the introduction second after the title and before the abstract because writing an abstract is much easier once the introduction has been written. The best way to write an introduction is to follow Keith Head's (2020) introduction formula.

I remember coming across that formula while in graduate school (and so it has been around since at least 2006) and thinking "I know how to write, I don't need this." Do not make that mistake. Even if you (think you) know how to write, the beauty of Head's formula is that it removes all uncertainty as to the order in which an introduction's sections should be presented.

The formula—and really, all credit goes to Keith Head for articulating it—is as follows:

• *Hook*. A good introduction starts with a good "hook," i.e., something that grabs the reader's attention and makes them want to keep reading. Here, the closer one can get to the reader, the better. Likewise, the broader one can go, the better. Bad hooks tend to appeal to the literature: "A long literature in economics has looked at . . ." Then why should anyone put up with your attempt to make that literature any longer? Good hooks tend to relate to the real world: A lot of the food we buy at the grocery store is grown in the context of long value chains. What does the first link in that value chain look like? What does participating in those value chains do for the people who actually grow the food we eat? The hook should be one or two paragraphs long.

• *Research Question*. After hooking the reader in and setting the stage, it is time to state your research question as clearly as possible. I like to do so by stating my actual research question as the first sentence of this part of my introductions. To carry on with the example in the previous bullet point: "What is the impact of participation in contract farming on the welfare of those who participate?" The more clearly this is stated, the better, because fewer are the occasions for the reader to be disappointed. This should be one paragraph long.

• *Antecedents*. After stating your research question, it is time to relate it and what you are doing to the existing literature. Here, relate your work to the five to ten closest studies (the closer to five, the better) in the literature. What the relevant literature—the antecedents—is will obviously depend on the question at hand. If you are lucky enough to work in a literature that has seen a lot of activity, you may have a hard time narrowing it down, and you will need to judiciously pick the five to ten closest studies. If you are working on a problem that no one has really looked at, or that no one has looked at in a long time, you might have to go back in time a bit further or expand your parameters for what counts as antecedents. Here, what counts is to tell a bit of a story; no one wants to read a bland enumeration of studies: "Johnson (2011) found this. Wang (2012) found that. Kim (2013) found something else. Patel (2015) found something else altogether." For every topic, the intellectual history of that topic can be told in an interesting way.

- *Value Added*. This is where you need to shine. What is your contribution? How does your paper change people's priors about your topic? Ideally, your paper will have three contributions. For instance, you may be improving on the internal validity front for the question you are looking at by having a better identification strategy. You may also be improving on the external validity front by having data that cover a broader swath of the real world, or you may be performing a mediation analysis that allows identifying what mechanism m the treatment variable D operates through in causing changes in y. Finally, you may also be bringing a small methodological improvement to the table. This is not necessary, as even papers with fewer than three contributions deserve to be published, provided at least one of their contributions is important enough.
- *Roadmap*. Finally, you should provide your reader with a roadmap to your paper. This section usually starts with "The remainder of this article is organized as follows," and it lists sections and what they do in order. So for a typical paper, it would go: "The remainder of this paper is organized as follows. Section 2 presents the theoretical framework used to study the research question and derives this paper's core testable prediction. In section 3, the empirical framework is presented, first by discussing the estimation strategy, and then by discussing the identification strategy. Section 4 presents the data and discusses some summary statistics. In section 5, the empirical results are presented and discussed, followed by a battery of robustness checks and a discussion of the limitations of the results. Section 6 concludes with policy recommendations and suggestions for future research." I have seen some economists on social media state that they have had papers rejected for many reasons, but never for want of a roadmap section. Fair enough. In most cases, however, it is simply easier to include such a roadmap section and delete it at a reviewer's request than to not have one and have to write one when asked to revise and resubmit a paper, not to mention the fact that some readers will simply expect there to be a roadmap, since the majority of applied economics articles include them. Anything that signals that you know what the unspoken rules and norms of the profession are is a good thing for your article's chances of getting published.

It is best to start writing a paper's introduction as soon as there are some empirical results. After the title and the abstract, the introduction is where most people will decide whether (i) they think your work is interesting enough to keep on reading, and (ii) whether they think your work is of a good enough quality for them to believe your findings. I would guess that the fate of at least 75 percent of articles—whether they get sent out for review, or whether a revision is solicited by the journal when they do get sent out for review—is driven by the introduction. As such, the introduction should be rewritten every time the file is worked on by any of the authors. I would guess that, for most of my papers, I have gone over the introduction at least a few hundred times.

A good introduction works because it sets your readers' expectations just right. If there is one thing that will make a reviewer recommend a rejection, it is a bait-and-switch (i.e., when an introduction overpromises and the rest of the paper underdelivers), or when an introduction is unclear as to what the paper does and how it does it.

As mentioned earlier in this chapter, a busy reader will typically read: (i) your title, (ii) your abstract, (iii) your introduction, then skip to (iv) your tables of results, then read (v) your conclusion, going back to the other sections if and only if they have questions about what you are doing, or how you do it. A good introduction minimizes (or eliminates altogether) a reader's need to flip through the paper in search of answers to her questions.

In addition to Keith Head, Claudia Sahm and David Evans both provide advice on how to structure the introduction of an economics article. In her advice to job-market candidates, Sahm (2019) suggests the following order of sections for papers in macroeconomics:

1. Motivation
2. Research question
3. Main contribution
4. Method
5. Findings
6. Robustness checks
7. Roadmap

Though her suggested structure is close to Keith Head's, it is worth noting that Sahm suggests a more precise content for Head's "value added" section, namely, you should tell your reader what empirical methodology you use to answer your research question as well as how you make sure your results are robust.

Similarly, after analyzing the introduction of "the most recent empirical microeconomic development papers from a range of top journals,"

Evans (2020) suggests the following structure, as well as a suggested length for each "section" of the introduction:

1. Motivations (1–2 paragraphs)
2. Research question (1 paragraph)
3. Empirical approach (1 paragraph)
4. Results (3–4 paragraphs)
5. Value added (1–3 paragraphs)
6. Robustness checks, policy relevance, limitations (optional)
7. Roadmap (1 paragraph)

Although Evans' advice stems from analyzing empirical development articles, it broadly overlaps with the advice given by both Keith Head and Claudia Sahm, and there is a payoff to adopting a common structure for your introduction: McCannon (2019) analyzed the papers published in the *American Economic Review* from 2000 to 2009 by looking at their readability score, and found that the papers that were hardest to read suffered a statistically significant decrease in their citation count of 0.20 standard deviation.

2.7.3 Abstract

Having chosen a good title and having written a good introduction, the task of writing your abstract should be relatively easy. Typically, it is possible to write a solid draft of your abstract by keeping only the first sentence of the hook, research question, and value-added sections of your introduction, and by polishing up the resulting paragraph some.

A good piece of advice I received from a senior colleague early on in my career was that except for the requisite terminology (e.g., RCT) difference-in-differences, regression discontinuity), your abstract should be intelligible to any smart, college-educated person who is not an economist. This is especially true for an empirical paper in economics. After all, we are writing about real-world phenomena that are of interest to policy makers or business managers, so your abstract should be intelligible to someone with a master's degree in public policy or in business administration, depending on what you are doing. In other words, do not make the mistake of confusing lack of intelligibility with intellectual rigor; this is economics, not French postmodern philosophy (Sokal and Bricmont, 1999).

Ultimately, your goal is not only to get your papers published, but to get them read, and to get them cited. The measure of a scholar's impact in any discipline is her number of citations.[13] If your title is not repellent, and if your abstract is intelligible to people who are not experts in your field and to people in other disciplines, you have just considerably expanded the scope of your citations—for better or for worse, a lot of people cite a lot of articles they have only read the abstract of.

2.8   Literature Review and Background Sections

You may have noted that Keith Head's introduction formula includes its own (mini) literature review. Although master's theses or doctoral dissertation chapters should include a separate section reviewing the literature to signal that the student is clearly familiar with the literature she is working in, such a section is almost always entirely unwarranted in a paper to be submitted to an economics journal.

The reason is simple: most readers have only very little time on their hands, and most readers will want to get to a paper's contribution sooner rather than later. As a result, a mini literature review discussing how a given paper relates to the five to ten closest studies in the literature is much more effective than a separate section reviewing an entire literature.

Moreover, most people are not good enough writers to pull off writing a literature review section that is worthy of being read, which requires telling a compelling story about the development of an idea or method. Though most researchers know their topic well enough to be able to identify all or almost all of the relevant related studies, few are able to aggregate the knowledge derived therefrom and coherently write up the intellectual history of the topic at hand. In any case, literature reviews are best written by senior scholars—who are more likely to offer a unique perspective on a topic because they have thought about it for a long time—and to theses and dissertation chapters. For the majority of applied economics articles, unless a reviewer asks for a separate literature review section, a mini literature review in the introduction is enough.

What about background sections? Those are a different story. When a topic requires a good amount of background knowledge, a separate background section can be very useful. This is especially the case when

---

13. One is tempted to add "in any discipline *except* economics," as it is only in economics that it is seemingly more important to please five to ten gatekeepers so as to get in the right journals than it is to actually have an impact.

the details of some legislation need to be kept in mind when assessing the effects of some part or all of that legislation on some outcome of interest. Likewise, in empirical industrial organization studies, it is common for authors to include a background section that describes the industry they are studying. As with anything else in an economics article, the background section should tell the reader what she needs to know—no more and no less.

2.9   Writing for the Right Journal

All of the foregoing is geared toward writing papers that can be submitted (and hopefully published) in peer-reviewed journals. Though I will have more to say in chapter 4 about where to submit on navigating the peer-review process, this naturally raises the question of whether you should write with a specific journal in mind.

Some people say that you should write with a specific journal in mind; others say you should just write the paper, see how it turns out, and then think about where to submit.

I do not really have an opinion on the matter, except for the following: I strive to write for an (imaginary) audience composed of PhD economists, but an audience of PhD economists who are not familiar with my field. Here, think of your classmates during your first-year core courses, most of whom probably ended up in different fields. As such, I tend to write for a more general reader. I am convinced that even when you end up submitting an article to a field journal,[14] writing for a general audience helps. The editor, for instance, might be in your field, but might not be familiar with your specific topic, so writing for a general audience can help convince her that your work is of general enough interest within your field. Likewise, writing for a general audience might help you attract readers who would otherwise not read your article by making it accessible to them, which ultimately leads to your work being cited more often.

If you want to write for a specific journal, however, here are a few general guidelines, in no particular order.

If you plan on submitting to a field journal, make sure that you actually cite a good number of articles published in that journal or close

---

14. Field journals are defined in relation to general journals. Whereas the latter might be open to publishing articles on most if not all areas of economics, the former publish articles in a given field (e.g., agricultural economics, economic history, monetary economics).

substitutes (e.g., *Economic Development and Cultural Change* for the *Journal of Development Economics*, or *Labour Economics* for the *Journal of Labor Economics*) and in that field over the last five years, and more recently if possible. This does two things. First, citing articles published in that journal serves to convince the editor, who has to decide whether to desk reject your paper or send it out for review, that your paper should be sent out for review because it is likely a good fit with what the journal publishes. Second, citing articles recently published in that journal helps the editor select reviewers for your paper.

If you only cite older articles published in your target journal, odds are the journal has moved on from publishing on that topic (probably because the topic is no longer of interest to readers), which makes it more likely that the editor will desk reject. If she does choose to send your paper out for review, it might be difficult for her to find the right reviewers, because the people who have published on that topic in her journal are likely to have moved on to other topics and to get cranky about having to review papers on it.

If you do not cite articles in your target journal, even if the editor decides that it is a good fit for that journal, you run the risk of getting reviewers suggested by a keyword search. For instance, I once had to handle a trade manuscript which only cited the works of Jagdish Bhagwati, Paul Krugman, Marc Melitz, and so on, without citing any work in the journal I was handling it for (or in any close substitute journal, for that matter). When they are not familiar with a given topic, editors start thinking about reviewers by looking at the references of a paper. Here, the issue is that Bhagwati, Krugman, and Melitz probably do not have time to referee for field journals, especially field journals that are not ostensibly about international trade. So how did I get reviewers? By doing a keyword search (e.g., "international trade") in the editorial system. This returned a few hundred candidate reviewers, and I selected two or three of them. But I am pretty sure none of those reviewers had seen the paper before. And therein lies the rub: one of the unfortunate, unstated truths about this profession is that network effects sadly matter, and reviewers are more likely to be favorable toward your paper if they have seen it before, preferably in a seminar or at a conference where they had an opportunity to ask their questions about the work.

If you plan on submitting to a field journal, it is thus important to cite articles that have been published recently in that or closely related journals. How about general journals? Here, opinions differ. When submitting to a top-five journal,[15] it is best to minimize the number of citations to field journals, because some general-journal editors conclude when they see that an article citing too many articles in field journals that that article also belongs in a field journal.

Given the foregoing, two approaches work reasonably well. The first approach is that you write your paper with a specific target journal in mind, because you know that that journal has recently been publishing articles on your topic.

The second approach is to just write the paper without a specific outlet in mind, but still keeping the average economist in mind. Once you are "done" writing your paper, you then look at your list of references. If there are some field journals you cite more than three times, those are all good candidates regarding where to submit. Once again, if your work improves on both the internal validity and external validity fronts, you should start with a more general economics journal. Know, however, that even the very best papers have a low probability of getting into those journals, as the competition is fierce—and it is getting fiercer.

2.10   The Act of Writing

A chapter on writing papers would be incomplete without discussing the act of writing itself.

I cannot claim to be a good writer, but I have managed to become a competent one over the years. To carry my earlier analogies further, no one can become a good film director who has not watched a lot of films, good and bad, and no jazz musician can become proficient at improvising over chord changes who has not listened to a lot of other musicians doing it. It is the same with writing, and the best way to become a competent writer is to spend time reading. Here, almost anything will do—just find something you enjoy reading, and which has been professionally produced. English is my second language, so when I made the conscious decision to improve my written English during my first year of college, I settled on taking the *The Economist* and the novels of Robertson Davies with me on my daily subway ride to campus. Reading

---

15. Traditionally, the top five journals in economics have been, in alphabetical order, the *American Economic Review, Econometrica*, the *Journal of Political Economy*, the *Quarterly Journal of Economics*, and the *Review of Economic Studies*.

regularly will provide a solid foundation upon which to build your own writing skills.

Beyond that, there are a number of excellent resources on how to improve your writing. Among the ones I have benefited from are Strunk and White's classic *The Elements of Style*, Zinsser's *On Writing Well*, best-selling author Stephen King's *On Writing*, and Phillips' *Ernest Hemingway on Writing*.

Generally, however, the following rules of thumb can help you become a better writer:

1. *Briefly embrace mediocrity.* When trying to write anything, anyone but the most self-delusional of narcissists will typically hear a voice in their head immediately criticizing anything they write once they write it. In a now-famous section of her 1995 book *Bird by Bird* titled "Shitty First Drafts," Anne Lamott outlined a very useful strategy to become more productive as a writer, which is as follows: When we write the first draft of anything, we should do so fully expecting that nothing good will come out of it, and knowing that the first draft will be, well, shit. But once you have a first draft, you can improve upon it—no one will ever see how bad your first draft was, and you can just keep polishing it until you have a product you like. The same cannot be said of a draft that never gets written and remains an idea in your mind because you could not briefly embrace mediocrity.

2. *Writing is rewriting.* Speaking of polishing, as much as people like to believe urban legends about this or that famous writer who wrote their *magnum opus* in one fell swoop,[16] the bulk of writing anything consists in rewriting it to make it better. As I have mentioned when discussing above how to write introductions, this act of rewriting is what ultimately can take a mediocre first draft and make it good.

3. *Write every day.* Though this seems like a tall order—who actually has time every day to dedicate to writing?—it really is not when you think

---

16. The most famous of such urban legends is probably that surrounding Jack Kerouac's *On the Road*. From a story on National Public Radio (Shea 2007): "Legend has it that Kerouac wrote *On the Road* in three weeks, typing it almost nonstop on a 120-foot roll of paper. The truth is that the book actually had a much longer, bumpier journey from inspiration to publication, complete with multiple rewrites, repeated rejections and a dog who—well, *On the Road* wasn't homework, but we all know what dogs do."

about it. Unless you make a point of not responding to email (say, because you are on vacation), every day you spend in this profession will bring an occasion for you to make the decision to deliberately write well in some form, even if that form is responding to email. Though some productivity tips and other "life hacks" encourage you not to worry about proper capitalization and grammar when writing email (presumably in an effort to add a whole five minutes of productivity to your day), I would encourage you to see everything you write as an occasion to write clearly and concisely—in other words, to write competently. If you want more occasions to write, the habit of keeping a daily journal builds writing time into your day.

2.11   Writing Papers for General-Science Journals

Increasingly, economists interested in improving the visibility of their work submit to and publish in general-science journals such as *Nature*, *PNAS*, and *Science*. Writing for those journals, however, is dramatically different than writing articles for economics journals. I thus briefly discuss how to do so to close this chapter.

General-science journals care much more about your findings and their implications than they do about methods. Methods are important, but they are relegated to the end of the paper (or to supplemental materials), for specialists who may be interested in seeing them.

Structure-wise, a paper in a general-science journal has four sections: (i) introduction and motivations, (ii) results, (iii) discussion, and (iv) methods. In the results section, you should only report results. The interpretation of those results should be kept for the discussion section, where they can be put in context. You can even afford to speculate, since unlike in an economics journal, not everything you state needs to be backed up by a number of robustness checks. But even in general-science journals, your core results need to be robust, and speculation should only be relied on to explain the implications of these results.

Understand: it is very challenging to write for general-science journals, as you will need to appeal to researchers beyond economics. As a colleague with experience publishing in both top general-economics and general-science put it: "Publishing in *PNAS* requires just as much effort as publishing in a general interest economics journal. Don't wing it."

3

Giving Talks

After writing papers, presenting them—giving talks—is the second most common form of communication in which economists engage. Even an economist who has no intention of ever joining academia will almost surely have to prepare at least one research presentation in her career— her job talk, or a presentation of her research for an audience of people who are considering hiring her as a colleague.

Like writing papers, how to give talks is something the average economist is expected to learn on her own, learning both from others and by doing, with little to no formal guidance except the odd blog post. This chapter provides guidelines for giving talks, from your first presentation at your department's graduate-student brown-bag seminar to full-fledged invited seminars, and from technical disciplinary research talks to outreach talks given to people who know little or nothing about economics.

Presenting a paper involves the distillation of the results in that paper, so much of the advice given in the previous chapter for writing papers (e.g., structure, content) naturally extends to giving talks. One difference between presenting and writing—indeed, one advantage of giving talks over writing papers—is that giving a talk is an occasion to engage in a dialogue with would-be readers, and maybe even with potential editors and reviewers.[1]

3.1 Invited Seminars

I use invited seminars as the benchmark against which I will compare other types of talks, because an invited seminar is the ideal format for a

---

1. Anecdotally, reviewers tend to be more favorable to papers they have seen presented at conferences or in seminars, because that has given them a chance to ask all of their questions. In other words, it has given them a chance to engage in a dialogue with the author about the paper.

talk in that it allows you to present a paper fully, or nearly so. Moreover, it is a format most economists will be familiar with from presenting at departmental brown-bag seminars.

An invited seminar lasts anywhere from 60 to 90 minutes,[2] and the presenter is expected not only to present a paper but also to answer the audience's questions about that paper. As such, it is the ideal setting to communicate the contents of a paper from start to finish.

Thus, the first step involved in successfully giving invited seminars is to know precisely what the norms are in the department that has invited you to present your work. Though this obviously includes asking how much time you will have to present, it also involves asking what the ground rules are regarding questions. It used to be a distinguishing trait of economics seminars that questions would be asked and answers given in a free-for-all format,[3] but that is no longer the case as some seminar series have moved to a format where no questions are allowed, say, for the first 15 minutes of presentation to allow the speaker to set the stage for her work, or to a format where only clarification questions are allowed throughout the talk, with more substantial questions being relegated to a formal question-and-answer session at the end.

Generally speaking, an updated version of the one-slide-per-minute rule of thumb applies to giving talks. Though a 75-minute seminar will rarely need as many as 75 slides, a 15-minute conference presentation should have no more than 15 slides. Thus, the updated version of the rule is something like "You should only have as many slides as you have minutes to present, and the shorter the talk, the more likely this constraint is to be binding."

Although the advice given to people making their first deck of slides is invariably of the "less is more" variety when it comes to making each individual slide, economists tend to be more comfortable with more text on slides as well as with fewer images than, say, business executives. It is thus perfectly acceptable for slides to have three to four bullet points, each containing a full sentence. This serves a dual purpose: First, it means that the speaker wastes no time memorizing what she wants to say. Second, it

---

2. Norms vary, however, and sometimes you may have as few as 45 minutes including questions from the audience.

3. Indeed, some departments have become infamous, perhaps unfairly, for barely letting speakers get past their introduction slides before asking questions as well as for not allowing some presenters to give the entirety of their talks due to the high frequency of questions.

also helps the audience understand what is going on in the paper, which in turn helps the speaker by giving her more time to present instead of answering clarification questions.

Like a paper, a talk—whether an invited seminar, a conference talk, or any other kind of talk—is not a murder mystery. As such, a talk on a given paper should be structured just like the paper it is meant to introduce to a new audience. Specifically, an invited seminar presentation should generally have the following structure:

1. *Title.* A single title slide with the title of the paper, the name of the authors, and perhaps the date and location of the talk. If you do choose to include the date and location of the talk, make sure it is up to date.

2. *Introduction.* Do not make the mistake of assuming your audience cares about what you are talking about just because you were invited to give a seminar. It is your job to convince audience members that your question is important, and that they care about the answer more than they had hitherto realized. Use descriptive statistics, broad trends, stylized facts, and so on to motivate your work. Your introduction should consist of as many slides as necessary to motivate the talk for the audience it is delivered to. Generally, an invited seminar draws people from all kinds of fields, so motivating the talk identically to how the paper motivates what it does is fine. One way to draft the introduction slides is to take the first sentence of every paragraph in the introduction and turn it into a bullet point, perhaps shortening it in the process. If a paper is written so that each paragraph introduces a separate idea (or a separate piece of an argument), taking the first sentence of each paragraph should yield a workable draft of the introduction slides, with only a few gaps left to be filled. Taking Keith Head's introduction formula as an example, the introduction slides should be separated into a broad hook meant to make the audience care, a clear statement of the research question the talk is meant to answer, a short (i.e., one- or at most two-slide) discussion of antecedents (i.e., the five to ten most relevant related contributions), a clear statement of the paper's value added (i.e., how it improves on those related contributions), and a roadmap slide outlining the remainder of the talk. Much like the roadmap paragraph at the end of the introduction, opinions vary as to the usefulness of the outline slide. My view is that it is better to include it and skip over it than not have it and have some audience members confused about where they are in the talk. It is

also ideal to give a preview of your results, just in case people have to leave early, or in case you cannot make it through your entire talk.

3. *Theoretical Framework.* Presenting a theoretical framework in support of an applied paper can be tricky. A common mistake is to go into so much detail that one ends up in the weeds, and thus wasting time with details that are, at best, left for the curious to read for themselves. Another common mistake when presenting theory—one that typically stems from the speaker's insecurity, and so one that is especially common among graduate students and early-career researchers—is to go too quickly over the theoretical framework in an effort to prevent audience members from criticizing it. A middle-of-the-road approach works best. First, this section should introduce the primitives, or basic building blocks of the theoretical framework (i.e., the agents considered, the commodities under study, the structure of the market, the agent's preferences or the technology they are using to produce, the various constraints they face, and so on) as clearly and concisely as possible. Second, the various assumptions made about those primitives (e.g., whether a utility function is concave, whether a production function exhibits constant returns to scale, and so on) should also be stated clearly. Finally, the relevant results should be stated roughly in the form "If assumptions 1, 2, . . . are satisfied, the following result is obtained." That's it. This is not the place to show how much tedious algebra you needed to do to get at a specific result. If you feel the need to include a specific proof, the place for it is your slide deck's appendices, which you can refer to in case someone asks for it.

4. *Data and Descriptive Statistics.* This section should present, in bullet point format, all of the details necessary for an audience member to understand the empirical work that follows and its limitations. Where do the data come from, both geographically (e.g., India) and institutionally (e.g., the US Census Bureau)? What was the initial purpose of the data collection effort that led to the data set? What is the basic unit of analysis? How were the units selected for inclusion in the sample? What time period(s) do the data cover? Were units followed over time, or is part or all of the sample in a time period freshly sampled? For longitudinal data sets, how much attrition was there between the beginning and the end of the sample? Were the units that attrited replaced by new ones and, if so, how were those replacement units selected? What is the final

sample size? Which observations, if any, were dropped? Which variables are transformed using a common transformation like a logarithm? After answering those questions, it is customary to present a slide of descriptive statistics. Only the variables retained for analysis should be included here—outcomes, treatments, controls and, if applicable, instruments and mediators—no more, no less. As with the outline slide at the end of the introduction, the descriptive statistics slide tends to be skipped ("Unless anyone insists on seeing these, I am going to skip directly to my empirical framework") unless the speaker wishes to bring attention to any specific feature of the data. This section also should feature slides for the relevant balance tests, and the talk should clearly discuss the results of those tests—and their consequences for the empirics. The one sin many commit here is to present the tables in the paper "as is," which is to say much too small for anyone not having preternatural eyesight to see. Unlike in a manuscript, it is perfectly fine here to break tables into several slides for readability. Finally, this section is also where limits to external validity should be discussed.

5. *Empirical Framework.* As with papers, the empirical framework should be divided into two broad sections, namely estimation and identification. The estimation framework should show the core equations whose results are presented in the following section, how those equations are estimated (i.e., least squares, maximum likelihood, generalized method of moments) and which estimator is used (e.g., linear probability model, probit, logit), clearly define each variable used in those equations, clearly explain what the subscripts (and superscripts) refer to, and so on, just as in the paper. One thing to be aware of in this section is how variable names are chosen, with the norm being either to use variable names exactly as they are used in the theoretical framework or to use fresh new variable names for the empirics. A common mistake is to repurpose some variable names used in the theoretical framework to refer to something completely different in the empirical framework; for instance, to use x to refer to quantity demanded in your theoretical framework, and then use x to refer to your vector of control variables in your empirical framework. After presenting the estimable equations, there should be a thorough discussion of identification—that is, of the source of (plausibly) exogenous variation used to estimate the causal effect of interest, and why the results about to be presented have a shot at being internally

valid. For papers featuring a lab or field experiment, this can be kept short. But for papers that rely on a feature of observational data (e.g., the staggered rollout of a program, a discontinuity in the data, some naturally occurring source of variation), the onus is on the speaker to convince her audience that that feature allows (getting as close as possible to) estimating a causal effect as possible. Often, this section of the talk is where much of the dialogue between the speaker and her audience will take place.

6. *Results and Discussion*. This section is in principle the *pièce de résistance* of any empirical talk, and so special care should be put into making sure that the figures and slides are self-explanatory and legible from the back of the average conference room. One thing that many empirical economists do is to present empirical results that omit control variables. Opinions are divided as to whether that is a good thing or not. On the one hand, it makes it easier to focus on the relationships of interest by not fitting (almost) all of a regression's coefficients and standard errors onto one slide. On the other hand, the results for the control variables can help diagnose specific problems with the results for the relationships of interest. I suppose a middle-of-the-road approach is to both (i) show slides that omit the control variables as part of the main presentation and (ii) have detailed slides as part of the appendix. The ideal scenario is one where there are so few controls that everything can fit on one slide. Here, it is probably best to show all of the core results as well as the main robustness checks, but to keep the more offbeat robustness checks for the appendix. This section is also where, before presenting any results per se, the ancillary results necessary to make the case that the identification strategy does what it purports to do are presented: graphs of regression discontinuities, tests of the parallel trends assumption, maps showing the rollout of a given program over time, and so forth, should be featured early on in this section.

7. *Summary and Concluding Remarks*. It can seem like a waste of time to have to summarize the paper you have just finished presenting. And to some extent, it *is* tedious to do so, but the old saw "tell 'em what you're gonna tell 'em, tell 'em, and then tell 'em what you've told 'em," however cliché, is nonetheless useful, if only because some people may have gotten lost during your presentation and this is a way to bring them back. Much like jazz musicians playing a standard will typically play the melody, take

turns soloing over the chord progression, and then play the melody once again to conclude, one should summarize the paper—play the melody one last time—before offering some concluding remarks.

8. *Appendix*. Not everyone realizes that, just like a paper can have dozens of pages of appendix materials, a slide deck can also have dozen of slides of appendix materials. Those materials tend to be things that are included just for those curious audience members, and are not meant to be presented in the course of a normal seminar. Think of these appendix materials as you would the extra features on a DVD: they consist of interesting bits of material such as experimental protocols, tables of additional robustness checks, extra test results, visual aids used during fieldwork, as well as derivations and proofs of theoretical results. If you have had the opportunity to give a talk often, you are likely to have heard the same questions a number of times, so the appendix slides can even contain answers to some of the most commonly asked questions.[4]

Once again, giving an invited seminar is not only a chance to publicize one's research findings, it is also a chance to engage in a dialogue with other researchers about those findings and to get feedback which will ultimately improve the paper. They should thus be approached as such rather than as a monologue. You are there to talk *with* other researchers, and not *at* them. Before moving on to job talks, I should discuss how to get invited to give seminars. Obviously, reputation matters, and the more you become known for your research, the more you will get to give invited seminars. But reciprocity also matters, as does being entrepreneurial. On the former, if you volunteer to organize seminars at your own institution, you can invite people who may be in a position to invite you to give a seminar at their institution later on. This obviously means that you should not only invite superstar researchers from top departments, but also people from comparable departments. On the latter, a colleague who is excellent at networking suggested the following: if you know you will be in a given city or region, you can get in touch with the departments in that city or region and politely offer to give a talk. This will not always work, and your success rate is likely to be strictly decreasing as the quality of the department you offer this to increases, but it is a strategy whose expected payoff is nonzero.

---

4. This last point can make a job-market candidate look especially thoughtful and polished.

3.2   Giving Job Talks

As I noted in the introduction, this book generally steers clear of giving job-market advice, both because the job market is changing rapidly, and because there are much better resources on that topic. I nevertheless wanted to bring up the topic of giving job talks for those aiming to transition back into academia after spending a few years outside of it, for those going on the market as senior assistant professors, or for those going on the market at mid-career.

Most of the advice given in the previous section about giving invited seminars holds for job talks as well, but job talks are different enough that they require their own section.

In *The Obstacle Is the Way*, Holiday (2014) tells the story of how George Clooney stopped being ignored by the directors he auditioned for when he realized that instead of going into an audition hoping to get the job, he should go into an audition with the idea that he was the solution to the problem the director was trying to solve. In that spirit, one strategy that makes a candidate stand out is when she takes the first three to five minutes to talk about herself, and explain why she is a good fit for the position.

Likewise, if a candidate presents herself as the solution to the interviewing department's constrained optimization problem, odds are she will be seen more favorably than her competitors, which will in turn raise the likelihood she receives the first offer (or an offer). How does one do that? One thing to realize is that if you are invited to give a job talk, the time you are allocated for your talk is yours, so that you can certainly take the first five minutes of your job talk to introduce yourself to your audience.[5] Those first few "About me" slides should ideally have a slide that lists (i) where you got your PhD, (ii) which (relevant) positions you have held, and (iii) any big-ticket, noteworthy item your audience should know about (e.g., major awards or professional honors). A second slide can also have a few bullets explaining how you fit the position—here, a bit of legwork beforehand to find out why they are hiring for this position and why they are doing so now can go a long way. Finally, a third slide should feature what you have worked on and what you are currently working on other than the paper you are there to present, as

---

5. Do not count on anyone having looked at your CV ahead of time, and much less on them having read your job-market paper.

this shows that you have both a proven track record and a proper pipeline, and that you will not stop being productive if and when you get the job.

One piece of advice about giving talks which I personally have found to be overrated when applied to job talks is the "know your audience" mantra. For whatever it is worth, and as the preceding paragraph makes clear, my view is that the audience should know *you* instead. When I first went on the job market in 2006, I gave job talks in four economics departments and at one policy school; when I went on the market in 2013, I gave job talks in three agricultural economics departments and at one policy school. Even though I presented fairly technical papers in both 2006 and 2013, I never felt the need to change my talk for interdisciplinary audiences at policy schools. My view was always that if they did not like what I do, warts and all, then it would not be a good match, and not getting an offer was simply an easy way of knowing early what would not be a good match. This is certainly not a foolproof way of screening out bad matches, but it does help reduce the likelihood of one.

One thing many people consistently get wrong in presentations is the level of technique. You can never go wrong assuming you are presenting to an audience of smart college graduates with no experience in your field. This means you should emphasize the motivations and intuition, and define technical concepts in plain English.

That said, even when presenting technical material, you should try to provide as much intuition as possible. If you can keep someone not in your field interested in your presentation for the entire duration of your talk, that person will be much more likely to vote for you when the department has to choose who to make an offer to. There are few worse offenses than that of wasting people's time; for an academic, there are few things worse than sitting in a seminar where the speaker has made no effort to be understood by as many people as possible.

When interviewing for senior (i.e., post-tenure) positions, one strategy which I have seen work well in the past is to present an overview of one's research agenda (either in whole or on a given topic if interviewing for a more narrowly defined position) instead of a job-market paper. For instance, I recall seeing a colleague who applied for a global health position presenting her entire research agenda on HIV/AIDS in China. This worked well for her because it allowed her to both show that she had been (and would remain) productive in an important area of global health, and thus that she was the solution to our constrained maximization problem.

3.3 Conference Presentations

Whether you have previously presented a paper as an invited seminar or are presenting it for the first time at a conference, preparing a presentation for a conference is not much more difficult than preparing it for an invited seminar.

The main difficulty here is to ensure that you prepare just the right amount of material. Indeed, although conference presentations tend to be much shorter (i.e., 10 to 20 minutes) than invited seminars, it is not uncommon for busy academics to show up at conferences and present using the same deck of slides they would use for an invited seminar—only three to four times faster. Here, it behooves the presenter to put himself in his audience's shoes, and to understand that few people, if any, enjoy listening to relatively complex presentations at triple or quadruple speed.

Obviously, the key lies in determining which parts of the longer, invited-seminar version of the presentation can go. The advantage of presenting a paper at a conference is that the audience for a conference talk tends to be more selected than the audience for an invited seminar. In the former case, the conference is often dedicated to a specific field (e.g., the annual conference of the Society of Labor Economists or the various NBER Summer Institutes), whereas in the latter case, the audience is much more heterogeneous, especially in departments where there is a strong social norm about attending seminars. This means that a lot of material meant to convince a general audience of research economists that your work looks at an interesting research question and educate them about how things are done in your field need not be made explicit for a conference. Even for general conferences, such as the annual meetings of the American Economic Association (AEA) or the annual congress of the European Economic Association, the audience for a specific session will tend to have selected into attending your talk and thus require considerably less handholding than at an invited seminar.

In the case of a conference presentation, the one-slide-per-minute rule is useful, so if your talk is to last 15 minutes, aim for 15 slides, and aim for 20 slides if you are given 20 minutes. If you go over your allotted time when giving a seminar, it only impacts you, and audience members who need to leave can always leave before you are finished. If you do the same at a conference, however, you have directly taken time away from the other speakers.

It is thus crucial to figure out how much time you will have to present before you sit down to make your slides. Here is how you should go about making conference slides:

1. *Title.* No difference from the title slide for an invited seminar.

2. *Introduction.* For a selected audience, your hook is not as important, and you can often state the research question right away since the audience will immediately understand why it matters. You can also keep the antecedents—the mini literature review—rather short, because once again, your audience is likely to be familiar with the literature.

3. *Theoretical Framework.* Again, Thomson (2011) discusses how to give talks about theory papers. When presenting an empirical paper, a brief (i.e., one-, at most two-slide) presentation of your primitives, variables, assumptions, and of the optimization problem before presenting the main predictions to be tested is fine.

4. *Empirical Framework.* A brief (i.e., ideally one-slide) presentation of your estimable equations(s) and definitions of the included variables, and a two- to three-slide discussion of your identification strategy. Though you may ideally need 15 minutes in an invited seminar to render justice to your identification strategy and discuss its subtleties, it is best to focus on the strict minimum here, and to leave further discussion for after your talk.

5. *Data and Descriptive Statistics.* In the ideal case, the data you use will be so well known to your audience (e.g., the Panel Study of Income Dynamics) that you will not have to dwell on your data sources other than to mention which rounds or waves of data you are using. In other cases (e.g., when presenting a paper relying on primary data) you will have to go into more detail. Here, too, brevity is the soul of wit, and your audience only needs the necessary information. Although you may be justifiably proud of (and have unforgettable memories from) having spent a significant fraction of your life in sub-Saharan Africa overseeing an RCT in difficult conditions, this is not the time to go into needless details. You should have slides of descriptive statistics and balance tests, but those should be skipped unless there is something crucial in them (e.g., randomization was not done correctly and the balance is off on more covariates than one should be comfortable with), and are thus only included for the curious who want to see them after the talk.

6. *Results and Discussion.* You have obviously worked hard to estimate all of the relevant specifications and to conduct all of the robustness checks one could possibly want to see, so it may be tempting to show all of those tables. Please refrain from doing so for a conference talk,

and show two to three tables of core results (whatever that means in the context of your paper), and then show a slide with a list of short bullet points explaining what your results are robust to (e.g., "Results are robust to: linear trends instead of time fixed effects; quadratic trends instead of time fixed effects; region-year fixed effects; . . .")

7. *Summary and Concluding Remarks.* This is idiosyncratic, but my view is that conference presentations are short enough that this section is not necessary, and that this is more true the shorter the presentation. What I like to do is to prepare a proper two-slide (i.e., one slide summarizing the research question and findings, and one slide with implications for policy or business strategy and directions for future research), but to say something like "In the interest of time and of letting you ask your questions, I'll just skip this." If you prefer to go through a proper conclusion, there is no harm to doing so, but realize that it is directly taken out of your allotted time.

8. *Appendix.* If appendix slides are your secret weapon when presenting at an invited seminar, they can be even more so when presenting at a conference. All of the material that had to be taken out of the long-form, invited-seminar version of your presentation can (and should probably) be put in your appendix so that you may refer to it when audience members ask you to go into more depth about specific parts of your presentation.

There is one crucial distinction between an invited seminar presentation and a conference presentation: whereas an invited seminar is a primarily an occasion for you to engage in a dialogue with your audience and only secondarily an occasion to add something to your CV, the short clock on a conference presentation means that there is much less dialogue, and that such talks are more of an occasion to market your work and add a line to your CV, with the bulk of the dialogue taking place between sessions over coffee and during meals than for an invited seminar. So while you may expect your audience to make game-changing comments about your work at a conference, if and when you get such comments, you are more likely to get them after your session is over than during your allotted time. For early-career researchers, knowing this can be quite liberating.

3.3.1 Serving as Discussant
Some of the most valuable conferences from the point of view of improving your work are those that feature discussants. Serving as a discussant

is a good opportunity for you to learn about others' work and help them improve it. But as with everything else, there is a set of best practices related to serving as a discussant.

First of all, you should read the paper as you would when serving as a reviewer for a journal. This does not necessarily mean that you should read the paper down to the footnotes and appendices. If you have a clear sense that you would recommend that the paper be rejected at a field journal, it may not be necessary to read the entirety of a paper before you can formulate high-level comments that can help the authors improve their chances of getting a revise-and-resubmit.

Second, depending on how much time you have for your discussion (typically five, at most 10 minutes), you should prepare a short presentation with a view to helping the authors improve their paper. The best way to help the authors improve their paper is by focusing on those things they can do which will have the highest possible return at the margin. Your presentation should include the following sections:

Summary of the Paper. In contrast to my idiosyncratic preferences regarding how conference presentations should omit the conclusion, I have seen many discussants whose slides included a summary of the paper presented skip that summary by saying "We just saw the paper being presented so I'll skip this." While a summary of one's own paper immediately after presenting one's paper tends to be redundant, a summary of a paper by someone else can be immensely valuable: no matter what the authors say their paper is about in their abstract and introduction, the reader will occasionally think that the paper is about something else. So providing a summary of what you got out of a paper can be very helpful to the authors.

Comments. As I mentioned above, focus on what will have the highest possible returns at the margin. This means you should avoid discussing the quality of the writing, or details that are either cosmetic or stylistic. Do not mention typos (almost every working paper in existence has them, and more than a few published papers do as well).

Ask yourself: Is there another available identification strategy which would allow the authors to examine the same research question and assess the robustness of their results? Do you know of another data set that would allow answering the same research question in order to improve the external validity of the authors' results? Can the authors get to the same result by relaxing an assumption, thereby making their work more general? Can you think of better motivations—meaning either more general ones or simply more convincing ones—for their work than what they currently have in the paper? Can you think of ways to simplify the authors' argument, their theoretical framework, or their empirical framework? All of these higher-level, higher-return comments are fair game when you are a discussant.

One way to think about serving a discussant is the following: if you had to write a referee report about this paper, what would your major comments be—those things you would want the authors to do before you could recommend the authors be given a chance at revising and resubmitting or accepted?

Some advice about discussing a paper it to pick your best three comments about the paper and stopping there (see, for instance, Blattman 2010), because anything after your top three comments will not be as good. While I understand that reasoning, serving as a discussant is an act of service, and if you have a number of constructive comments for the authors, you should not hide your light under a bushel, and you should aim to mention all those comments in one sitting. Relatedly, serving as a discussant is not "gotcha" journalism. Your job is not to find a fatal flaw in what the author has done, but rather to help improve the work. If there is a fatal flaw, the best way to let the author know is in private conversation after your discussion of their paper.

In no case should serving as a discussant be about you. If you can formulate a set of brilliant, game-changing remarks on a paper, you should certainly do it. Though there is no shortage of brilliance in the economics profession, there is often a shortage of generosity. If you really wish to stand out, be generous and constructive—whether you are serving as discussant or performing some other professional task.

3.4   Online and Hybrid Talks

As a result of the pandemic, much of the professional life of economists has moved online.[6] For better or for worse, this includes seminar and conference presentations, which can now be entirely online or hybrid, with some people tuning in online and others congregating in person, either in the same room as the presenter or somewhere else.

While it can be nice to give a research talk from the comfort of your own home, giving online talks involves its fair share of problems, depending on the format.

---

6. This is hopefully temporary, but I expect we will see more online talks in the future as they allow featuring a greater diversity of speakers to a broader audience at a low cost.

The ideal format is one where you only have to focus on giving your talk, and a moderator is in charge of monitoring the chat for questions and interrupting you at opportune times to allow specific audience members to ask questions. A less ideal format, at least for audiences larger than about 20 attendees, is one where audience members un-mute themselves when they feel like asking a question.

At a minimum, you should arrange with the seminar or conference organizers to log on five to ten minutes early to make sure that the technology being used works and that you are familiar with it. Another thing to keep in mind is that because our professional lives have moved online, we all spend more than enough time online, and so no one will ever fault you for using less than your allotted time. In fact, because participants tend to ask fewer questions during online seminars, you should make a point of finishing early. With that said, the format of an online talk should be the same as for an equivalent in-person talk.

3.5   Other Talk Formats

Invited seminars and conference talks are the two most common formats for a research talk, but there are other talk formats. This section discusses what to keep in mind when preparing a lightning talk or a poster presentation.

Lightning Talks. If preparing a conference talk from an invited seminar presentation involves trimming some of the fat off of your longer talk so as to make it presentable in 15 or 20 minutes, preparing a lightning talk involves making deep cuts to your conference talk so as to make it presentable in three to five minutes. Something to keep in mind for lightning talks is this: If you had 5 minutes entirely to yourself to sell a research paper to someone, what would you focus on? And perhaps more importantly, what would you leave out? This means you should focus on answering a single research question even if your paper answers two or three, and only provide information that is strictly necessary to understand how you answer that research question and what you find. Put differently, this means turning your one- or two-page structured abstract into a presentation. That presentation should have one slide each for your title, motivations and research question, data, empirical framework, and results, for a total of about five slides. Here, one should avoid the temptation to cram as much information as possible on each slide. A good commitment device for this is to not let your presentation software adjust your font size downward as you include more and more information on a slide.

Poster Presentations. I must confess to having never prepared a poster for presentation at a conference. Although posters are common in other disciplines, where papers are not quality-differentiated by whether they are accepted as presentations or posters, in economics posters are often for papers that are a step down from presentations in terms of quality. Here, the best strategy seems to be to prepare a poster that tells someone who reads it what they need to know about your research question, methods, and findings if they only read it without you being there to explain anything, to use a vertical template that has two columns, and to break each column into three or four "slides." The major advantage of a poster presentation is that you can include much more text on each slide than you would for a conference presentation, and so your poster can include some of the details you would relegate to your appendix slides when giving a conference presentation. But because a poster presentation is inherently more visual, it helps to tell your story in pictures, if possible, and to include figures to make points that you would otherwise make verbally (when presenting at an invited seminar or a conference) or in writing (in the paper). For instance, while a flowchart would never be deemed acceptable as a theoretical model in a paper, a flowchart can help convey your theory of change quite well on a poster.

3.6   Talks for Lay Audiences

Sooner or later, a researcher will be asked to talk about her research to a lay audience—that is, an audience composed in part or in whole of people who do not have a PhD in economics or related disciplines. This could be a research talk given to a multidisciplinary audience, a talk given to policy makers or business decision-makers, or an outreach talk given to a trade group, politicians, members of one's community, or at a local school. This section discusses what to keep in mind when giving such talks.

Multidisciplinary Research Talks. When they congregate with researchers from other disciplines, there is sometimes an unpleasant tendency among economists to think of themselves as the smartest people in the room. But let us get one thing straight: if markets are efficient—or even just minimally *in*efficient—there will be really smart people in every discipline. Therefore, when giving a multidisciplinary research talk, it helps to think of your audience as being composed of the smartest undergraduates you have encountered. It also helps to realize that such audiences generally care more about your findings and the external validity of your findings than they do about internal validity. Indeed, whereas you will have to work hard to make a general economics audience care about your work, a multidisciplinary audience will usually have selected to come to your talk because they care about the topic. They are unlikely to care, however, about the intricacies of your identification strategy, and compared to an audience of economists, they are more likely to trust that you know what you are doing. This does not mean that these details should be kept from them if they ask (for example, smart undergraduates can understand why a valid instrumental variable can yield causal identification when it is clearly explained to them). Ultimately, what matters to such an audience is how they can use your findings in their own work. In the best of cases, giving good multidisciplinary research talks can lead to opportunities to do interdisciplinary research, if that is something you are interested in doing.

Policy or Business Talks. Much like a multidisciplinary research audience member cares about how she can use your findings in her own research, an audience of policy makers or business decision-makers will care about how they can use what you tell them in their own work. The difference is that policy makers and business decision-makers will often be interested in more than what a single, necessarily narrow research paper does. Rather, they will be interested in the sum total of what your field has had to say about a specific problem they are grappling with. So if it helps to think about a multidisciplinary research audience as an audience of the smartest undergraduates you have encountered, it helps to think about a policy or business audience as your average group of undergraduates. Here, unless you have been asked to talk about a specific paper, stylized facts and broad descriptive statistics tend to be useful to your audience, as are specific stories and anecdotes conveying the points you want to make.

Outreach Talks. Every once in a while, you may be asked to do some outreach. Typically, this means giving a talk to non-academics about something you are more qualified to talk about than the average individual. This can take several forms: a talk at a government or international agency, a briefing to political staff, a testimony to lawmakers, a presentation to industry experts, or even a short presentation of what it is that you do for work at a local school. But outreach can also take on other forms, such as appearing on the radio or on television to comment on current events.

In most cases, outreach involves sharing your expertise with people who are likely to benefit from your doing so. What "sharing your expertise" means can vary wildly from one context to another. At one extreme, you might get paid a princely sum for presenting some descriptive statistics that are only somewhat related to your core research interests to industry experts.

In my experience, the one principle that ties all of these activities together is this: if you enjoy doing the kind of outreach you have been asked to do and would like to get asked again, be as clear as you can, and do not be sloppy.

When I write "be as clear as you can," understand that though you might get further in some corners of the economics profession by being arcane, simplicity and clarity are what you were asked to do outreach for. Can you take a complex concept or empirical finding and explain it to someone who has never taken an economics class? That is the level at which to pitch a lot of outreach activities.[7]

When I write "do not be sloppy," what I mean is that you should make sure that what you say is backed by rigorous research, and be mindful of the fact that in some cases, your words can have drastic consequences on someone else's welfare. To give one extreme example, in *Texas Beef Group v. Winfrey*, TV show host Oprah Winfrey and one of her guests were sued by beef producers under food libel laws (specifically, Texas' *False Disparagement of Perishable Food Products Act of 1995*) for linking the consumption of beef to mad cow disease after beef futures and beef prices fell significantly the day after they made those statements. So when I was asked by the *New York Times* to write an op-ed about my findings on farmers markets and foodborne illness, I hemmed and hawed for a moment while I double-, triple-, and quadruple-checked my data, code, and findings to make sure that what I was saying was backed by a rigorous analysis.[8] After that experience, a colleague who does a number of live media appearances (where it can be trickier to ensure that every claim you make is backed by rigorous research) recommended I get business insurance, which covers you in case you get sued for things you do that are work-related but not your work itself. Though that kind

---

7. In the case of media-type outreach, get in touch with your institution's public relations office if there is one, as those people will usually be able to help you translate your research into op-eds, send out news releases about your work, and coach you on how to be a more effective communicator on the radio or on television.

8. Luckily in this case, I found out from the *New York Times'* legal department that I was well clear of food libel, which requires that you point to a specific commodity to take effect.

of insurance may not be available in every country (if only because most countries are nowhere near as litigious as the US), if you plan on doing a lot of outreach or consulting, it may be wise to look into getting that kind of insurance, which costs about as much as a reasonably priced intercontinental flight.

3.7   Giving Keynotes

Eventually you may get to a point where you are prominent enough in the profession to get asked to give keynote addresses at conferences.

Because there will typically be only a handful of keynotes per conference, giving one is an honor, and it should be treated as such. In most cases, being asked to give a keynote means that the conference organizers will pay for your travel, food, and lodging during the conference, and that you may get an honorarium for your trouble.

Given the foregoing, it is only fair that, as keynote speaker, you give special attention to what you will be talking about in your keynote. The only thing worse than attending a "keynote" wherein the speaker uses the occasion to present their paper *du jour* is attending the same kind of presentation during a conference dinner, because in the latter case, the audience is captive.

So when you are asked to give a keynote address, think about *why* you were asked. In most cases, people will want to hear about much more than your latest paper. How do you see the field evolving over the next five to ten years? In which direction do you see a research agenda—not *your* research agenda, but *a* research agenda that includes yours—headed? If you were just starting to write your dissertation, what would you be investing in, or what would you be working on? What else would you do differently if you could go back to the start of your career? What are some of the big questions in your area of research you wish you had time to look into, and would like to see the answers to?

With prominence in the profession—especially with the kind of prominence that gets you invited to give keynote addresses—you must come to the realization that you have "arrived." Instead of pushing for one more peer-reviewed article, it is now your job to lift other people up.

3.8   Whether and How to Practice Your Talk

Should you practice giving a talk? On the one hand, it is always better to give a polished rather than an unpolished talk. On the other hand, there are only 24 hours in a day, and early-career researchers tend to both keep themselves busy in view of getting tenured or promoted and be kept busy, as early-career researchers also tend to start their careers around the time most people move in with a partner, get married, or have children.

The broad answer to whether you should practice your talk is "maybe," and the answer depends on several factors which you should weigh carefully. These factors include whether English is your first language, how effective a public speaker you are at baseline, how much time you have, and how important it is to you that you give a talk that is polished. If you were a member of the debate team in college or are a member of Toastmasters International, your baseline level of public speaking is probably pretty good, and so you likely need less practice than others. If your first language is not English, you will almost surely need more practice than a native speaker of English. Similarly, if English is not your first language, but you are asked to give a talk about your research in your native language, odds are you will need to make slides in your native language, or at the very least look up the English-to-your-native-language translations of words you may have learned only in English. For shorter talks (i.e., 20 minutes or fewer), one way to make sure not to go over is to practice your talk with a view to staying within the time limit. And finally, although I sincerely believe that if a job is worth doing, it should be done right, some talks are simply more important than others—at least in the short run. This means that job talks should probably be practiced more than other kinds of talks, given that a job offer may depend on your performance.

Practicing talks, however, can be a double-edged sword. For one, it is a good thing for a talk to be polished, but not to be *too* polished. One quirk of the economics profession is the sort of countersignaling wherein we tend to put a bit too much stock in appearances, to the point where between a speaker wearing a suit and tie and one wearing jeans and a Led Zeppelin t-shirt, *ceteris paribus*, the former will tend to be viewed with suspicion ("What is he compensating for by wearing a suit and tie?") and the latter with an endearing attitude reserved for eccentric geniuses. Similarly with over-polished talks, which can give people the impression that you do not value your time. This is admittedly a small concern, and one that is not first-order, but it is nevertheless a concern in highly competitive environments.

Should you choose to practice your talk, the best way to do that is in front of other researchers, perhaps in the context of a brown-bag with other graduate students or of a seminar at your own institution. Failing to do that, practicing in front of an imaginary audience (or an online audience consisting of colleagues who owe you a favor) will have to do.

Time yourself, either by using your phone's timer, or maybe even going so far as setting alarms at specific points (for instance by giving yourself five- and three-minute warnings). If you can record yourself practicing your talk, that can help you fix some of the things that might be annoying (most of us rely on verbal quirks and tics that we fail to notice in everyday conversation, and which can be really distracting).

3.9   How to Answer and Manage Audience Questions

Your first reaction may be to think "I don't need a book to teach me how to answer questions; I know how to do that." And in all likelihood, you have a good idea how to do it. But I have seen enough bad answers to audience questions by speakers at seminars and conferences that I thought this deserved its own section.

First off, you should always have a pen and some paper to note down your audience's questions and comments, both because it can be difficult to remember multi-part questions and because you may want to refer to those questions and comments when you update your work. And indeed, a speaker who is not noting down his audience's questions and comments at best looks like he is only there to add a line to his CV, and at worst come across as though he does not think any interesting question or comment will formulated by the members of this specific audience. Either way, it is not a good look.

Second, it should go without saying that whatever you do, you should remain respectful of your audience. You may be asked a question that you think is stupid, but the questioner may simply not have expressed herself clearly, or you may not have understood her question. In both cases, it helps to restate the question in your own words, and give the questioner a chance to either agree with your restatement or reformulate the question.

One thing which I have seen annoy audiences is some speakers' tendency to begin answering questions before those questions are finished and thus to speak over the questioner. You may have given your talk 20 times and be able to anticipate exactly where a question is going, but resist the temptation to start answer the question before it is over, both because no one likes getting interrupted, and because your questioner might decide to add on a second question at the end of that first one.

Third, a good thing to keep in mind when answering questions at seminars and conferences is that economics (and science in general) is a collective enterprise, and so this is meant to be a conversation. The seminar culture in economics tends to be more blunt (but not necessarily more adversarial) than in other disciplines, but only in rare cases are questions asked out of malice (though they certainly often arise out of a desire on the part of the questioner to impress their colleagues). In the vast majority of cases, questions are asked in earnest, out of a desire to either learn or understand something or to make the speaker's work better. Therefore, approaching the question-and-answer period as you would a conversation at happy hour about your work helps.

Finally, if you do not know the answer to a question, do not try to hide your ignorance. Just admit that you do not know, and speculate about how you might go about answering the question if given the time or the means to do so. If someone asks a question that is clearly beyond the scope of your work or that is too narrowly focused on the questioner's own interests, or if the questioner has already asked two or three questions, it is perfectly fine to tell them that the two of you should chat after the seminar, either in person or by email.

4

Navigating Peer Review

After writing up your paper and presenting it to diverse audiences at invited seminars and conferences, the time has come to submit it for publication. In economics, journal articles—not books, not chapters in edited volumes, not peer-reviewed abstracts in conference proceedings, and certainly not op-eds or blog posts, but *articles in peer-reviewed journals*—are the coin of the realm. This means that a research economist's professional reputation primarily depends on a combination of the quality and the quantity of the peer-reviewed articles she has published.

But unless you grew up in a family of academics, odds are you are not familiar with how to navigate the peer-review process before you submit your first article for publication. This chapter aims to serve as a guide for the perplexed when it comes to the peer-review process—and it certainly can be perplexing to deal with such a unique process early on in one's career.

4.1 Why the Peer-Review Process?

Before anything else, it is certainly worth asking: Why has much of modern day academia—or, at the very least, those academic disciplines that aim to be scientific—settled on the peer-review process? Why does the fate of our work have to be at the mercy of a handful of peer reviewers who often rely on the veil of anonymity to make obnoxious remarks? And indeed, every once in a while, I see discussions on social media of how the peer-review system is "broken." But just as often as I see the word "broken" used in the economics of food systems—one of my areas of research—to mean "generating outcomes that I do not like," I suspect that a lot of the claims that the peer-review system is "broken" are made by well-meaning individuals whose work has recently been rejected—perhaps unfairly or unjustifiably so.

One of Winston Churchill's famous quips is "democracy is the worst form of government except for all those other forms that have been tried from time to time." And so it is with the peer-review process. It is not a perfect system. It can take a very long time to hear back from a journal after submitting. The reviewers may not have read your work very carefully, even after you gave them every reason to do so. The editor might not have read their reviews very closely or at all, or she might not have read your paper very closely. Ultimately, however, peer review has been adopted by all the scientific disciplines and by all the journals within those disciplines without any effort at coordination within or across disciplines for one reason: because however imperfect, peer review works better than the alternatives.

A simple example can illustrate my point. At a conference in 2012, I took part in a small-group dinner in which the editor of a top journal in my field also took part. Having recently seen a discussion on social media about the peer-review process, I suggested to the editor that we should put an end to the anonymity of the peer-review process. He responded by asking me "Would you be willing to write a fair but critical review of a paper written by a senior member of the profession and recommend that it be rejected? How about the same for a paper written by a senior scholar from whom a letter might be solicited to evaluate your case when you go up for tenure?" Similar arguments against other would-be "improvements" to the peer-review process can be made. At the end of the day, the peer-review process is also like democracy in one other way: You might not like it. You might not like the outcome of it. But you knew the rules when you decided to play, and the system is unlikely to change in your lifetime.

That said, by and large, the peer-review process does lead to better scholarship. Though we all sooner or later have to deal with grumpy reviewers, most reviewer comments lead to better manuscripts in my experience, both as an author having published over three dozen peer-reviewed articles and as an editor having solicited reviews for hundreds of manuscripts. In recent years, the term "gatekeeping" has acquired a bad reputation due to its use in reference to some people appointing themselves as arbiters of who does or does not belong in a given hobby community, and I have seen that term thrown around on social media by academics complaining about reviews they disagreed with. But academic research is no hobby (at least not unless you are fortunate enough to be independently wealthy) and so gatekeeping in the form of peer review is a necessity. This is especially so in a discipline like economics, wherein research findings may end up informing public policy, thereby affecting the welfare of individuals who, more often than not, are from vulnerable populations.

4.2   When to Submit?

As I noted above, after writing up your paper and presenting it to diverse audiences, the time has come for you to submit it for publication. How do you know *when* the time has come? There is an optimal time at which to submit your work for publication—the time where the marginal cost of polishing starts exceeding the marginal benefit of doing so—and that time depends on a variety of factors related to the work itself, where you are in your career, when in the academic year you submit, how many other people might be working on similar ideas, and where you want to submit.

The work itself. You should submit your work when it is ready. When is that? One thing I was told in graduate school was that your paper is ready to be submitted for publication when you keep hearing the same comments about it when presenting it, or in conversations with colleagues about it. That advice, however, is somewhat incomplete. For instance, you may have a paper whose way of measuring the outcome of interest is deeply flawed, which means you are likely to hear over and over when presenting that your outcome of interest is not measured well. If there exists a way to fix that problem, this does not mean that your paper is ready to be submitted! So perhaps a more useful statement is:

> Your paper is ready to be submitted for publication when you keep hearing the same comments about it when presenting, or in conversations with colleagues about it, and those comments are about things you cannot do anything about except acknowledge them in the paper.

If you have a chance to present your work widely, at a number of seminars and conferences, you should do so. It is very helpful to take a paper on the road for a while before submitting it for publication, both because this means you may receive comments that will help make your work better, and because this means your would-be reviewers may have had a chance to see it—and ask their questions about it.

Where you are in your career. The earlier it is before a big deadline where your publications will matter (in the US, there are three such times, typically: when you go on the job market, when you go up for tenure, and when you go up for promotion), the more you can afford to wait and perfect the work. One important thing to bear in mind when considering how long to wait before submitting is that the time between submission and acceptance can take anywhere between one and five years, depending on where you are submitting. The best-case scenario is one where the first decision on your paper is conditionally accepted or accepted with minor revisions after a first round of review, and where the review process is quick (i.e., fewer than three months elapse between the moment you submit and the moment you get a decision on your submission).[1] Generally, however, if your department has its PhD students write a second- or third-year qualifying research paper, you should submit it for publication with the hope of having a publication before going on the job market. Likewise, you should aim to have your job-market paper submitted before you start teaching when starting in a tenure-track position—if anything follows Parkinson's Law ("Work expands to fill the time available for its completion"), it is teaching.

When you choose to submit in the academic year. One thing many researchers are unaware of is that journal submissions are not uniformly distributed throughout the year. Most academic economists tend to "finish" articles in the few weeks after classes end (between late April and early June in the US), in the few days before their semester starts (between mid-August and mid-September in the US), and over the winter holidays (between mid-December and mid-January in the US). But those are also the times when editors and reviewers are most likely to be on vacation or taking time off to be with family (at least in late summer–early fall and over the winter holidays), which may lead you to conclude that the review process is slower than it actually is.

Where you submit. Although where you should submit your work is the topic of the next section, where you submit will affect when you should submit. Typically, the higher-ranked the journal you are aiming for within economics, the longer a successful process will take. As a senior colleague put it to me when I started on the tenure track, "getting a paper published in a top-five journal is a five-year process." General-science journals like *Nature*, *PNAS*, or *Science* tend to have a very short review process (i.e., at most two months on average) relative to economics journals. There

---

1. Even after doing this job for almost 15 years, I have never experienced such a lucky event, and after handling roughly 1500 articles at two journals, my recollection is that I have only accepted one article after the first round of review.

are also journals (such as *Economic Inquiry*) that offer the opportunity to submit under an "up or out" system, where the first decision will either be an acceptance (perhaps with minor revisions) or a rejection. Bear in mind, however, that journals that have a fast-track, up-or-out submission track in no way lower their quality threshold for papers submitted on that fast track.

4.3   Where to Submit?

I have already briefly discussed in chapter 2 the difference between writing for a field journal versus writing for a general journal. This section is about where you should consider submitting a paper in general: should you go for an economics journal, and interdisciplinary journal, or a general scientific journal? If you go for an economics journal, should you submit to a general or field journal? How should journal rankings figure in your decision?

Before anything, I want to convey one important thing as clearly as possible: never, ever submit to predatory journals. Generally, a predatory journal is a journal that will publish (just about) anything in exchange for money.[2] A journal that does that is called predatory because it preys on unsuspecting authors who need to publish to get tenure, be promoted, and so on.[3] But tenure and promotion committees tend

---

2. See, for instance, Mazières and Kohler (2005). The authors having had enough of receiving solicitations from the *International Journal of Advanced Computer Technology*, they submitted a paper titled "Get Me Off Your Fucking Mailing List" to it. The paper, which consists of nothing but the title phrase repeated over and over for 10 pages, was accepted and subsequently published by that journal. See Stromberg (2014) for the broader story behind Mazières and Kohler's paper, as well as for other examples.

3. Do not confuse journals that have author processing charges (APCs) with predatory journals. On the one hand, some legitimate journals, like *PNAS*, will charge authors for the costs of processing and producing an article if and only if that article makes it through their review process. On the other hand, predatory journals will publish just about any article for a fee. You can usually tell whether a journal is legitimate or predatory by looking at whether it is indexed on RepEc or EconLit or other bibliographic databases, whether it has an impact factor (or other measures of impact), or whether the authors who publish in it are people whose names you recognize from having read their work in legitimate journals. You can also ask your advisors or your more experienced colleagues what they think of a given journal. When in doubt, it is best to err on the side of caution, and assume that a journal is predatory.

to be composed of people who know a predatory journal when they see one.[4]

Generally speaking, you should approach journals like Groucho Marx resigning from the Friars' Club: "I don't want to belong to any club that would accept me as one of its members." Likewise, most journals (or presses, or conferences) that write to you soliciting your work should be viewed with suspicion. In the vast majority of cases, that will be a predatory journal (or press, or conference). In a small minority of cases, you may receive a legitimate request to contribute one of your articles a special issue of a well-known peer-reviewed journal in your field, or an inquiry from an editor at a reputable press asking whether you are thinking of writing a book. But when that happens, you will usually receive the solicitation of your work from a guest editor for that special issue who will be a leading scholar in your field whom you have almost surely heard of, if not someone you know personally.

So much for those journals you should not submit to. When it comes to choosing from among journals you should submit to, you should keep in mind the fact that any publication adds value to your CV in two ways. First, it determines your odds of getting tenured, promoted, getting an endowed chair, and so on within your own institution. Second, it also determines your reservation wage by affecting the type of job you could hope for if you were to go on the market. When considering the latter, a good rule of thumb is to aim to publish in the best possible journals in the eyes of those who will be looking to hire when you go on the market. When considering the former, you should aim to publish in the best possible journals in the eyes of those who will be evaluating you for tenure, promotion, and so on. The two sets of individuals will never completely overlap, and it may well be the case that your internal incentives (i.e., the incentives you face within your institution) differ from your external incentives (i.e., the incentives you face on the market at large).

Although external incentives tend to be much too varied and depend on too many factors to be discussed here usefully, when it comes to your internal incentives, ask your department and college whether they have a

---

4. If you are not sure, though a simple search-engine search will typically yield the results you want, you should also consult with your advisors or more experienced colleagues. There are also a few online resources dedicated to helping researchers avoid falling prey to predatory journals; as of this writing, Beall's List of Potential Predatory Journals and Publishers (http://beallslist.net) is the best-known such resource.

specific list of journals or a journal ranking they use for tenure and promotion. While such lists are not common at R1 institutions, they are very common at doctoral/professional universities and at liberal arts colleges.[5] This is because many of those departments are smaller, and so they do not have multiple people in one field who are able to vouch for the quality of a given journal, and where most of the time, people are not publishing in top field or top general journals. As a result, the department or school builds its list of journals to target from various sources (e.g., Scimago, RepEc, Web of Science).

4.3.1   Economics Journals versus Other Journals

The first question you should ask yourself is whether you should submit to an economics journal (e.g., the *American Economic Review*, *Econometrica*, the *Journal of Public Economics*), an interdisciplinary journal (e.g., *World Development*, *Global Environmental Change*, *Health Services Research*), or a general scientific journal (e.g., *Nature*, *PNAS*, *Science*).

Ideally, you should choose the broad category of journal—economics, interdisciplinary, or general scientific—you want to submit to before you start writing your manuscript, because these different categories aim to appeal to different readerships, which means that your article will have to be written differently for these different readerships. Chapter 2 explained how to do so.

Which of these three broad categories to submit to will depend on your paper itself, on your preferences and what you value, as well as on factors external to you. In terms of preferences, what kind of scholar do you want to be? Do you aim to speak to a smaller group of people who are highly respected experts in your field or in economics? Then go for an economics journal. Do you aim to speak to a broader audience of social scientists who work on a set of related policy issues (e.g., climate change, health care, international development)? Then go for an interdisciplinary journal. Or do you aim to speak to the broadest possible audience— social scientists *and* natural scientists—working on those policy issues? Then go for a general scientific journal.

---

5. I will return to this classification in chapter 5, but for our purposes, this follows the Carnegie Classification of Institutions of Higher Education. According to that classification, there are R1 universities (doctoral universities with very high research activity), R2 universities (doctoral universities with high research activity), D/PU universities (doctoral/professional universities), and so on. See https://carnegieclassifications.iu.edu/ for a complete classification.

Not every paper has the potential to be submitted to all three categories, no matter how much rewriting you do. General scientific journals will tend to want clear connections to questions of broad scientific interest, and they tend to value linkages to scientific debates and external validity much more than they do internal validity. Thus, a paper that most applied microeconomists would deem unacceptable (say, a paper that relies rather mechanically on fixed effects to "deal with endogeneity") but which uses satellite data on all cultivated plots in the world to look at soil degradation has a much better chance of being interesting to *Science* than the results of an RCT on water quality in 50 communities in Lesotho.

Relatedly, if you want to maximize the expected number of citations to your article you should favor, in order, general scientific journals, interdisciplinary journals, and then economics journals. For all of the cult-like veneration of the top five economics journals within economics, those journals tend to have low impact factors relative to interdisciplinary journals and general scientific journals.[6] For instance, in development economics and policy in 2019, the *Journal of Development Economics* had an impact factor of 2.649, but *World Development* had an impact factor of 4.410, *PNAS* had an impact factor of 10.620, and *Science* had an impact factor of 41.845.

The expected number of citations to your work is a factor that is both internal to you—you may or may not value citations—as well as external to you—as I have already mentioned, people from other disciplines (including those at the college and university levels, who will make recommendations about whether you should get tenure or be promoted) are familiar with impact factors, but they are almost surely unfamiliar with the subtle difference between an article in the *Journal of Monetary Economics* and the *Journal of Money, Credit and Banking*.

The other external considerations to keep in mind are what kind of job you want to go for (if you are submitting as a graduate student),

---

6. Unless otherwise noted, I refer to a journal's simple impact factor when I write "impact factor." A journal's simple impact factor is the number of citations to articles in that journal in the Clarivate/Web of Science Journal Citation Reports during a given year divided by the number of articles published by that journal over the previous two years. As with any performance measure, a simple impact factor is not perfect. It is nonetheless a proxy for a scholar's impact that is widely used across all scientific disciplines, and thus favored by college- and university-level tenure and promotion committees.

and what your colleagues and the people in your area of research and in your field (who will be called upon write your external review letters for promotion and tenure) value. Graduate students should probably stick to economics journals, since those are the journals they are trained to read articles in (and, in some cases, write for). If you already have a job but do not have tenure, then your goal is to please your colleagues and your letter writers. If you are in an economics department, this very likely means that you should submit to economics journals. If you are in a multidisciplinary outfit (e.g., a business or policy school), then do your best to find out what your colleagues value and what kind of scholar they are likely to solicit external review letters from, and adjust your strategy based on the preferences of those two non-overlapping sets of scholars.[7] Finally, if you have yet to go up for promotion to full professor, you are generally free to choose your path, which can be anything from doing more of the same things that got you tenure in the first place to aiming for more interdisciplinary or general scientific scholarship, and even to writing books.

One unspoken rule you should know about when submitting to journals within economics is this: economists prize efficiency, which means that beyond enforcing page limits, instead of having authors waste their time formatting their manuscripts to some arbitrary (and often borderline unreasonable) specifications, journals are willing to wait until a journal is conditionally accepted before having the authors go through the rigmarole of properly formatting their article to the journal's specifications. If you are just starting out, this is good to know, because time is of the essence, and you are unlikely to have an afternoon to waste on properly formatting your article. The rule of thumb is that if your paper looks like a working paper as laid out in chapter 2 and you do not go beyond the journal's page limit for submitted articles, you are unlikely to be told to go format your paper per the journal's specifications before it gets sent out for review.

With that said, one of the anonymous reviewers who reviewed the proposal for this book noted that they had recently spoken with a professor at a top-five department who had told them that in practice, the appearance and aesthetics of a paper are often influential in determining

---

7. Another strategy in such cases, if it is available to you, is to look at the research portfolio someone who has gotten tenure in your school or department in the last two or three years.

which papers get read, which candidates are invited to interview, which submissions get past the desk rejection threshold, and so on. There are best practices for making figures, tables, and slides. You may think of these things as minor details. That is entirely your prerogative, but if this is even remotely true, it is well worth working hard to ensure that the look of your paper conforms to what you see in working papers by the best and the brightest.

4.3.2   General versus Field Journals

In most cases, you will have chosen to submit to an economics journal, so the question will be: Should you submit to a general journal (e.g., the *American Economic Review*) or to a field journal (e.g., the *Journal of Health Economics*)? Again, the decision will depend on several factors.

First off, how much time do you have ahead of you? If you have just started in a tenure-track job and you have anywhere from four to six years before you have to apply for tenure, you have enough time to submit to one, maybe two, maybe even three general economics journals before submitting to a field journal where your paper is considerably more likely to be accepted. But please do not let my use of "considerably more likely" fool you: the acceptance rate at top general economics journals was between 2.5 and 5 percent in 2017, down from between 12 and 24 percent in 1980 (Card and Della Vigna 2018). In a recent Twitter thread, *American Economic Journal: Applied Economics* editor David Deming reported that his acceptance rate since he had started as co-editor had been 4 percent. Field journals are better in relative but not necessarily absolute terms: in development economics, one of the fields I am familiar with, the acceptance rate at the top journal—the *Journal of Development Economics*—was 6 percent in 2016, 5.3 percent in 2017, and 8.3 percent in 2018. At the *American Journal of Agricultural Economics*, the acceptance rate was 10.8 percent in 2019 and 10.2 percent in 2020. All of this to say that even in the best-case scenario, your paper faces difficult odds, and it is best to gird your loins for what is a long process—this is not a profession for those who want instant gratification.

Second, there is the question of what your colleagues (who may or may not know your field, but who will still be voting on whether you should be getting tenure or be promoted) and external letter writers (who know your field very well, and will be weighing in on whether you should be getting tenured or be promoted from outside your institution) will want to see. The closer you get to being at a top department, the more your colleagues will expect you to publish in top-five journals—and probably more than once. In case you are not told exactly what is expected of you by the time you go up for tenure or promotion, the best way to find out what your colleagues will expect is to ask your department chair and your senior colleagues. Only in some rare cases will you get a clear answer, because fuzzy incentives ("You need to publish well enough") tend to foster higher effort than bright-line ("You need at least one article in a top-five journal and four or five more articles in top field journals") incentives.

Third, is your paper of sufficiently general interest? It can be particularly difficult to answer that question if you are an early-career researcher. After all, you would probably not have spent all that time on your paper if you did not think it was of general enough interest. And yet, to paraphrase scriptures, it is almost easier for a camel to get through the eye of a needle than it is for a paper to make successfully through peer-review at top general journals. Recall what I mentioned about acceptance rates at those journals a few paragraphs earlier; that, combined with the fact that good referees are hard to find and thus over-committed, means that editors will typically be looking for a reason to desk-reject your manuscript, and "not general enough" is often it.

I do not yet have a top-five publication, but what I have reliably been told by a close colleague who has a friend who is editor of a top journal is that the following rule is used by some editors at top general journals to determine whether a paper is of general enough interest. When they receive a paper, those editors look at the list of references. If there are too many references to field journals, they desk-reject, telling the author their paper is not of general enough interest, and to send it to a field journal. This is second-hand information, so I cannot be sure that it is true, but looking at lists of references for the papers published in top journals on topics I am familiar with, I have no trouble believing that this rule of thumb for knowing whether a paper is of general enough interest is widespread among the editors of top general journals. And though you may think that this is not a good way to determine what counts as general interest or not, an ounce of prevention is worth a pound of cure.

One unspoken fact of life in the economics profession is that if you want to publish in top journals, it significantly helps to be "in the club," meaning that it helps to have attended a top PhD program, to have been invited to be a member of the NBER, to be on first-name basis with the movers and shakers at the very top of your field—that is, those economists at top-20 departments who actively publish in your field—and to have presented your work to them at the right conferences.[8] As I mentioned in the previous chapter, it really helps if your reviewers have seen you present your paper at a conference or seminar, because that will have given them a chance to ask their questions, and they will therefore trust your results more.

4.3.3 General-Science Journals

Publishing in general-science journals is not easy. Though some economists often imply that it is easier to publish in general-science than in economics journals, this is misleading.

Most general-science journals are much more punctilious about formatting, the length of your paper, its structure, and so on than economics journals. Often at general-science journals, before an editor even looks at your paper, it has to satisfy the journal's formatting guidelines. This is not a cause for rejection, but it will slow down the entire process. A colleague recently submitted a paper to PNAS as a brief report, which allows no more than three pages in typeset format. He exceeded that limit by one line, and the journal sent the manuscript back to him asking that he fix the problem before assigning it to an editor.

It is common to send pre-submission inquiries to general-science journals. In other words, unlike at economics journals, it is often acceptable to write an email to an editor to ask whether they would be interested in seeing your paper. Keep those brief and polite.

At general-science journals, cover letters actually matter. In economics, it is often the case that you will not have to submit a cover letter unless you want to. For general-science journals, however, the cover letter is not just a formality. In most instances, an editor's decision of whether to send a paper out for review or not is made on the basis of reading the cover letter. Make that letter at most two pages long. In addition to briefly summarizing the paper, explain its contribution and why the paper is timely and of broad interest to the scientific community, and not just to economists.

At many general-science journals, you will be able to suggest (if not select) who you would like as editor. Select your editors carefully. Most general-science journals have large editorial boards, which means picking your section (e.g., behavioral science, sustainability science) is important,

---

8. See Kleemans and Thornton (2021) for evidence on the determinants of NBER membership.

as is selecting an editor within that section. A mismatch here likely means your paper will get desk rejected.

4.4   What to Prepare Before Submitting

Having chosen where to submit and having prepared your manuscript in view of submitting it there, what else do you need to prepare before submitting? Unfortunately, there are as about as many precise answers to that question as there are journals in existence, and even journals in the same discipline that fall under the same publisher may request different things from prospective authors. What follows is a nonexhaustive list of all the things you may be requested to submit, and what they typically entail, beyond the paper itself and its various appendices.

Cover Letter. Not all journals require a cover letter. Some journals will have a box in which you can write specific comments to the editor if they are required or if you have them, and where you can direct the editor's attention to the important stuff (e.g., "The data we use is proprietary, and we cannot share it beyond descriptive statistics"). Generally, however, cover letters for economics journals are best kept short: "Dear colleagues, I am delighted to submit our paper titled [title] for publication in [journal]. My coauthors and I wish to confirm that this paper is not concurrently being submitted anywhere else, and that it consists entirely of original work. Sincerely, [Author]." A cover letter is not the place for you to restate your paper's findings, to explain why it is important, or to note that it has already received media coverage. At most, you can note some specific things you want the managing editor to know about (e.g., "This is a resubmitted version of a paper which [editor] had previously rejected, but which she said she wanted to see a thoroughly revised version of under a reject-and-resubmit"), but nothing more.

Title Page. Many journals—those that retain a double-blind reviewing policy[9]—will ask for a separate title page. This should include your

---

9. "Double-blind" here refers to those cases where the reviewers are anonymous to the authors, and the authors are in principle anonymous to the reviewers— "in principle" because the working-paper culture of economics, combined with search engines, means that it is generally easy to figure out who wrote what. "Single-blind" refers to those cases where the reviewers are anonymous to the authors, but the reviewers know who the authors are. On the basis of experimental evidence, Tomkins et al. (2017) show that single-blind reviewing disadvantages authors who are not famous or who do not work at prestigious institutions.

paper's title, the names and affiliations of the authors, the abstract, as well as an acknowledgments footnote where you thank your sources of funding, and colleagues who have actually taken the time to read your paper and comment on it,[10]

Manuscript. This is self-explanatory. Whether you should include the title page or leave it out altogether will be specified on the journal website. A useful tip: in cases where you are asked to submit your manuscript without the title page, include the title and abstract on the first page of your manuscript, just before the introduction begins. This is because you want to make sure the reviewers actually see your abstract. If your abstract only shows up on the title page and the journal has a double-blind policy, you run the risk that the reviewers will not know what to expect going into your paper. As discussed in chapter 2, managing the editor's and the reviewers' expectations is key in getting your work published. One more thing I would encourage you to do: if you have appendix materials, include them here, in the same document as the manuscript, even if the journal's editorial system has a separate slot to upload your appendices as well. I have seen cases where appendices were not sent to reviewers, and where the reviewers got annoyed about that fact and did not think of asking the editor whether those materials were available, and recommended a rejection. It is much better for you that the reviewers get your appendix twice than they do not get it at all. The same goes for pre-analysis plans and other ancillary materials.

Appendices. Anything you want your reviewers to see but which you do not feel is directly of interest to the more general reader should go in here. Do not feel like (or worse, state that) anything should be left out "in the interest of brevity," or "omitted but available from the authors." Your appendix is where you can stretch your wings and show all of the work you can show in making your case for your results. As far as etiquette

---

10. Here, it might be tempting to thank your significant other or family members, as they have almost surely supported morally or financially while you were working on your paper. It is customary, however, not to do so. Similarly, you may have discussed your paper for a few minutes with a famous economist when she visited your department, or with a Nobel laureate at a conference. Unless those people have made game-changing comments—the kind of comment that profoundly changes your work—refrain from wanting to be seen as associating with the good and the great by thanking them. The fact that you once discussed your paper with Paul Krugman will not make your paper more likely to be sent out for review or accepted for publication. If anything, it may even set unreasonably high expectations about it.

goes, do not include output from the software you use, both because those can be difficult to read—your reviewers will not have the patience to figure out what var3 refers to, or they may simply not be familiar with the specific software you are using—and because it is simple courtesy to provide the reviewers with tables that are easy to interpret. But you can include experimental protocols, pre-analysis plans, and so on here.

Disclosures. Thanks in part to the Great Recession, which highlighted that some economists making policy recommendations also had major conflicts of interest (Berrett 2012), many leading journals—certainly all of the of the AEA journals—now require that authors fill out a disclosure form before their paper can be sent out for review. Because some of the findings published in economics journals directly influence policy, the aim of requiring these disclosures is simply to reduce the likelihood of conflicts of interest. If you do not have any conflict of interest, you still need to fill out a disclosure form, but doing so is relatively simple. If you do have a conflict of interest, fill the disclosure form truthfully to avoid problems down the road.

Code and Data. After emphasizing the internal validity of economic findings, the Credibility Revolution of the early 2000s (Angrist and Pischke 2010) has more recently led to an emphasis on transparency and replicability in the interest of credibility (Christensen and Miguel 2018). Some journals now require that you turn in your code and data when submitting an empirical article for publication, and we can reasonably expect that more and more journals will require that you do so. Entire guides have been written about how to properly prepare replication files (among the earliest such guides, see King 1995), and the AEA has resources on its website regarding how to prepare replication materials (American Economic Association 2020). Another useful resource is the entire portion of the International Initiative for Impact Evaluation (better known as 3ie) website dedicated to replication (International Initiative for Impact Evaluation 2020). Ideally, you should include what is necessary for a reader to conduct a "push-button" replication of your paper. That is, to run your code with your data and reproduce each table and figure in your paper and its appendix in order.

Highlights. Some journals require authors to also submit highlights of their article. Those are a series of three to five bullet points that explain what your article does, with each bullet kept short.[11] A good list of

---

11. As of writing, only Elsevier journals require highlights, and they require that each bullet be 85 characters or less, including spaces.

highlights mentions at least three things: (i) what the research question is, (ii) how it is answered (i.e., using which data and method), and (iii) what the core finding is. After spending years working on an article by refining its arguments and polishing the empirical work it contains, it can be very frustrating to have to boil down your paper to a list of bullet points, especially since those highlights are only ever prepared by authors when they have to, namely when submitting. As such, it may be tempting to cut corners. Resist that temptation and approach these highlights thoughtfully, both because some busy readers (e.g., journalists looking for new research findings to write about, other researchers conducting a review of the literature) might only look at your highlights, and because those highlights are used by search engines to link to your article in response to certain keyword searches.

Other Materials. It is impossible for a list such as this one to cover all the possible idiosyncratic things some journals will require. The more you stray from economics (i.e., general and field) journals to go toward policy journals, interdisciplinary journals, and journals outside of economics, however, the more likely you are to be asked for things not covered in this list. For instance, I was once asked for a tweet-length summary of one of my papers for a journal's social media account, and many journals now encourage authors to submit a graphical abstract—a figure summarizing the paper—if possible.

4.5   How to Maximize Your Chances of Getting Good Reviews

For better or for worse, economists have a reputation in academia for being particularly unkind to one another and uncaring of one another's feelings. Part of that is certainly the byproduct of good intentions: as a profession, we value stating things as clearly as possible. But part of it comes from a less well-intended place, as we have all witnessed the back-in-my-day-we-suffered-through-x-and-it-only-made-us-better attitude of some senior scholars, according to which because they had to face certain hardships, others should, too. Also, part of economists' reputation as being unkind and uncaring almost surely comes from more toxic traits, though whether that is the result of selection into the profession or the result of acculturation into it is anybody's guess, given the reflection problem (Manski 1993). The end result, however, is that a lot of the tone used by economists when commenting on each other's work can be off-putting to someone outside the economics profession, to someone new to it, or even to those of us who have simply grown to accept it as a common (but still discouraging) practice.

Imagine, then, what happens to that (seemingly) unkind and uncaring tone when an interaction not only does not take place face to face, but is also anonymous—and often only anonymous in one direction!

Given the nature of the economics profession as characterized above, there are two things you can do. The first is to brace yourself for reviews which at best might willingly (if not willfully) misunderstand the arguments in your paper, and at worst be insulting and contain personal attacks.

So how can you maximize your chances of getting good reviews, or at least minimize your chances of getting bad reviews? Having served as editor at two field journals, I can offer some insight. From what I have seen, you should generally try to avoid the following situations:

Submitting to a journal that has not published on the topic of your manuscript in more than five years. One thing you should be aware of is that once they decide to send your manuscript out for review, most editors will begin their search for reviewers for your manuscript by looking at your bibliography.

Specifically, they will look at whether (i) you cite their journal and related journals, and (ii) you cite articles published recently in those journals. For instance, if you submit to the *Journal of Econometrics* in 2020, they will likely look to see whether you cite articles in the *Journal of Econometrics*, but also possibly the *Journal of Business & Economics Statistics*, the *Econometrics Journal*, *Quantitative Economics*, and so forth, published between 2015 and 2020. Why? Because this allows the editor to draw up a list of would-be reviewers by looking at who has recently published on your topic (and thus remains interested in that topic, and has not moved on from it) in similar journals (and are thus willing to review for the journal you are submitting to), or at the very least who has published on closely related topics, and can thus provide knowledgeable comments on your paper.

Pain is the best teacher, so it is perhaps more useful to illustrate what happens when you fail to follow that advice. When I am assigned a manuscript on a topic which the journal I edit (or related journals) has not published in five years, I immediately ask myself two things. The first is "Is this a topic that is no longer at the frontier of research?," in which case I take a careful look at how the authors justify revisiting that "old" topic. In some cases, they have a good story for why they do so in that they bring a serious innovation to the table. But in many cases they do not, and this makes me likely to desk-reject the manuscript. The second thing I ask myself is "Who, among those who have worked on this topic in the past and have published in this and related journals, is likely to still want to review manuscripts on this topic?" Though it may be hard for an early-career researcher who has spent all of their time in the economics profession working on one topic to believe it, most senior scholars' research agendas have had more than one phase, and once they are done with a given topic, they may not want to see another paper on it ever again. And when they do agree to review on their "old" topic, they may not be familiar with current methods.

As an editor, when I receive a manuscript (i) on a topic on which we have not published in five years or more, (ii) that does not cite our journal or related journals, or (iii) both, if I choose to send the manuscript out for review, I then have to draw up a list of would-be reviewers by keyword search. In other words, I may have to choose reviewers going by your keywords, or by your article's *Journal of Economic Literature (JEL)* codes, which means that I then end up with reviewers who are only sort of, kind of, maybe qualified to review your article. This is exactly who you do not want as reviewers, because the further away a reviewer is from your topic, the more likely they are to misunderstand what you are doing, fail to see the point, want you to write an entirely different paper than the one you submitted, or feel like they are wasting their time reading something they are not a priori interested in—and thus to be negatively inclined toward your manuscript, and recommend a rejection after writing a review that is not very useful.

To ensure that you get the right reviewers, then, make sure that you submit to a journal that has recently published on the topic you are working on (or that related journals have), and make sure that you cite those relevant articles in those relevant (and related) journals.

Citing only famous economists. This is related to the previous point. If your manuscript cites only famous economists, and if editors start making a list of would-be reviewers for your manuscripts by taking a glance at whose work you cite, this is a surefire way to maximize your chances of getting reviews written by referees found by a keyword search.

I realize that citing only famous economists might make you feel like your paper is in the same league as those famous economists' papers, but one thing you have to understand is that often, like referees like. In other words, if you are an early-career researcher, odds are your paper is getting reviewed by early-career researchers, and if you are a very senior researcher, odds are your paper is getting reviewed by very senior researchers. This means that even if you submit your paper to a top-five journal, your citing leading economists still does not mean that your paper is going to get reviewed by those leading economists. The bottom line is that although you certainly should cite famous economists wherever appropriate, you should aim to cite those economists who (i) have worked on topics similar or close to your topic, and (ii) are likely to referee for the journal you are submitting to. Only you can answer who fits the bill for (i). As for (ii), a good rule of thumb is whether those would-be reviewers have published in the journal you are targeting.

Strategically avoiding citing certain people. The findings in your paper might run counter to the priors (or worse, the ideology) of some of the people doing the gatekeeping in your field. Or you may have a personal conflict with someone in your field. One unfortunate feature of the peer-review process—especially in economics, where single-blind reviewing has become the norm at top journals—is that it involves human beings, and thus human frailties. This means that if you step on the toes of someone who is more senior than you, and whose ego is invested in a particular qualitative finding (e.g., "School vouchers are bad"), you will predictably want to avoid having them (or their cronies) as reviewers, which makes it tempting to avoid citing their work. Avoid that temptation as much as possible. While drawing those people as reviewers is certainly not ideal, a worse outcome occurs when you get caught strategically citing the literature, which is at best interpreted as you not knowing what you are doing and at worst as you trying to obscure some part of the literature. The only right way to act here is to cite honestly, and use your writing skills to simultaneously signal to the editor (who makes the final decision, and can often see through people's biases when given a reason to do so) that you are stepping on some toes and to soften the blow of your findings to your reviewer's ego.

Here is an example. I once wrote a paper looking at the relationship between farmers markets (number of farmers markets per capita in a given state) and food-borne illness (aggregate number of outbreaks and cases of food-borne illness per capita in a given state, and then the same broken down by types of illness). The identification was obviously not up to randomization standards, but it was pretty good, and we even supplemented our core identification strategy (state fixed effects with a battery of means of accounting for time: year fixed effects, linear time trends, state-specific linear time trends, census region–year fixed effects, and coarsely controlling for violations of the stable unit treatment value assumption) with a weather shock-based instrumental variable. No matter which way we approached the data, we kept finding the same thing: there was a positive relationship between farmers markets and food-borne illness.

But we also kept running afoul of one specific reviewer who hated our finding because that reviewer was invested in the goodness of farmers markets, to a point where they simultaneously told us, in the same referee report, that (i) our results were likely spurious, and that (ii) we were looking at "too many" outcomes because we disaggregated. We resolved that problem in our cover letter, by telling the editor that the reviewer was at best not being earnest and at worst a crank when we wrote:

> So we are in a *Catch-22*: If we hadn't conducted a disaggregated analysis by illness, we would have been told that our findings are likely to be spurious. Now that we do conduct such a disaggregated analysis, we are exposing ourselves to the "multiple hypothesis tests" criticism. This really makes us wonder whether anything we do or say will satisfy [that reviewer].

Ultimately, the editor saw through the reviewer's bias, and decided to accept our manuscript for publication. Though you should not write as candidly in a manuscript as we did in our cover letter, it is still possible to write your introduction in such a way as to communicate to the editor (and the other reviewers) that your work, though it may contradict someone else's pet findings, is worthy of publication.

4.6   When to Propose Reviewers and Associated Conflicts of Interest

Some journals will allow you to suggest the names of a few reviewers whom you think would do a good job reviewing your paper, and some journals will even allow you to list the names of scholars whom you would rather not have as reviewers. This is a practice that is mainly found outside of economics, but some economics journals have adopted it.[12]

Here, it is obviously tempting to list friends, advisors, and coauthors in the "wanted" category, and it is just as tempting to list scholars whose findings yours go against, or with whom you've had personal conflicts in the "unwanted" category, because you may think that the former will be especially kind to your paper and the latter will be especially unkind to it. While there is nothing fundamentally wrong with letting the editor know who you would rather not have as a reviewer, it is more ethically fraught to list advisors, friends, and coauthors as would-be reviewers. First off, ideally, the peer-review system relies on the opinions of peer researchers who are not invested in your research getting published or in your being

---

12. For instance, in economics, the *Journal of Economic Behavior and Organization*, the *Journal of Economic Growth*, and the *Journal of Human Resources* ask you to list would-be reviewers. Outside of economics, general science journals like *PNAS* and *Science* ask you the same.

successful one way or the other. Second, the risk with listing people who are close to your research as peer reviewers is that if the editor finds out about those close links (and often, people on your "wanted" list will reveal those links themselves), this gives them an occasion to think that you are less than forthcoming about things, including perhaps the validity of your findings. There is thus an incentive for truth-telling here.[13]

4.7   Whether and When to Contact the Editor in Charge

Once you have submitted your paper, the wait for a decision on your manuscript begins. For all of the talk of how long it takes to hear back from journals, things are significantly better than 15 years ago. In the old days, you submitted a paper by mailing it to the editor in charge by postal mail. In those days, physical manuscripts would sometimes get lost in the mail, or there would be delays in mail delivery, or worse—that editors or their assistants would misplace a manuscript, and you would not know about it until you sent a polite inquiry to the journal six months to a year later, only to be told that they could not find your manuscript.

Fortunately, everything is done electronically nowadays, which means that manuscripts rarely (if ever) get lost, and that authors are no longer at the mercy of postal delays. As a result, the transaction costs associated with submitting manuscripts for review have gone down significantly, which has had both good and bad consequences. On the one hand, the process is significantly more streamlined and efficient, which tends to speed things up. On the other hand, and as anyone who has read a modicum of New Institutional Economics knows, lower transaction costs lead to more market activity at the margin (Williamson 1975). This, combined with the fact that there are now many more research economists than a mere 20 years ago, means that on the whole, the peer-review process is not significantly faster than it was back then, and you can expect to wait on average about three to six months for a decision on a paper that does not get desk-rejected.

Understandably, you are champing at the bit to hear from the editor about whether your manuscript has a chance to get published in the journal you submitted it to. So when should you contact the editor in charge? Should you *ever* do so?

---

13. Likewise, if you are asked to review a paper whose author you are close to (say, because they were one of your advisors, or you are coauthors), it is best to let the editor know that you have a conflict of interest, and let them decide for themselves whether they are okay with it.

Before answering those questions, let us get one thing out of the way: editors do not keep track of how often you check the status of your manuscript on their journal's editorial system, and doing so will have no impact on the fate of your manuscript.[14] And there is sometimes valuable information to be drawn from your manuscript's status.

Indeed, if your manuscript is "with editor" for more than a month, you can send a polite email asking the editor about the status of your manuscript, as that might nudge her to get to make a decision one way or the other (i.e., desk reject, or send for review) about your manuscript. Similarly, if your manuscript is "under review" for more than six months, you can also email the editor asking the same. If a manuscript is "under review" for a while, then the system says that it is "ready for decision," but it then goes back "under review," it usually means that the reviewers were split, and the editor is soliciting additional reviews. Or it can mean that one of the reviewers let the editor down by not submitting a review, and your manuscript has gone to a new reviewer.

One category of emails I would discourage the readers of this book from sending consists of what I have come to call "protest" emails. Those emails are usually sent in response to a rejection or desk rejection, but they are not formal appeals—they merely consist of the authors protest-ing the reasons for the rejection. My attitude to those emails is to file them away without responding unless the authors specifically request an appeal (more on those below), since editorial decisions are meant to be final rather than opening gambits in a negotiation.

Finally, if you do get a favorable decision, you may be tempted to email the editor back to thank them. That is certainly nice, but it is by no means necessary.

4.8 Understanding Editorial Decisions

The various types of editorial decisions can be confusing at first, especially for people who have hitherto spent their entire scholastic lives being at or very near the top of their class, and who have rarely been told that their work was anything less than very good, if not perfect. This section aims to clarify what each type of editorial decision means.

---

14. Technically speaking, there probably is a way to keep track of how often you log on to an editorial management system, but I have yet to find an editor who had so much time on their hands (or cared enough) to keep track of that.

Desk Rejection. A desk rejection occurs when a paper is rejected by an editor without getting sent out for review. These decisions tend to occur quickly, and are usually the result of a manuscript being a poor fit for a journal. This occurs either because the topic of the manuscript is too far off from what the editors are currently interested in publishing, or because the quality of the manuscript is too far below the journal's quality threshold, or simply because the topic does not fit the editor's vision of what the journal should publish. When you get a desk rejection, if the editor gives you any actionable feedback on your work, you may try to incorporate that feedback before submitting your paper somewhere else. It sometimes happens, however, that an editor will see a fatal flaw in your work. If and when that occurs, remember the sunk cost fallacy, and consider abandoning that manuscript to work on something else.

For instance, I spend a good amount of my time rejecting manuscripts that are best labeled "determinants of" papers. Those are papers where the authors had some data (almost always cross-sectional data) but no research design to speak of. Even so, the authors decided to run some regressions, look at what was significant, and take a heroic step from partial correlations to causation by speculating about the mechanisms behind those findings. Almost always, those manuscripts include policy recommendations. In such cases, the authors should work on something else: though that kind of analysis was certainly novel and interesting in the 1980s, standards of evidence have changed considerably over the last four decades, and that kind of paper would not pass muster as a term paper in a field course.

Rejection. A rejection occurs when a manuscript is sent out for review and gets rejected after the editor has received anywhere from one to five reviews on it. Though the norm at most journals is for authors to receive two or three reviews as part of a decision, nothing holds any one editor to that norm. Many manuscripts get rejected once one clearly negative review has been submitted (this is especially likely when the editor likes to have unanimous support for a manuscript before giving a revise-and-resubmit, and would prefer not wasting the authors' time by waiting for another review, or when the editor was somewhat negatively inclined initially, but wanted to see what the reviewers thought of the paper). At top journals, an editor will sometimes solicit additional reviews.[15]

---

15. At the *American Economic Review*, for instance, it is not uncommon for authors to receive five reviews.

Revise and Resubmit. Revise-and-resubmit decisions (R&Rs) come in two broad varieties, strong and weak, also respectively called minor and major revisions (so-named because a strong R&R entails minor revisions and less work than a weak R&R, which entails major revisions). For those cases where what the reviewers and the editor ask from you seems feasible within the amount of time you are given to submit a revision, see below on how to prepare a successful revision. If you think the revisions are feasible but you believe you will need more time than the deadline you are given in the decision letter, you should ask for more time. In many (if not most) cases, deadlines for revisions are arbitrary, and editors understand that life events (e.g., changing jobs, moving, welcoming a new child into the world, caring for an ailing family member) can get in the way of research productivity.

Unless you know for a fact that the revisions required from you are impossible to undertake to the reviewers' and the editor's satisfaction, you should always jump on the chance to resubmit a revised version of an article when you get an R&R. The probability of getting a manuscript accepted at a journal, conditional on that journal having requested a revision, is significantly higher than the unconditional probability of a getting a manuscript accepted at another comparable journal.

One brief word about what you should *not* do when given a chance to revise and resubmit your manuscript. After getting an R&R where the comments are so good as to make the paper significantly better, you may be tempted to incorporate those good comments and submit the revised version of your paper to a higher-ranked journal without letting the original handling editor know, thus leaving the window open for you to resubmit. Do not do that. This is highly unethical (the peer-review system is already stretched thin by an excess quantity of manuscripts relative to the quantity of decent-quality refereeing time available), and you can quickly get a reputation for unethical behavior if you get caught doing so.[16]

---

16. You may think you are unlikely to get caught, and that if you do, it will not matter. In my experience, authors tend to view editors much like undergraduate students view their professors. That is, as entities that are entirely independent from one another. But just as professors tend to know each other and will sometimes talk to each other about specific students, editors tend to know each other and will sometimes talk to each other about authors. As for thinking that it will not matter if you do get caught, because you can just coast on the high quality of your work, that is a risky gamble. Though there certainly are a number of successful toxic people in economics, those people are successful *in spite* of their being toxic, and they almost always fail to realize that they could be even more successful if not for their toxicity.

When you are offered the chance to revise and resubmit your manuscript, it is customary to update your curriculum vitae (CV) so that it states for this manuscript that a revision has been requested by the journal that gave you the R&R.

Reject and Resubmit. This category of decision tends to puzzle those who are on the receiving end of it, both because it is uncommon and because of its neither-fish-nor-fowl nature. Indeed, a reject-and-resubmit is neither a revise-and-resubmit nor a rejection, but rather a rejection with an invitation to submit a significantly different version of the paper. Such a resubmission after a rejection is then treated as a fresh new submission, and it will likely have new reviewers if the original paper went out for review. This kind of decision is typically made when the editor feels as though the original submission contains the kernel of a good paper, but the current version is so unsatisfactory as to practically require a brand new paper.

When you get a reject-and-resubmit from a journal, the odds of getting the paper ultimately accepted in that journal are much less than if you get an R&R, but they still tend to be slightly higher than for a fresh submission at a comparable journal. Indeed, though a reject-and-resubmit offers no guarantees, in giving you a reject-and-resubmit the editor has specifically told you the kind of paper she would like to see in her journal, and there is a good amount of information in that signal.

When you get a reject-and-resubmit, do not update your CV like you would for an R&R. For all intents and purposes, your manuscript was rejected by the journal, and in no case should your CV state that a revision was requested.

Acceptance with Minor Revisions. This type of decision, also known as a conditional acceptance, means that the editor likes the paper enough so as to be able to accept it subject to your making a few revisions. Typically, those revisions will be stylistic or cosmetic in nature. This decision usually comes after one or more revise-and-resubmit decisions. It might also happen that an acceptance with minor revisions or conditional acceptance will be the first decision you get on a manuscript, but that is very uncommon.

When your paper is accepted subject to minor revisions or conditionally accepted, you should list the paper as such in your CV.

Acceptance. This is the Holy Grail of editorial decisions. It means that your paper is now forthcoming in the journal that accepted it and that you should take time to celebrate. This decision usually comes after one or more revise-and-resubmit decisions and a conditional acceptance.

Such a decision can also in principle occur upon the initial submission of a manuscript, but that is exceedingly rare.

When your paper is accepted, it is customary to list it in your CV as "forthcoming" in the journal that accepted it. In an effort to generate buzz for forthcoming articles, many journals will publish manuscripts online before they do so in physical form. When your article is published online, it should remain as "forthcoming" in your CV until it is assigned volume or issue numbers (or both) as well as page numbers, unless you are publishing in a journal that is only published electronically, in which case it should be published in an issue of the journal soon after it is first made available online.

4.9   Dealing with Rejection

Anyone who is in the business of publishing peer-reviewed work—most academics, and many scientists in government, industry, or at think tanks—will sooner or later almost surely face rejection.

And hopefully, you will (or already have) too, because even though getting rejected is never good news, it is a sign that you have been productive and that you are ambitious and hopeful about the quality of your work.[17] So first: if you are planning on doing research in economics for a career, you will get rejected. You will get rejected *a lot*. In many cases, you will disagree with the reasons why you were rejected, at least initially, before you have had time to think carefully about the reviewers' or the editor's comments. In some cases, the reason why you are rejected will be nebulous ("We receive more manuscripts than we can publish"). Rarely if ever will a rejection be for personal reasons. Thus, the first thing to understand is that a rejection says nothing about you, and it most likely says nothing about your overall ability to do or write about research. All that it says is that this paper—more accurately, this version of this paper—was deemed as either not a good fit for or not up to the quality level of the journal you submitted it to.

One particular quote which I have found to accurately describe how I felt in my first few years as an assistant professor is the following quote from Ira Glass, probably the most successful public media personality of this generation:

---

17. If you never face rejection, it is either because you submit everything to journals whose quality standards are too low or to predatory journals. In either case, you owe it to yourself to be more ambitious.

All of us who do creative work, we get into it because we have good taste. But there is this gap. For the first couple years you make stuff, it's just not that good. It's trying to be good, it has potential, but it's not. But your taste, the thing that got you into the game, is still killer. And your taste is why your work disappoints you. A lot of people never get past this phase, they quit. Most people I know who do interesting, creative work went through years of this. We know our work doesn't have this special thing that we want it to have. We all go through this. And if you are just starting out or you are still in this phase, you gotta know its normal and the most important thing you can do is do a lot of work. Put yourself on a deadline so that every week you will finish one story. It is only by going through a volume of work that you will close that gap, and your work will be as good as your ambitions. And I took longer to figure out how to do this than anyone I've ever met. It's gonna take a while. It's normal to take a while. You've just gotta fight your way through.

Glass is the host and producer of *This American Life*, a radio show that tends to have little if anything to do with frontier research in economics, but as researchers, we are engaged in creative work, especially when we decide which research question to spend our time on and when we write up our research results. For every additional year I am fortunate to spend in this profession, I find the above quote more and more accurate, both because of my own experience and because it finds echoes in the experience of all of the early-career researchers I know.

Indeed, it is not uncommon for an assistant professor to have no publications (or no new ones since starting on the tenure track) at the end of their third year, but for them to publish anywhere from five to ten articles in their fourth, fifth, and sixth year on the job.[18] Knowing that, it is important not to let those first few years—those difficult few years during which there is a gap between your taste and the quality of your work—get you down. And there will likely be times where you will want to give up and look for one of those well-paying private-sector jobs where there is little to none of that publish-or-perish nonsense.

For most people, getting rejected does not get better with time, with tenure, or with successive promotions. Linearly interpolating from that, I suspect getting rejected also does not get better if and when you are named fellow of your professional association. For this reason, it is best to develop a thick skin, and learn to take rejection in stride.

---

18. This is because most early-career researchers start out ambitiously, by submitting their first few papers to journals that are significantly higher-ranked than the journals that will eventually accept those papers. Most researchers eventually develop a good instinct about where a given paper will eventually get published, but that instinct is a byproduct of experience.

4.10   Whether and How to Appeal an Editorial Decision

When you receive a rejection which you believe is unjustified, you can always appeal the editor's decision. Some journals have a formal appeal process in place,[19] whereas others tend to deal with appeals on a case-by-case basis.

Just because you can always appeal an editor's decision, however, does not mean you should.

First, if you wish to appeal an editorial decision, make sure that you have as good a case as you can possibly have for doing so. If your paper was rejected on the basis of its fit with the journal's aims and scope, there is no use in telling the editor that you disagree with her interpretation of those aims and scope and that you think your paper is a good fit for the journal. If that is the basis for your appeal, you are likely to be told—deservedly so—that you are entirely free to reinterpret the journal's aims and scope when you are chosen to be editor of that journal.

A good case for an appeal is one where one of the editor's stated reasons for rejecting your paper is grounded in a clear mistake that the editor (and possibly the reviewer who brought up that reason to the editor) made about your manuscript. For instance, a colleague once told me about the following successful appeal. That colleague and his coauthors had run an RCT to test the impact of some intervention and submitted it for publication to a journal. This was in the mid-2000s, when RCTs were not as widespread (and their mechanics and properties not as well known) as they are now. The authors had randomly assigned observations to treatment, but treatment take-up was voluntary, so that it was not possible to recover an average treatment effect, but only an estimate of the intention to treat (ITT). To make things worse, the authors had been somewhat unclear about that. When the reviewer brought up the fact that even though treatment assignment was experimental, treatment take-up was endogenous, the editor read no further, and rejected on the vague basis of endogeneity of the authors' results. The authors decided to appeal, arguing that even though their research design only allowed the identification of an ITT instead of an average treatment effect (ATE),

---

19. At the journal I am currently editing, for instance, appeals are handled by a different editor than the one who handled the original submission, and the appeal editor usually looks at the entire correspondence folder (manuscript, reviews, decision letter, appeal, and any other relevant documents) before making a decision, which sometimes might involve soliciting advice from additional reviewers.

their findings were of interest nonetheless, if only because theirs was the first experimental study in that literature. Ultimately, the editor agreed with the appeal, and the paper was published.

Where things get murkier, and where you have much less of a case for an appeal, are those cases where the editor or the reviewers misunderstood something in your paper. Here, even though you could appeal and explain to the editor the mistake they or the reviewers made in understanding your work, you are likely to be told that the onus of being understood is entirely on you, and that you had one shot at it. In other words, there is an unspoken rule here that peer review is not a proofreading service, that you should submit a manuscript that clearly explains what it does and why it does it, and that if anything is unclear, that is as good a reason as any to reject your manuscript. This may seem unfair to you (doubly so if English is not your first language; see chapter 7), but forewarned is forearmed.

You should clearly avoid appealing when you feel as though the reviewers were positive about your work, but the editor chose to reject nonetheless. This is so for two reasons. First, because you have only read the reviews, and not the reviewers' confidential comments to the editor, which are often much more candid and straightforward than the reviews themselves—believe it or not, many reviewers try to write their reviews so that their comments are kind and constructive. Thus, no matter what you (think you can) infer from a review, you are only getting part of the story. Second, because editors have their own preferences, too. They may not have been crazy about your paper, but in their humility, they nevertheless chose to send it out for review to see whether actual experts on your topic would like it. In that case, reviews that were mildly positive but not overly excited about your work might have been enough to confirm their initial suspicions, and cause them to reject.

Generally speaking, I would encourage you to avoid appealing editorial decisions, even in those cases where you feel like you might have a good basis for an appeal. First, and as I alluded to above, editors may not always give you the whole story behind a rejection. Second, you especially do not want to acquire a reputation for being the kind of person who appeals editorial decisions. The economics profession is composed of a relatively small number of people who interact repeatedly, and while positive information about specific individuals tends to travel through networks slowly (if at all), negative information tends to travels fast. This is even more so within specific fields of economics, or within groups of researchers working on the same topic within a field.

Rejection stinks, but it is best to err on the side of assuming that the editor had a good reason to reject your work, whether they communicated it clearly to you or not, and move on to your next target journal.

4.11   How to Prepare a Successful Revision

Once you have been given a chance to revise your manuscript for and resubmit it to a given journal, what do you do?

Victories are few and far between in this profession, so the first thing you should be doing is to make plans to celebrate this little victory as soon as possible. If you fail to celebrate the wins as they occur, next thing you know you will be mourning a loss, so make sure you do something nice for yourself, whatever that means to you—going for a long run, eating at your favorite restaurant, going out of town for a weekend, getting yourself a new book, watching a film, and so forth.

The next thing you should do is to read the reviews once, then put them away for a week. I realize that, given how rare R&R decisions are, and how much of a difference a publication can make to your career, it is difficult not to want to start working on an R&R right away. Realistically, however, waiting one week is unlikely to make a difference to your career. Perhaps more importantly, setting those reviews aside for a week gives your subconscious mind a chance to process them, so that when you look at them again after a week, they do not seem as daunting. This is something I have noticed time and again when getting R&Rs: upon first reading the reviews, I tend to get defensive, and I tend to think the revisions will be more difficult than they objectively turn out to be.

When I read the reviews after a week, however, I immediately start noting the ways in which I will address the comments. The bottom line is that reading the reviews once when you get them and setting them aside for a week seems to be a good way to spark your creativity when it comes to how you address reviewer comments.[20]

---

20. If that process was good enough for French mathematician and polymath Henri Poincaré, it should be good enough for most of us. In an article on creativity in science and art, Holton (2001) writes: "Poincaré analyzed [his] intuitions in these terms: 'Most striking at first is this appearance of sudden illumination, a manifest sign of long, unconscious prior work. The role of this unconscious work in mathematical invention appears to me incontestable . . . It seems, in such cases, that one is present at one's own unconscious work, made particularly perceptible to the overexcited consciousness.'"

Once you get back to the reviews, it is time to sketch out a broad plan for successfully addressing the reviewers' comments. Read the reviews once to get a high-level view of what you will need to do, and to write one, maybe two sentences next to each reviewer comment telling yourself how you plan on addressing said comment. This stage involves thinking about things like what you were asked to cut (and whether it makes sense to do so in light of your paper's argument), what additional results you are asked to generate (and whether they should be in the main body of your paper, or whether they can go in the appendix), whether you are asked to include a theoretical framework, and any other big change that will require that you reorganize your paper's tables or sections.

After that first step, it is a good idea to write down and contrast two outlines on a single piece of paper: one for the version of the paper that you submitted and which received an R&R, and one for the planned revised version. This will allow you to think more clearly about what needs to be done in going from one to the other. More generally, it helps looking at whether the planned outline of the revision makes sense to you, and thus to prospective readers, especially your reviewers and the editor. This is worthy of note because sometimes a reviewer will ask you to move things around or cut something out in a way that does not make sense to your core argument.[21]

When sketching out the outline of the revised version, I would recommend following the rough order in which a paper is written, which I discussed in chapter 2. You should go over each section of your paper, ask yourself whether it needs to be revised and, if so, what needs to be done to successfully revise it, and whether this has consequences for the other sections of the paper. Because each of the sections in the following rough order tends to feed into the next, you should aim to revise in order the

---

21. For example, when I finally got an R&R on my job-market paper after six years of submitting and getting rejected, the statistical test I was running to investigate my research question rested pretty heavily on the theoretical model I had developed to guide the empirical work, and the test clearly involved regressing the outcome variable on the slope of a function of an observable variable rather than on the variable itself (Bellemare 2012). When a reviewer asked me to cut out the theoretical model (and the editor agreed with that reviewer), my first inclination as a pre-tenure academic was to do everything the reviewers asked for. But when I realized that taking out the theoretical framework would remove any sound basis for my empirical test, the compromise I settled upon was to put the theoretical framework in an appendix.

1. Theoretical Framework
2. Data and Descriptive Statistics
3. Empirical Framework
4. Results and Discussion
5. Summary and Concluding Remarks
6. Introduction, and possibly
7. Literature Review and Background

You should also aim to prioritize tackling the major comments first—those comments which reviewers will label as major, which they will tend to list first in their reviews, or which they will tend to clearly signal are the big, nonnegotiable things they want you to do before they can recommend that your manuscript be accepted for publication. It is always tempting to start with the easy stuff, and to begin by fixing typos and adding the references the reviewers felt were missing from your manuscript. Avoid that temptation, if only because a lot of the easy stuff might just fall by the wayside and no longer be relevant once you have taken care of the big stuff. For instance, Reviewer 1 might want you to add a reference when you discuss the literature, but if Reviewer 2 wants you to completely reorient your motivations to place your paper in an entirely different literature, you would be wasting your time if you started with the former instead of the latter.

Once you have a good idea of how you will respond to each comment, it is time to start preparing two types of document. The first type consists of your responses to reviewer comments. The second one consists of your cover letter to the editor.

You should prepare a single document for each reviewer. Each document should clearly indicate in the title which reviewer it responds to, so a title like "Responses to Reviewer 1," or "Responses to Referee 2" at the beginning works well. Then, because all academics are busy and time is the scarcest of commodities, it is customary to thank the reviewer for taking her time to read your paper and comment on it. Even if you did not like their comments, it is simply common courtesy to thank people when they dedicate some of their time to reading your work. And even if their comments were insulting, you can still take the high road and express your gratitude for what they probably thought were great comments.

After that, it is best to just tackle each reviewer's comments in the order in which they appear in their review. What I like to do is to reproduce in my response to a given reviewer each of that reviewer's comments in boldface font, and then write my response under each comment. For example:

2. In your application, you cluster your standard errors at the community level because that is the level at which households were randomly selected. But following Abadie et al. (2017), you should cluster your standard errors at the household level since that is the level at which randomization took place.

<u>Response</u>: You are entirely right, and we now cluster our standard errors at the household. This does not change our results.

3. Instead of interacting your treatment variable with the gender of the individual who is getting treated, I would rather you present two sets of estimation results, i.e., one for women, and one for men.

<u>Response</u>: Done. You can find the results by gender for what used to be Table 4 in what are now Tables 4a and 4b.

As with everything else, clarity of communication is key. This means you should never assume that your reviewers will understand why you did something, and for each comment, tell them how you addressed their comment, and *show them*. Do not just write "Done" or "See page 14." in response to a reviewer's comment. Write "Done. On page 14, we now have added the following paragraph in response to this comment," and quote the full paragraph. That way (and in the spirit of what I said in chapter 2), you are writing so as to not be read: writing your response, that is, so that the reviewers hopefully do not feel the need to look at your paper too closely this time around.

When preparing responses to the reviewers, it is not uncommon for each such reviewer-response document to be ten pages or more if you reproduce each reviewer comment and copy the relevant sentences, paragraphs, and tables from your paper, or if you show additional results that the reviewer wanted to see, but which did not go in the paper.

That said, there is an optimal amount of work to do in response to reviewer comments. You want to do what they ask you to do, and not less, because then it might make the reviewers suspicious that you are hiding something, and thus more likely to recommend a rejection. You also want to do no more than what they ask to avoid wasting their time having to read things they did not ask for.[22]

---

22. Related to this point, you will sometimes receive comments from friends and colleagues on your paper after you have received an R&R on it. Very often, it might be tempting to implement some of the changes those comments suggest you should make. Resist that temptation! I see a revise-and-resubmit as a near-binding contract wherein the editor tells you that she is likely to accept your manuscript if you do everything she and the reviewers ask for—no more, no less.

If any of the reviewers' comments are unclear, you should still do your best to address them. This obviously means reading and re-reading that comment to try to understand it, but it also means having colleagues have a look at those comments. Very often, you might be coming at a problem a certain way, but a reviewer might be coming at it a different way, and the same words (e.g., "identification," or "exogenous") might take on different meaning. For instance, someone who is used to doing causal inference using reduced-form methods is unlikely to have the same meaning of "identification" as someone who does time-series econometrics.

If you disagree with any of the reviewers' comments, it is still a good idea to do what they are asking for, and to keep your disagreement for your cover letter to the editor, which I discuss below. When it comes to refusing to do what reviewers ask, a simple rule of thumb is this: if you must do so, do so no more than once on any given paper, and make sure you have good reasons behind your refusal. I recently handled a manuscript where the reviewers, quite reasonably, asked the authors to present versions of their regression results where the outcome variables were in logarithms instead of in levels. The authors refused to do so, telling me that "papers are getting too long these days." After fighting my inclination to reject the paper because the authors were not being reasonable (the paper did contain interesting findings, after all), I sent the manuscript back to the authors, explaining to them that this was not a negotiation, and that as long as they did not address that comment, the paper would not move closer to publication.

If reviewer comments are contradictory, once again, you should do your best to address them. Very often, this will mean picking whichever one you feel is the best of the two comments, and telling the reviewer whose comments you did not incorporate about that contradiction (and really, do not invoke this defense without it being true, because reviewers can almost always see each other's comments), but leaving open the possibility to change the manuscript if they can find a way forward by writing something like: "Reviewer 3 asked us to do something that is in direct contradiction with this comment, and we felt their comment made for a stronger manuscript. If you can provide a suggestion for how we might be able to accommodate both your comment and theirs, we would be happy to do so in the next version of the manuscript." Likewise with comments that are rather vague, like "The authors are missing some key citations to the literature in their review of the relevant literature" (in my experience, this is usually brought up by reviewers who are upset that you did not cite more of their work). Here, it is perfectly fair game to tell the reviewer that you would be delighted to cite the right papers—if they tell you which papers they would like you to cite.

Once you have addressed all of the reviewers' comments to the best of your ability, it is time to write a cover letter to the editor explaining how you have addressed those comments as well as the editor's own comments, if she made any. Your cover letter should start by telling the editor what you have done in response to her comments. That part of your cover letter should follow the structure of a response to a reviewer, as outlined above. Then, you should discuss what you have done to address each of the reviewers' major comments in broad strokes. That is, you should tell the editor how you have addressed each major comment, rearranged the manuscript, whether and how your qualitative findings have changed, and so forth, in one or two sentences. If the editor wants to know the details of how you tackled a specific point, she can look at your responses to the reviewers. Generally, that letter will not be shared with the reviewers, so if you feel that a reviewer was particularly obtuse, this is the place to mention it.

After submitting the revised version of your article, the wait for an editorial decision begins once more. In the best-case scenario, the editor chooses not to send your revised article back to the reviewers, and accepts it after having had a look at it and at your responses to the reviewer comments. The second-best scenario occurs when the editor accepts (or conditionally accepts, i.e., accepts subject to minor revisions) your article after sending it back to the reviewers. The third-best scenario occurs when you get another R&R decision, as it is not uncommon for articles to go through additional rounds of revision after the initial one before it gets accepted.[23] Obviously, the worst-case scenario is for your article to be rejected after R&R—a situation that is increasingly likely the closer you get to the top of the journal rankings.

---

23. Some editors refuse to accept a paper until all reviewers are *completely* satisfied with everything, going up to five rounds of revision. Such an editor can be the bane of the existence of someone on the tenure track, for whom time is of the essence, because drawing that editor will often mean a manuscript will be with a journal for three years or more before it is finally accepted. But editor types vary. I know what I like in a paper, so my own preference, if at all possible, is to make the authors suffer no more than one round of (substantial) revisions unless there is something fundamentally wrong with a revision, and to treat reviewers as working for the journal instead of the other way around. If time is of the essence for you, discreetly asking around whether a given editor is the kind to entertain several rounds of revision can save you some precious time.

4.12   Once Your Article Is Accepted

When your article is accepted, you should again make sure to set time aside to celebrate by treating yourself to something you would not normally do. As I mentioned earlier, those little victories are rather scarce, and if we fail to celebrate them as they happen, soon enough we are mourning another loss. Once you are done celebrating, the wait begins for your article's galley proofs—the draft version of your typeset article. Those proofs will typically be sent by the journal publisher's production department, which tends to be almost entirely orthogonal to the journal's editorial team. Consistent with that orthogonality, the production people will typically require that you return your corrected proofs, along with your answers to their own queries (e.g., "When you cited Stiglitz (1974), did you mean Stiglitz (1974) in *REStud*, *QJE*, *AER*, or *JPE*?")[24] in most cases within 48 hours.

Here, my one recommendation is to arm yourself with patience. Manuscripts are typeset by people who are neither economists nor writers. Very often, because of outsourcing, they are typeset by people for whom English is a second language. To make matters worse, each publisher now requires you to make corrections to your galley proofs using an unusually cumbersome online system which does not necessarily allow you to see what your article will actually look like on paper. It can be extremely frustrating to have to explain basic grammar to the one person standing between you and a published article, and it can be maddening to have to figure out how to align an entire column of coefficients and standard errors along the decimal point on a web-based application you are unlikely to use more than five times in your entire life. But the incentives are clearly aligned for you to do the best you can, and to do it within 48 hours.

4.13   Publicizing after Publishing

Though the goal of every junior researcher is to get their papers accepted, one should take the long view and consider what matters in the long run. Yes, the quality of your articles and the journals they're published in as well as the quantity of publications you have all matter for the welfare of your career. Once your position in the profession is relatively secure (say,

---

24. The query is fictitious, but the example used for it is not: Stiglitz really did publish articles in four of the top five journals *in a single year*.

because you have tenure or have been promoted), however, what matters for the next step in your career more often than not has to do with your impact as a scholar.

For better or for worse, impact is nowadays measured in terms of the number of times your work is cited on the usual citation aggregators—generally, Google Scholar or Web of Science. Citation counts are especially useful when comparing scholarly impact between disciplines, or between fields within a certain discipline. And for all of their imperfections—for instance, they do not account for quality of the source citing the work, nor do they account for whether the source citing the work is critical of it—they remain the most democratic and objective measure of scholarly impact.

How do you ensure that your work receives the right amount of attention? Obviously, scholarly impact is heavily dependent on decisions made months if not years ahead of publication. Empirical articles that provide a credible finding about a policy question that is on people's minds at the moment the article is published will tend to be more relevant than an umpteenth proof of Arrow's impossibility theorem, no matter how simple the former, and no matter how elegant the latter.[25]

There are steps you can take, however, as late as right before an article goes to production if you want to increase its scholarly impact. The easiest of such ways is to go with a good title. Here, clear trumps clever, and the shorter your title, the better in terms of citations, it seems. Though their empirical methods would not be convincing to most economists, Letchford et al. (2015) discuss descriptive evidence according to which papers with shorter titles get cited more frequently.

Next, except for the really technical terms (e.g., dynamic stochastic general equilibrium model, regression discontinuity design), your abstract should be intelligible to a college-educated reader. Similarly, your introduction should be *mostly* intelligible to a college-educated reader.

---

25. That said, scholarly impact concerns focusing on citations should probably only drive your choice of topics and research questions after getting tenure. Because citation numbers are extremely noisy for people who are only five to seven years post-PhD, citation counts are rarely all that relevant to tenure decisions, and what matters at that stage is a sufficient number of articles (e.g., at least five articles) in journals whose quality is above a certain threshold (e.g., top field journals or better), as well as other potentially nonlinear adjustments (e.g., at least one top-five). I would thus encourage you to focus on an article's expected impact—citations or otherwise—for those articles which you expect to be counting for what lies beyond tenure.

Having your title, abstract, and introduction (and perhaps your conclusion) intelligible to people outside your field, outside your discipline, and ideally outside of academia altogether can do wonders for your scholarly impact. As I mentioned in chapter 2, people "read" papers inspectionally, which means that if you want your work to have impact, the parts they read should be accessible to them. You can lead a horse to water, but you cannot make it drink. Nothing prevents you, however, from bringing water up to its mouth once you get to water!

One thing that often gets overlooked in terms of expected impact is search engine optimization (better known as SEO), which is about how search engine algorithms will look for keywords and organize searches as a result. Though repetition makes for less elegant writing, it is better for your title, highlights (if applicable), abstract, keywords, and introduction to consistently use the same keywords to denote the same concepts. In other words, a web page that has the word "apple" 100 times in it will rank higher in search engine search results than a web page with the word "apple" only 10 times on it, *ceteris paribus*. For instance, I have done a lot of work on the economic institution of contract farming. Many people refer to contract farming arrangements as "outgrower schemes," or "grower–processor contracts." In the interest of writing elegantly, it was tempting to write my abstracts so that they would cycle through those various names for the institution. But because of the way search engines rank-order various pages, it was much better to consistently use "contract farming" in my titles, abstracts, highlights, keywords, and my introductions, because doing so moved my articles on the topic significantly up in searches for "contract farming." I obviously will never know the counterfactual, but I believe this has translated into more citations to my work.

Once your article is accepted for publication, it is wise to post a pre-print (i.e., the version of the paper you submitted and which was finally accepted for publication) on your website, though not all publishers will allow that, as some publishers embargo papers until they are published. When in doubt, consult the journal or the publisher's policy on pre-prints.[26]

---

26. It may pay off to know the publisher's policy on pre-prints before submitting. In a sad cautionary tale about working papers, Dionne (2011) tells the story of how she had an acceptance at a top public health journal rescinded after the publisher discovered that her paper had been posted in a working paper series.

One obvious way to make your work easily accessible is pay for open access, either through choosing to publish in journals that are entirely open access (e.g., *PLoS ONE*) or by choosing open access for your work that gets published with traditionally paid-access publishers (e.g., Elsevier, MIT Press, Wiley). Either way, you will need to have substantial research funds at your disposal in order to be able to publish open access. That said, funding agencies (e.g., the European Research Council) and donors (e.g., the Bill & Melinda Gates Foundation) increasingly require the research they fund to be published open access; the good news is that this means that they also tend to provide you with the necessary funds to do so. In a recent working paper, Staudt (2020) exploits the National Institutes of Health's Public Access Policy (PAP) as an instrumental variable for whether an article is public access. His estimate of the local average treatment effect—in this case, the effect of open access on citations *for those articles that were made open access as a result of the PAP*—is positive, and shows an increase in citations of up to 50 percent. Taking Staudt's results at face value, the relevant trade-off is between your article's (expected) increase in citations against a publisher's price for open access.

Another way to publicize your work and get it in front of the eyes of the people who are likely to be most interested in it is through social media. The beauty of social media is that on social media, people's networks tend to be rich in researchers who are working both within their fields and disciplines but also in researchers who are working on related topics across disciplines, and so it is well worth cultivating a professional social media presence if you want to increase your work's scholarly impact. I will have more to say about using social media in chapter 6.

One way to publicize your work which I would caution against is through a mass-email list, both because there is too much email already and because the impersonal nature of these emails tends to turn people off. That being said, thoughtful individualized emails (e.g., "Given your earlier work on the topic, I thought you might be interested in this new paper of mine") certainly work well.

If you care about real-world impact, one place to start is with your university's media relations office. Much of the work done by economists nowadays can be argued to have ties to what goes on in the real world, and your institution's media relations folks will be able to write up a press release about your work and circulate it to the media if you take the time to clearly explain to them what your work is about, what it says and what it does not say, and why it is important. At wealthier universities, the media relations office can even assist you in writing an op-ed about your work and shopping it around to various media outlets. If you care about having policy or business impact, this is probably the most fruitful way to have such an impact.

4.14   Author Ethics

There are numerous resources available at any PhD-granting institution for you to learn about academic integrity in general. If you have not familiarized yourself with them yet, take a moment to do so—depending on what the social norms were during your pre-PhD training, some of the current social norms surrounding academic integrity may be surprising to you. About a decade ago, for instance, a well-known economist published four articles on roughly the same topic in four different journals and, in at least one case, without citing the other three articles. At the time, accusations of self-plagiarism spread like wildfire (Shea 2011), and some of the hitherto highly respected economists involved became pariahs whose names will forever have an asterisk next to them.

Self-plagiarism can take subtler forms. For example, it is often the case that people write two or more papers with the same data set. Every one of those papers, however, has to present and discuss the data, and so it can be tempting to cut and paste from an earlier paper that uses the same data. Though this kind of self-plagiarism falls into more of a gray area than the four-papers-on-the-same-topic case discussed above, do not let the "self" part of "self-plagiarism" do all the lifting—self-plagiarism is still plagiarism. It is not fun to have to tell the same story two or more times differently each time, but it is a small price to pay in comparison to having to collect brand new data or to having your reputation put into question because you reused some of your own writing.

5

Finding Funding

Thirty years ago, when a much larger share of economists were doing theory, finding funding was less important than it is now. With advances in computing power, the falling cost of data, and the Credibility Revolution, however, economics has become much more of an empirical discipline (Backhouse and Cherrier 2017a, 2017b; Angrist and Pischke 2010), which means one often needs funds to get data.

Although grants are almost always a necessary condition to fund primary data collection (e.g., lab or field experiments and surveys conducted by the researcher herself), it is not uncommon for researchers to have to buy the data they want (e.g., data collected by market-research firms). Even a researcher who is interested in building a data set from scratch using publicly available sources (e.g., by combining socioeconomic data from one source with geographic information from another) is likely to have to fund the tedious work of merging the various kinds of data together, and so she will need funds to pay someone else to do that.[1]

Before proceeding with this chapter, I should define some of the terms I will be using throughout. According to the Carnegie Classification of Institutions of Higher Education,[2] the various categories of institutions of higher learning in the US include, for the purposes of this discussion:

1. R1 universities, or doctoral universities with very high research activity.

---

1. Moreover, in some departments, the graduate student funding model is closer to that used in the natural sciences, wherein a graduate student's stipend, tuition, and fees are funded by faculty members' grants, in which case students are admitted in the program to work on specific research projects and with specific faculty members.

2. See https://carnegieclassifications.iu.edu/ as the reference for this discussion.

2. R2 universities, or doctoral universities with high research activity.

3. D/PU universities, or doctoral/professional universities.

4. Master's colleges and universities, which "includes institutions that awarded at least 50 master's degrees and fewer than 20 doctoral degrees during the update year." These institutions are divided in tiers M1 (larger programs), M2 (medium programs), and M3 (smaller programs).

5. Baccalaureate colleges, which includes "institutions where baccalaureate or higher degrees represent at least 50 percent of all degrees but where fewer than 50 master's degrees or 20 doctoral degrees were awarded during the update year."

6. Baccalaureate/Associate's Colleges, which includes "four-year colleges . . . that conferred more than 50 percent of degrees at the associate's level."

All of this matters because the category an institution falls into will often determine the type of grant researchers at that institution can apply for. For instance, many National Science Foundation (NSF) grants will not accept applications from institutions outside of the R1 and R2 tiers. Many grants are available only to researchers at undergraduate teaching institutions or liberal arts colleges. As a result, researchers at R1 and R2 institutions will tend to go for large, nationally recognized government-sponsored grants, whereas researchers at D/PU institutions will tend to rely more on grants from foundations since that they are unable to apply for big-ticket governments grants such as those awarded by the NSF or the National Institutes of Health (NIH). Likewise, researchers at undergraduate teaching institutions and liberal arts colleges tend to target a different set of national grants of lower monetary values, and which usually are not to be used to purchase equipment or data unless undergraduate research is involved. Thus, before you put in the hard work of applying for a grant, make sure researchers at your institution can apply for that grant. If you are not eligible for a given grant (say, because your institution is not allowed to apply for specific grants, or because you do not have the necessary administrative support), it is often possible for you to apply for it as a sub-awardee or as a consultant on someone else's grant who is at an eligible institution.

Likewise, different fields get grants from different sources. Researchers in agricultural economics, development economics, environmental economics, and industrial organization are often funded through government grants. Health economists rely on both government grants and foundation grants, with the most prominent such foundation being the

Robert Wood Johnson Foundation. Monetary economists are almost entirely funded through think tanks. Experimental economists tend to be funded through foundations as well; this is especially true of behavioral economists, whose work is often funded by the Russell Sage Foundation. Given how each field has its funding idiosyncrasies, and given increasingly stringent funding disclosure rules at many journals, I suggest reading the acknowledgments footnote of the papers published in your field for indications of where research funding comes from in that field.

5.1 Internal versus External Funding and Indirect Costs

A useful dichotomy when it comes to funding is internal versus external funding. "Internal funding" refers to grants and other sources of funding within your institution, whether at the level of the department, school, college, or university. The higher internal funds are within your institution's hierarchy, the harder they are to get, both because you will face more competition for every dollar of funding and because your proposal will be read by people who are further removed from your area of research.[3]

"External funding" refers to grants and other forms of funding outside of your institution. Any funding from local, state, and federal governments or their agencies (e.g., NIH, NSF), from foundations (e.g., Ford Foundation, Pew Charitable Trust, Rockefeller Foundation), or from international organizations (e.g., the Consultative Group on International Agricultural Research) is external funding.

Beyond defining those terms, why is it useful to know the difference between the two? Because typically in a job where grants are seen as outputs more than inputs (i.e., in a job where grantsmanship is an explicit tenure and promotion criterion, and where there are clear incentives to get funding), a dollar of external money is worth more to your career than a dollar of internal money given that it is both more difficult to compete for external funds (and submitting grant proposals and being successful at getting funds is a form of peer review) and literally worth more to your institution because typically, for every external grant dollar

---

3. For many internal sources of funding, you are more likely to get funded if you can clearly explain that you plan on applying for external funding later on, and make a credible case for why you think you are likely to receive that external funding. In that sense, many internal sources of funding are intended as seed money, i.e., as funds to be leveraged to get more funds.

you bring in, your institution will have you pay up to an additional 60 percent. This means that if you need $100,000 for a given research project, you will have to request $160,000 from the funder to cover these so-called indirect costs.

For most economists, this system of indirect cost recovery (ICR) can be rather frustrating. This is because the stated reason for universities to recover indirect costs—the university has to be able to host your research project and provide the relevant physical and administrative infrastructures—is less likely to apply to economists than to some other disciplines. Unlike natural scientists, who often need expensive laboratories occupying valuable space in university real estate, most economists can do their research on a laptop with a reliable Internet connection. Moreover, when they do change, ICRs almost always go up. As I write these lines, the ICR at my own institution is 54 percent, but it will go up to 55 percent next academic year.

There are various ways to reduce the amount paid in ICR. First and foremost, if you are applying for funding with a team of coauthors, it is worth asking them what the ICR rate is at their institution, and go with the one that has the lowest rate.[4] Second, if you can argue that a significant portion of the work done as part of the grant will be done off campus, you can request to pay the off-campus rather than the on-campus ICR. I already mentioned that my institution's (on-campus) ICR is 54 percent. But if I were to get a grant to run an RCT in another country, for example, I could lower my ICR to the off-campus rate of 26 percent if I could argue that more than half of the work done as part of that grant would be done off campus.

5.2   How Much Funding Do You Need?

The first question to ask yourself is "How much funding do I realistically need?" Although we are trained from the very beginning as economists to think that utility is increasing in money, and so your immediate answer

---

4. That said, bear in mind that the spread of those rates will be rather tight. In a 2014 survey of ICRs at the top 50 institutions in terms of funding received from the NIH (Datahound 2014), New York University had a whopping 69-percent indirect cost rate. The lowest ICR in that survey was the University of Florida's 49 percent. A colleague who teaches at a liberal arts college tells me the ICR at her institution is 39 percent, but that the ICR at another liberal arts college across town is much higher, and on par with the figures quoted earlier.

to this question might be "As much as possible!," it is worth noting that additional grant money always comes at a cost, that a grant is a contract between the funding agency or donor (as principal) and you (as agent), and to recall that in contract theory, the agent's cost of effort is almost always assumed increasing *and convex* in effort for a good reason. In other words, the expected benefits you derive from grant funding should not exceed the certain costs of getting that funding, starting with the considerable fixed costs involved in preparing grant proposals. The variable costs include the cost of doing the research, the opportunity cost of your time (which you can sometimes cover with your grant, but only up to a point), the cost of supervising grant personnel (sometimes across time zones, to the detriment of a healthy sleep schedule), the cost of managing the grant,[5] and finally the cost of preparing the deliverables.[6]

So how much funding do you actually need? Before applying for a grant, it is worth asking yourself the following questions:

1. *Are grants an input or an output in your research process?* I have alluded to this earlier in this chapter, but do you need to raise funds as an explicit criterion for tenure or promotion (i.e., grants as an output), or do you only need those funds for your research (i.e., grants as an input)? In the former case, you will need more grant funding (ideally both more grant dollars and more grants from prestigious sources of funding) than in the latter case—at least for tenure or promotion, if not for your actual research.

2. *How excited are you about this particular research project? How excited can you remain about it without working on it for a few months?* Not all research questions are created equal. You will be so excited about some research projects that you will wake up in the middle of the night wanting to work on them. Others merely fulfill someone else's need for an answer about something you are knowledgeable about, but have no particular interest in. Choose wisely, because although the payoff is

---

5. A colleague noted that this is generally independent of the size of the grant, and that managing a multimillion dollar grant is often no more costly than managing a $150,000 grant. This means that you are often much better off getting one big grant than cobbling together the same funds from many different sources.

6. The same colleague mentioned that the costs of applying for a grant can be significantly reduced if you are sub-awardee on someone else's grant proposal.

uncertain (you may not get the grant), you will bear the certain cost of applying for a grant.[7]

3. *Are there other ways to answer the research question at hand (or a nearly identical one) which do not require grant funding? Or are there other research questions you could answer instead?* I have done most on my research on a shoestring. Part of that involved decisions at the extensive margin (i.e., "I will not work on this question, because it would involve conducting an RCT, which I do not have the human-resource management skills for"), but some of it also involved decisions at the intensive margin (i.e., "Although it would be ideal to collect my own data on this, I can get close enough using an existing data set.") One of my PhD students, for instance, wanted to look at the effect of output price volatility on whether individuals exited the agricultural sector. After we discussed it together, she realized that no survey of agriculture recorded farm exits, and that any seeming exit could also simply be sample attrition. So instead of getting into a costly data collection effort, she decided instead to look at whether output price volatility drove rural households to make one of theirs migrate, presumably in search of wage work (Lee 2021).

4. *How much do you (dis)like managing finances, human resources, or both?* Some institutions (e.g., R1 universities) will have better administrative resources to help you with this, but getting grants often involves no uncertain amount of financial and human resource management skills. As Dean Yang noted in an interview for the book *Experimental Conversations* (Ogden 2017), such skills are not taught in graduate programs in economics or related disciplines.[8] If you are the kind of person who dreads doing his or her own taxes, whose eyes glaze over when discussing the details of a mortgage or of an investment strategy for retirement, who dislikes having to tell a subordinate that they are not performing well or, worse, that they are fired, you are better off not getting into the grants

---

7. A colleague also suggested a ratcheting-up strategy, wherein you get a small grants to test out an idea and establish a proof of concept, and if the idea works, scale it up by going for bigger grants.

8. A colleague who teaches at an R2 notes that at R1s, researchers can focus on the research design and have someone else do the rest, but in her case, she only gets minor help with budget-related stuff, which is a huge barrier to her getting external funding.

game. In the same interview with Ogden (2017) mentioned above, Dean Yang also added that although the skills discussed here are not taught in graduate programs in economics, they are not necessary to do good research. If there is one aspect of a research career where it is helpful to play to your comparative advantage, it is this one.

5. *How much do you (dis)like managing people?* This sounds the same as managing human resources, but it is not. Managing human resources refers to managing people who work for you. Managing people refers to managing personalities, egos, expectations, and so on of everyone involved in a grant, including those who are not your subordinates or who may be your seniors. Very often, writing grant proposals involves colleagues realizing that there are considerable pay differentials between them, which can lead to frustration with one's employer. In some cases, a grant team will involve people who dislike each other. If you tend to avoid socially uncomfortable situations, it is useful to know what you may be getting into.

5.3   Where to Look for Funding?

The ideal approach to scientific research involves observing some phenomenon in the real world, speculating about the causes or consequences of that phenomenon, generating some testable predictions about some of those causes or consequences, finding data to test those predictions (possibly with the help of grant funding), and then testing those predictions.

But in the real world where we live, not all scientific endeavors proceed in the way just described. Very often, "research" questions are answered because someone outside of the research community (e.g., a government agency, a firm, or a nongovernmental organization) has an interest in knowing the answer to specific questions and is giving out funding for it.

There are thus two broad approaches to research. The first starts from observation and then goes in search of funding to test whatever derives from that observation. The second is much like famous climber George Mallory's reason for climbing Mount Everest,[9] and it starts from there being some funding available to answer a specific research question posed by the funding source or to answer a research question in the context of the funding source's call for proposals.

---

9. "Because it's there."

Under the former approach, it helps to be on the lookout for calls or requests for proposals or applications (CfPs, RfPs, or RfAs; the US government uses RfP for contracts, but RfA for grants) coming out of various organizations. Many universities will have an entire web page dedicated to upcoming funding deadlines, often searchable by how soon the deadline is coming, by broad research area (e.g., natural vs. social sciences), or by topic. It also helps to be proactive in regularly looking at various prospective sources of funding's websites. Although what those sources are will obviously vary from field to field and from discipline to discipline, there are some aggregator websites outside of research universities that can be very useful. As of this writing, examples of those websites include the Grants.gov website in the US, the websites of the Marie Curie Fellowships, the European Research Council, and the European Commission in Europe, and the Economic & Social Research Council in the United Kingdom. Almost all if not all of those sources of funding will tend to have funding for broad research areas instead of narrower research questions.

Under the latter approach, catch as catch can, and getting funding becomes a matter of applying for any project you feel qualified to undertake and feel like you have the bandwidth for, keeping in mind the points raised in the previous section. This approach may be especially necessary if your position is a soft-money position wherein you have to raise some or all of your salary every year. Such soft-money positions are common in schools of public health (where the universe of obtainable grants is correspondingly much larger than in most areas of economics) and at multilateral institutions like the agencies that compose the CGIAR, such as the International Food Policy Research Institute.

5.4 Sponsored Project Life Cycle

The typical life cycle of a sponsored project goes roughly as follows:

1. *Pre-proposal stage 1.* Many institutions require all grants to be reported and processed through the institution for legal purposes, no matter the size or source of a grant. Your first step should thus be to let the people at your institution whose job it is to oversee such things know that you are planning on applying for a given grant. This is not a binding commitment, as it is common for such plans to fall through. It is merely a heads-up to the staff at your institution so they can plan accordingly. And given which institutions can and cannot apply for specific types of

funding, this is a good way to ensure that you are actually eligible for the grant you are targeting.

2. *Pre-proposal stage 2.* The most crucial step here is to read every detail that is provided to you by the funder, both in the CfP or RfP and in the documents available on their website. What will be required of you, and when? Can you deliver on what is expected of you? What do funded projects look like? Does yours come close to that description? Additionally, some funders (e.g., some think tanks) come with ideological baggage. Does the funder whose proposal you are considering applying to come with such baggage? If so, are you willing to live with having a reputation for doing ideologically driven work, even though that reputation may not be deserved? If you answer all of these questions in the affirmative, then you should submit a proposal. But if you have any hesitation, you should probably think twice about submitting a proposal, and wait for a better opportunity. A colleague who sits on the funder side suggested that you may even chat with the program officer to be sure you understand what the funder is looking for, as this may lead you to grasp some of the nuances of the research program being funded, which can in turn help with how you write your proposal.

3. *Set your budget.* This is the right time to set your budget, because (i) it forces you to make your collaborators list their budget needs within the grant, (ii) allows you to adjust your goals or number of team members if your budget is unrealistic, and (iii) the budget itself will determine the scope of the work done under the grant, and who is responsible for it. This is the time to figure out whether you can use your grant to pay part of your salary, get summer support,[10] or buy out of teaching a course, and how much it will cost to do so.[11] For more on writing your budget, see Pain (2017).

4. *Make a list of all of the documents you will need to prepare and assemble.* If you apply for a small internal grant, you will usually need nothing more than a short (i.e., two- to five-page) proposal, a short CV, and a budget. But if you apply for a big external grant, you will need a lot more

---

10. It is common for people on nine-month appointments to supplement their nine-month salary with one or two months of grant-funded salary.

11. At liberal arts colleges, buying out of teaching is often strongly discouraged if not impossible.

(e.g., a list of all of your current and past coauthors and collaborators, letters of support from research partners, a biosketch, a list of would-be reviewers, and many required forms). To keep track of everything and make sure everything is included and formatted the right way, you will almost surely need the help of professionals. Luckily, most research universities in the US have an office (usually called Office of Sponsored Programs, Sponsored Programs Administration, or some variant) that helps researchers do that. So when you do decide to apply for a large grant (e.g., an NSF or NIH grant), the first thing you should do is to get in touch with your institution's sponsored programs office to give them a heads up that you want to submit a proposal. That office will then assign a professional to your case who will help you navigate the often dazzlingly complex world of big grants.

5. *Assemble your team.* Many big grants will require a whole team composed of a principal investigator, one or more co-principal investigators, research professionals, graduate students, and administrative staff.

6. *Play to your strengths, and focus on the proposal itself; delegate the rest.* If you are reading this book, it is probably a safe bet to say that you are a research economist, and therefore that your comparative advantage when it comes to preparing grant proposals lies in developing the proposal itself. Focus on that. Delegate the task of filling the various forms required to submit federal grant proposals to your institution's sponsored programs specialists whenever possible.

7. *Get everything assembled at least two weeks before deadline.* For big external grants where you need to work with your institution's sponsored programs office, the institution, not the researcher, submits the grant proposal, and so the sponsored-programs professionals will typically need *at least* five business days to guide your proposal through the relevant channels before submitting on time to meet the deadline. That lead time is necessary not only to ensure that all of your *i*s are dotted and your *t*s crossed so your proposal does not get rejected because of some administrative detail, but also because other researchers at your institution are applying for grants of a similar caliber to the one you are applying to.

8. *Wait for a decision on your proposal.* Just because you have submitted your proposal does not mean you should sit back and not work on the research project you are seeking funding for. No research project is

ever "finished," not even when the main manuscript from it is accepted for publication. There is always something to be done. You can always think of more robustness checks, additional ways of measuring your outcome variable, and additional papers to be written with the data you are seeking funding to collect. You can get the manuscript started and draft the sections that you can write without seeing the data (e.g., most of the introduction, the theoretical framework, the empirical framework). Out of sight, out of mind; if you are anything like me and your present preferences for your future self are not your future preferences for your future self, this is a way to remain interested in this project and not lose your motivation to work on it if and when you do get the grant and must do the real work.

9. *When you hear the result of your proposal.* If you did not get the grant, look for the next source of funding. If you received comments on your proposal, you should use them to make it better for the next submission. Otherwise, you can often reuse a failed proposal for another CfP or RfP almost lock, stock, and barrel—the rules about self-plagiarism do not apply to grant proposals, as there is a broad understanding that such documents are not meant for public consumption, and so it is not necessary to reinvent the wheel. If you did get the grant, the real work begins. Reassemble your team and make sure everyone is still committed to their roles as stated in the proposal. Familiarize yourself again (because it has probably been months since you checked) with the rules about what you can and cannot spend your grant money on, the various reporting deadlines, and what the deliverables are. And *then* start spending grant money on your research project.

10. *Submit reports on time.* Most big, multi-year grants will require you to submit periodic reports on your grant-related activities, usually one such report every year. Those tend to be financial reports that keep the funders appraised of how you are spending their money, but some will also require a narrative about the progress made since the last report. It may be tempting to do a slapdash job on those reports. In the interest of maintaining a good relationship with those who hold the purse strings, avoid doing so. Also make sure you submit those reports on time; submitting them late (or not at all) on some federal grants can lead to hefty fines, if not jail time. If you do not spend the entirety of the grant by the end of the grant period, you can often request a no-cost extension. Make

sure you request those as early as possible before the end of your grant if you realize you cannot do everything before the grant period ends.

11. *Once the grant period concludes, submit your final report and other deliverables on time.* Most grants will require you to submit a final report, and possibly some deliverables (e.g., policy briefs based on the research the grant paid for). Again, it is tempting to do the bare minimum here and to focus instead on the research itself, but if you want to maintain a good relationship with and get more money from this funder, avoid doing so. One thing that is especially easy to overlook here is that knowledge of your bad actions with one funder are likely to easily spread to other funders, because program officers tend to move from job to job within their industry just like academics do, and so funder *B* may withhold funds from you because of your cavalier treatment of funder *A*. As with everything else in this profession, there are few players, you will repeatedly interact with them, and you do not know when the game ends. Act accordingly. For the final report and deliverables, those documents are more often than not for public consumption, so you should make an effort to write clearly and concisely, but the level of rigor required of you is nowhere near that of a journal article. This is where you will want to get into descriptive statistics and provide deep background as much as you can in order to tell a clear, accessible, and compelling story, just as you would do for a peer-reviewed article.

12. *Be grateful to the funder.* Many journals require authors to disclose any and all sources of funding for a submitted manuscript, and many funders will also require you to acknowledge their support in the work you publish thanks for their financial support. Even in the absence of such requirements, you always should include the funder (and the grant number, if applicable) in the acknowledgement footnote of each paper made possible by the work undertaken in the grant. This is true no matter how big or small the grant. Make sure you send your funders a copy of each article, book chapter, and so on which their funding made possible.

13. *Make yourself available to review proposals for this funder.* If the source of funding for your research relies on external reviewers to determine whether it should fund proposals, it is a matter of simple gratitude to make yourself available to review future proposals. Much like the peer-review process involved with publishing journal articles, you should

implicitly agree to review two or three proposals for every proposal of yours that gets funded.

5.5   Preparing Successful Grant Proposals

Having just seen the life cycle of a typical sponsored project, it is now time to discuss how to prepare proposals that maximize your chances of getting funded.

Once you have chosen to submit a proposal in response to a given CfP or RfP, the first thing you should do is ask the funder's contact person (usually their program officer) whether they are willing to make available examples of previous grant proposals, both successful and unsuccessful. Many funders will not be willing to do so, but you will not know unless you ask politely. If the funder is unwilling to make proposals available, you can try asking your institution's office of sponsored programs for examples of proposals submitted to the same funder. Even proposals on entirely different topics can be useful for you to learn how to structure your own proposal, what level of detail to go into, and so on.

Second, you should ask that same program officer about who is going to be evaluating proposals for this specific RfP or CfP. Will your reviewers be other economists in your field? Other economists who may or may not be in your field? A mix of economists and people from other disciplines? Or strictly people from other disciplines? Much like you would want to adapt how you write an article depending on whether you plan on submitting to a field journal, a general economics journal, an interdisciplinary journal, or a general science journal, you should aim to write your proposal with a view to your audience. An audience of economists will almost surely want to see equations when you discuss your theoretical framework, your empirical framework, or both. The same equations, however, are likely to antagonize an interdisciplinary audience.

Third, you should ask around to see whether anyone in your network has previously received the grant you are targeting. If they have, ask them whether they would be willing to share their insights about preparing a successful proposal for this grant.

Fourth, you should write out a rough sketch of your proposal that includes at the very least the following sections:

1. *Introduction and motivations.* Even once you have a good idea of whom your reviewers are going to be, it is a mistake to assume that they know everything you know. Motivate as broadly as you can given your

intended audience, state your research question as clearly as possible (e.g., "This project aims to estimate the causal impact of having an Asian name on the chances of getting called for a job interview by conducting an audit study in Minneapolis–Saint Paul during the period January 1 to June 30, 2021" is much better than "This project aims to investigate the effect of discrimination against Asian-Americans on the labor market"), explain clearly how your work innovates relative to what has already been done, and then explain how your work fits with the funder's objectives for this grant, which should have been stated clearly in the RfP, as well as with the funder's mission statement, which you can usually find on the funder's website. Some RfPs reference a specific literature when they discuss the goal of the grant. When that is the case, use that literature (as well as references that build on that literature) to motivate your proposal.

2. *Theoretical framework.* This goes by many names (e.g., theory of change), and depending on the grant you are applying for, it can be anything from a simple verbal conceptual model (in cases where the theory behind what you wish to study has already been explored, or in cases where you are writing for an audience that includes non-economists) to a hardcore theoretical model (in cases where the theory behind what you wish to study has not been explored or needs to be expanded *and* your audience consists of your peers). In either case, what should be crystal clear in your theoretical framework is what you wish to test using the funder's grant money. Perhaps more than anywhere else in your grant proposal, this is where it helps to know who your reviewers are going to be, at least in terms of their disciplines, and to write for the right audience.

3. *Research.* I realize this is vague, but it is necessary for me to remain vague given the breadth of work done by economists. Here, whatever you plan to spend the grant money on must be discussed, whether that means collecting survey data, purchasing one or more data sets, conducting lab or lab-in-the-field experiments, hiring research assistants, what you will be doing in exchange for the salary you may be paying yourself, or the course you may be buying out of using grant funds, and if the funder allows the following expenses: buying software or equipment required to do the work required by the grant, traveling to conferences to discuss the work done under this grant, paying for publication fees for articles

produced under this grant, and so on. Whatever methods the proposed research will use, here is where you have to discuss these in detail, clearly explaining why the methods you propose to use will lead to the best possible result for the funder's money.

4. *Timeline*. Most CfPs will require you to submit a detailed timeline. This is a year-by-year (and, if possible, month-by-month) rundown of what will be done in the context of the grant for the duration of the life of the sponsored project. A good rule of thumb here is to be pessimistic regarding how long things will take; if you think it will take you one month to develop an experimental protocol, budget two months for it instead of falling short on your own expectations and then having to play catch-up for the remainder of the grant's lifetime. Moreover, many funders now want the timeline to be embedded with a management plan discussing the people and tasks involved at every step.

5. *Other requirements*. Different funders will require sundry other things as part of the proposals they entertain. This can be as minor as a discussion of where you will place the funder's logo on the materials you give your subjects as part of the treatment whose effects you plan on studying, and as serious as a commitment to taking part in a conference where you present your results to the funder and other grantees.

6. *References*. Any grant proposal worth its salt will appeal to the literature to explain and justify its existence. This means your proposal should include a standard list of references. It also might not hurt to cite the relevant work that the funder has funded in the past.

7. *Anticipated outputs*. What documents or data sets will you receiving this grant make possible? Though you may be driven by the relentless pursuit of peer-reviewed articles (and you should be so driven if you have yet to get tenure or equivalent in your job), funders generally care less about peer-reviewed research. What they do care about will vary from funder to funder, but generally they will want you to prepare some report that can be circulated to stakeholders (e.g., policy makers) or to the general public, to make your data available for others to conduct their own empirical work, to make presentations at specially convened meetings of grantees or stakeholders, to write blog posts and op-eds on your research findings, and so on. Increasingly, funders will also want you to make the data collected under their aegis publicly available, so it helps to plan for that as well.

Whether it is an explicit part of the proposal itself or not, you will almost always have to submit a budget with your grant proposals. Indeed, it is exceedingly rare for a funder to give you a no-strings-attached lump sum of money to just go do research with. When preparing your budget for a grant, you should keep the following things in mind:

1. *It is fine to ask for the maximum allowed amount of money.* Sure, at the margin, between two proposals that differ only in how much funding they request, the one that is requesting less money is more likely to be funded. The problem with that reasoning, however, is twofold: *ceteris* is rarely ever *paribus*, and your proposal is unlikely to be the marginal proposal. So if a funder is willing to allow you to request up to $250,000, do not feel compelled to cut your budget in order to improve your chances of getting the grant. It may be especially tempting to cut the salary you are paying yourself out of a grant if you think it will improve your chances of getting funded. Avoid doing so: the funder would much rather know that you are getting paid for the work you are doing under their grant (and thus have an incentive to actually do that work and give it your best effort) than see you work for free (and thus have little to no incentive to perform the work, or treat it as an afterthought).[12]

2. *Provide precise dollar amounts.* It is imprecise to say that your plane ticket from Minneapolis to Lima will be roughly $1500, and it will make you look sloppy. It is much better to say that your MSP-ATL-LIM return trip on Delta Airlines' main-economy cabin departing August 15 and returning September 5 will cost $1438.00, as that has the double advantage of (i) allowing you to plan more carefully and precisely, and (ii) signaling that you are taking this grant seriously. It is a small detail, but one that will speak volumes about the kind of attention you pay to details.

3. *Think of everything you will need.* As a graduate student, I was fortunate enough to get an NSF doctoral dissertation improvement grant to conduct a survey in rural Madagascar. So in addition to flights from the US to Madagascar, I would need to pay for a visas, vaccines and prophylaxes, bug repellent, respondent payouts, software for data analysis, and so on.

4. *Do not skimp on anything.* The same logic that applied to the totality of your grant also applies to individual categories: it is better to slightly

---

12. Very often, the people in a foundation who will read your budget are not the same as the people who will read your proposal itself.

overestimate how much you will need for those categories where you cannot find exact prices *ex ante* just in case things end up being more expensive than you had initially anticipated. Cost estimates (instead of exact costs) are acceptable in cases where you simply cannot find an exact cost, or where there is cost uncertainty.

Figure 5.1 shows a sample budget for the Peruvian lab-in-the-field component of the experimental work we discuss in Bellemare, Lee, and Just (2020). Notice the precise dates and prices for air travel. Notice transportation costs both from the US to Peru, and also transportation costs in country. Notice the different per diems for different cities in Peru.[13] Notice how we factored in the cost of immunizations and pro-phylaxes given that we were traveling to areas with non-negligible health risks. Finally, notice how we only estimated costs for the things we could not be sure of, such as daily salaries for in-country employees.

5.6   Human Subjects

Many of the sponsored projects we work on as economists involve human subjects. This can be as simple as recruiting people for a survey with such innocuous questions as "What is your age?" to surveys with more intrusive questions like "Do you have HIV?" to downright invasive surveys where blood samples are taken from subjects to measure the level of iron in their blood.

In all cases where a sponsored project involves human subjects—and for economists, that is almost always the case—you will have to seek the approval of a recognized institutional review board (IRB), usually the one at your institution.[14] To make a long story short, ethical protocols surrounding research with human subjects emerged as a byproduct of the Nuremberg trials, which were held by Allied forces after World War II to prosecute not only Nazi leaders, but also Nazi scientists who had conducted abhorrent experiments with human subjects. The Nuremberg Code, which presents principles for ethical research with human subjects, was created so that such inhumane experiments with human subjects would never take place again.

---

13. You can find US government-approved per diems for most big cities in the US and in the world online.

14. In cases where researchers from multiple institutions collaborate, it is generally possible to seek approval from only one institution's IRB, and to make that IRB the IRB of record.

Sample Budget

Item	Price	Units	Total
Travel			
Roundtrip Tickets MSP-LIM June 24 to July 4, 2015	1293.34	2	2586.68
Roundtrip Ticket ITH-LIM June 24 to July 4, 2015	1436.84	1	1436.84
Roundtrips LIM-CUZ	368.93	3	1106.79
Per Diem for Lima	353.00	12	4236.00
Per Diem for Cusco	333.00	18	5994.00
Immunizations and Prophylaxes	200.00	3	600.00
Summer Support (Bellemare; Includes Fringe)	14707.00	1	14707.00
Summer Support (Lee)	5979.00	1	5979.00
Graduate Student Fringe (25.5%, Exempt from Indirects)	1525.00	1	1525.00
Fieldwork			
Daily Salary (Field Coordinator)	100.00	20	2000.00
Daily Salary (Head Enumerator)	70.00	20	1400.00
Daily Salary (Two Enumerators, $50 Each)	100.00	20	2000.00
Per Diem (Field Coordinator and Head Enumerator, $83.30 Each)	166.60	20	3332.00
Per Diem (Two Enumerators, $50 Each)	100.00	20	2000.00
Roundtrips LIM-CUZ (All Field Personnel)	368.93	4	1475.72
Internal Transportation (Head Enumerator)	235.00	1	235.00
Materials	83.00	1	83.00
Road Transportation to Selected Communities (Daily Cost)	117.00	10	1170.00
Experimental Payouts			
Average Payout Per Respondent	20.00	100	2000.00
Total Before Indirect			53,867.03
Indirect Costs			13,608.93
Total Requested			67,475.96

Figure 5.1
Sample budget

Now, most economic research involving human subjects is a far cry from what the Nuremberg Code sought to prevent, but because economists often collect sensitive data from or experiment with human subjects, the work that we do falls under the broad umbrella of human subjects research, and an economist interested in running a lab experiment to study how people behave in a public goods game is under the same restrictions as a team of medical doctors who are seeking to test the effectiveness of a new vaccine.

If you have never sought IRB approval before, you will first have to sit through about an afternoon's worth of training on how to approach human subjects—the history of human subjects research ethics, what counts as human subjects research, what you can and cannot do with human subjects, and how you should handle confidentiality issues. There are organizations that provide this training. The CITI program, for example,[15] offers such training for researchers at subscriber institutions (universities, for the most part, but also private-sector firms that conduct research on human subjects) who do not offer their own training. Even though IRB certification is required to apply for most if not all grants involving human subjects, oftentimes we rush through this training because it is just one more thing we have to do in order to submit a grant proposal. It is worth paying attention to what that training entails, however, both because it makes us more responsible researchers and because it makes us more informed citizens.[16]

What does tend to get more onerous is filling out the various required forms necessary to get IRB approval for your research with human subjects. This will usually consist of a form provided to you by your institution's IRB that you have to fill out with your answers to various questions (e.g., number of subjects, potential risk to your subjects, whether subjects will include children or members of vulnerable categories), the consent form you will use for your human subjects to give their free and full assent to being included in your research, as well as any translation in

---

15. See www.citiprogram.org.

16. Lest you think of having to get approval for research with human subjects as an antiquated procedure, as I write these lines in October 2020, the American media has just revealed to the public that the US government has allegedly been performing forced hysterectomies on migrant women at Immigration and Customs Enforcement detention facilities (Treisman 2020), and worse stories involving cruel experiments with human subjects have been percolating from North Korea for decades.

the language(s) spoken by your subjects, the various survey instruments, research, and experimental protocols you will be using (or advanced drafts thereof), and so on.

Because the details of any IRB application tend to be specific to a given research project, there is not much to be offered in the way of guidance other than (i) get started as early as you can on getting IRB approval, as the process can take several weeks,[17] and (ii) have patience with your institution's IRB staff, because they generally tend to deal with biomedical research projects instead of social science projects. For example, IRB approval was once withheld from me because the IRB staff deemed that the lab-in-the-field experiments I was planning to run were "gambling." After I politely explained that lab games were common in economics, marketing, psychology, and other disciplines, and that payouts were necessary for truthful revelation, IRB approval was granted.

---

17. It is sometimes possible to request an expedited review (instead of a full review) if the risk to your subjects is low. This is often the case with economics research, and so it is well worth asking for an expedited review whenever possible.

6

Doing Service

"Service" is the broad term whereby economics and other disciplines refer to activities that are aimed at providing the public goods necessary for researchers to be able do research. Service activities can range from the local (e.g., serving on the undergraduate committee in your department) to the regional (e.g., organizing a session at the annual meeting of the Southern Economic Association), and from the national (e.g., serving on the board of directors of the Canadian Economics Association) to the international (e.g., serving as treasurer of the European Economic Association). Even in a career outside of academia, opportunities for service will abound if you decide to remain involved in research.

If you are planning on a career in academia, it is best to realize sooner rather than later that in addition to doing good research and teaching well, you will eventually have to do your share of service if you wish to get merit raises and promotions.[1] Modern universities are in many ways different from other hierarchies (in the Williamson 1975 sense of the word), but one way in which they clearly differ is faculty governance. At most of the world's universities, a group of employees who are not professional managers but who instead have emerged from faculty ranks govern the hierarchy. Thus, whereas modern run-of-the-mill widget-making firms often hire someone with an MBA to manage the firm instead

---

1. Although many institutions will try to protect junior faculty from having to do any (or at the very least too much) service so that they may dedicate themselves to teaching and getting their research agendas off the ground, this tends to go out the window after tenure, when the service expectation often goes from none or very little to quite a bit. One rule of thumb when it comes to tenure (i.e., the move from assistant to associate professor in the US) and promotion (i.e., the move from associate to full professor in the US) is this: in order to get tenure, you need to excel in teaching and research. In order to be promoted to full professor, you need to excel in teaching, research, *and* service.

of promoting a widget-maker to the rank of manager, universities tend to be run by academics, from the president (or chief executive officer) and the provost (or chief academic officer) on down to department chairs and program directors. So if you hope to have a fruitful academic career, it is best to plan for doing service.

The bad news is that, as its name indicates, service tends to be either unpaid work, or work where the pay falls well short of marginal productivity of labor. The good news is that service comes in many shapes and colors, which means you typically can choose the kind of service that is right for you.

6.1   How Much and What Kind of Service to Do?

As I mentioned above, some departments, schools, colleges, and institutions[2] will deliberately try to protect their junior faculty's time by having junior faculty do little to no service. Whether this is a good thing or a bad thing depends entirely on the culture of the institution. I have closely observed institutions where the leadership was keen on saying to whoever would listen that they were protecting their junior faculty's research time by excusing them from service commitments—a statement which, while strictly true, also concealed a means of asserting existing power structures by depriving junior faculty of a voice when it came to faculty governance. At other institutions, people in leadership positions will say the same thing and mean it, but they will also let junior faculty do as much service as they feel comfortable with.

In some other departments, junior faculty will be asked to do their fair share of service. This is especially true in smaller departments (e.g., departments with fewer than 12 to 15 full-time tenure-track faculty members), where the fixed costs of running the department are borne by fewer individuals. In departments where junior faculty are asked to do their fair share, the best-case scenario is one where this is explicitly recognized come tenure time, and where standards of excellence in teaching and research are thus adjusted as a result. Unfortunately, the opposite scenario, where the senior faculty are completely checked out and expect junior faculty to do all the heavy lifting, is not uncommon.

How much service should you do, if you are given the occasion to do so? When starting out on the tenure track, you should do no more

---

2. For the remainder of this chapter, unless otherwise noted, I will use "institution" to refer to any or all of those entities.

service than what is expected of you, and when considering the marginal decision to take on one more piece of service, you should really consider a handful of factors. The first factor is that, like teaching, no amount of excellence in service can substitute for a research agenda that falls below your institution's threshold for what constitutes "good enough for tenure" when it comes to *both* research and teaching. The second factor is whether a particular piece of service gives you an occasion to become known to those who will weigh in on your tenure decision—your departmental colleagues, your colleagues at the college level, and your dean, but also your prospective external review letter writers—for doing good things. The third factor to consider is how onerous a given piece of service will be for you, and whether and how much you expect to enjoy performing that service.

From the foregoing, a few general principles emerge for pre-tenure academics:

1. *Everything else equal, between departmental- and college-level service, prefer departmental-level service, and between college- and university-level service, prefer college-level service.* This is because your departmental colleagues are going to be the ones to directly assess your performance for tenure, and serving on committees with them will give them an occasion to get to know you outside of looking at your publications and your teaching evaluations. Obviously, this assumes that you do a good job and pull your weight.

A useful if coarse and imperfect way of thinking about what kind of service to do is this: As an assistant professor, prioritize departmental service. As an associate professor, you can expand your service activities to college-level service. As a full professor, you can expand your service activities to university-level service and beyond.

2. *Avoid serving as program director.* Though most departments will avoid having junior faculty serve as director of undergraduate or graduate studies, some will not. For junior faculty, this is the kind of service that should be avoided like the plague. This is because although the vast majority of students, undergraduate and graduate, will require little to none of your time, the job of a director of undergraduate or graduate studies is to serve as backstop for problem cases, which can (and likely will) monopolize a great deal of your time.

3. *Prefer service that is concentrated in time.* For junior faculty, there is nothing better than serving on a committee that meets only a few times,

or doing service circumscribed to a given period of time. Graduate admissions committees tend to meet a few times from December until about February, with little or nothing to do the rest of the academic year. Serving as graduate placement director will usually require that you hold a few preparatory sessions for your department's job-market candidates in the fall, and serve as a resource for them between January and late March, if that.

4. *Prefer service that will allow you to become known to your prospective external review letter writers.* This comes in several flavors, namely local, and national, or international. One version of this is that if your department has a seminar series, you should volunteer to organize or co-organize it. It can be quite a bit of work to invite people to come give a talk in your seminar, coordinate their flights and hotels, take them out to dinner, and process reimbursements, but usually the size of the effort required is commensurate with a department's resources. That is, if your department has the resources necessary to invite four or five external speakers per semester on the one hand, then it has the resources to provide you with the help of an administrative assistant to do the paperwork, and you only need to select whom to invite and where to take them out to dinner on your department's dime. On the other hand, if your department only has the resources necessary to invite one or two external speakers per year, you will not have that much paperwork to do to make those one or two visits happen. The obvious upside is that by volunteering to organize a seminar series, you can choose to invite people who are likely to be asked to write your external review letters for tenure (e.g., editors of journals in your field, senior researchers who have written on the topics you are currently working on, and so on).

Another good service opportunity for early-career researchers is organizing a session on a given topic at a conference. Many international, national, and regional conferences solicit such sessions, where three to five papers on a given topic are presented in an effort to feature the state of the art on that topic. If you are an early-career researcher, this is can be a golden opportunity to get to know senior researchers in your area, and to get them to hear about your work.[3]

---

3. A closely related option, if you have the resources to do so, is to organize a small, two-day conference at your institution featuring a mix of junior and senior academics in your area of research.

By that token, you may be tempted to think of putting together a special issue of a journal. I would strongly caution anyone—especially junior faculty—against doing so, as there is little to no reward to be derived from it. In most cases, not only will the senior scholars who respond favorably to a call for or solicitation of papers for a special issue not submit their best work to that special issue, but your interactions with them will also often be of a purely virtual nature. Worse, deadlines are often soft for such special issues and people treat them as such, and as a junior scholar, you effectively have little to no coercive power over senior scholars who are ultimately doing you a favor by contributing to your special issue.

Everything I have said in the previous paragraph is multiplied tenfold for edited volumes.[4]

As your place in the profession becomes more secure once you get tenure, the scope for service increases, and once you get promoted to full professor, the sky is the limit. There are many ways to contribute to an institution's mission and service, though not as outward-facing as teaching and research, can certainly be very gratifying.

6.2   Institutional versus Professional Service

Opportunities for service will abound if you seek them out, and they will abound both at your institution and within the various professional associations you belong to (e.g., Economic History Association, Society for Economic Dynamics, Southern Economic Association). The question then becomes whether you should prioritize institutional service—that is, "local" service, or service at your home institution—or professional service.

Here is how I like to think about that question. When I started out on the tenure track, a senior health economist who was one of my colleagues told me "You will get no credit whatsoever for loyalty to the institution." And he was right: an institution will never love you back. We are all (academic) entrepreneurs whose research is to a large extent disembodied from the institution where market forces have come together to have us

---

4. A joke I once read—and I unfortunately cannot find a source for it—went something like this: "Scientists have finally proven that information can escape a black hole. They unfortunately could not prove the same for an edited volume." And indeed, my experience with them is that you should avoid contributing to them, and you should avoid having to edit them even more.

hang up our shingle. This is not to say that you should not be grateful that you have a job, and that you have a job where you currently work. The point is that one should keep things in perspective, and not invest things with a power that they do not have.

That being said, here is how I approach the institutional versus professional service dichotomy.

First, anything you do in terms of professional service will almost surely count outside of your institution, on the market at large. Conversely, a lot of what you do in terms of institutional service is unlikely to count outside of your institution. Therefore, between professional and institutional service, the former is much more likely to raise your reservation wage than the latter.

Second, even in places that try to protect their junior faculty from having to do too much service, your institution will expect you to do a modicum of service beyond attending departmental meetings. Thus, you likely face a binding constraint when it comes to institutional service, though where exactly that constraint binds is probably a bit fuzzy (i.e., "You should do some departmental service") rather than a bright line (i.e., "You need to sit on at least two of our seven committees.")

The conclusion is that at a minimum, you should do enough service to satisfy your local institutional constraint, and when it comes to professional service, you should do as much as you feel will benefit your career. One indirect benefit of taking on professional service (which is usually taken on on a voluntary basis) is that it can give you a get-out-of-jail-free card. That is, when you get asked to do institutional service which you would rather not do, it always comes in handy when you can point to all the professional service you are already doing as a reason for declining.

6.3   Reviewing

The one professional service task you are likely to be called upon to perform early in your career is reviewing manuscripts for journals. Reviewing (or refereeing; the two are interchangeable) is a thankless task. Ostensibly, beyond listing the journals you have refereed for in your CV, there is no outward glory in reviewing. In some cases, you may get an automatic email once a decision has been made on a manuscript you have reviewed informing you of the editor's decision, and thanking you for your service to the journal, but not all journals do that. Less commonly, a journal you have reviewed for might give an annual award to its best reviewers. Generally, however, only a handful of people will ever get to see the effort you put into your reviews, and among that handful of people, most of them will not know your name, and some of them may even resent you for it. In some rare cases, you may receive some symbolic compensation—usually just about enough to cover your share of a nice dinner out—if you return your review in time, but that remains uncommon.[5]

This last paragraph should have raised a number of questions in your mind, and so the goal of this section is to provide answers to those questions.

Why review manuscripts for journals if I am not getting paid for it? For the peer-review process to work, you have to give at least as much as you take. Let us consider the most optimistic of scenarios—so optimistic, in fact, as to border on fiction if you have any ambition: the first journal you ever send a paper to sends out your manuscript to two reviewers, and they both recommend that your paper be accepted "as is." This means that for your one submission, you have benefited from two reviewers giving your manuscript a thorough read. In this hypothetical scenario, for the system to work, you should perform at least two reviews.

Realistically, however, odds are your paper will be rejected after review a few times, that it will have more than two reviewers at some journals, and that when it does get accepted, it gets accepted after one or two rounds of revisions, so that your total debt to the peer-review system for that one publication is more like eight to ten reviews. That is why you should review manuscripts for journals even if you are not getting paid for it. As I have noted in earlier chapters, (almost) everyone is smart in this profession. If you really wish to stand out, contribute to public goods.

How do I get to review for a journal? In order for you to be asked to review a manuscript, the editor in charge of that manuscript has to know who you are and what you are qualified to review. Short of having an advisor who edits a journal, the best way for an editor to know who you are and what you are qualified to review is for you to submit to their journal, but there are also other ways. Very often, a senior scholar whom I solicit a review from will be unable to do so, but they will suggest their junior coauthor or a student of theirs instead. Less commonly, when you are at the start of your career, an editor will ask you to serve as reviewer

---

5. Getting paid to review is uncommon when reviewing manuscripts for journals, but it is more common when reviewing book manuscripts.

because a paper they are handling cites your work. Though you might be champing at the bit and be looking forward to refereeing, it is relatively rare that emailing an editor to tell them you would like to review for their journal will actually lead to the desired outcome.

I was asked to review a paper; what do I do? First, let the editor know whether you accept or decline the reviewing assignment as soon as you get their request. The peer-review process is slow enough in economics that you should not take days (or worse, weeks) after opening an email inviting you to review a manuscript before responding. The quicker you act on that email, the more you help speed things along for the authors.

Second, how do you decide whether you should agree to do a review or not? My own rule for myself, before I had any editorial duties of my own, was to never turn down a refereeing request when asked by a legitimate—that is, non-predatory—journal, because there is a great deal of value in reading bad papers, as I discussed in chapter 2. But I was in a privileged position at the time, with our daughter yet to be born, and with my teaching load never exceeding two classes per semester. As a rule, when it comes to refereeing, I would suggest doing as much as you can because there is a lot to learn from reviewing all kinds of papers.

"As much as you can," however, tends to vary both between and within individuals, and there are very good reasons to decline a review. If you have just had a child, are caring for an elderly parent, are seriously ill, or have any other personal constraint, it is perfectly fine to turn down a reviewing request. If you already have a pending review assignment for the same journal, that is also a good reason to decline doing a review. Another good reason is if you have three or more other reviews pending for various journals, or if you have a conflict of interest. Ultimately, any *good* reason to decline is fine, provided you let the editor know why you are declining so she does not think you are simply blowing her off.

Here are a few reasons to decline a reviewing assignment which I have been given as editor and which I would consider less than good. Here is one: "I am on sabbatical." This one is especially bad because if you are on sabbatical, it is presumably so you can delve into research. What better way is there to remain abreast of what is being done in your field than to serve as reviewer? Another: "This is not my research topic." Be that as it may, sometimes an editor wants to have the opinion of someone who is not an expert on a given topic, just to see if a paper will be interesting to more than the ten or so people in the world who care about a topic. And another: "I am too busy." There are very few people in this profession who are not "too busy," and yet things still get done.

Why does it matter that you give a good reason to decline when you do so? Because very often, the editors of the journals you submit to are among the handful of scholars whose external evaluations of your research *and* service records will be solicited when you go up for tenure or for promotion. Ideally, you want your external reviewers to want and be able to say good things (or at the very least, not have anything negative to say) about you in their letters. Though most early-career researchers may not realize it, getting tenure at your home institution is a by-product of getting tenure in the profession first and foremost. Even though economics has tolerated more than its fair share of jerks for far too long, being a good citizen of the profession can never hurt your career.

Additionally, if you have any hope of becoming an editorial board member, associate editor, co-editor, editor—all titles that unfortunately have different meanings at different journals, but which show that the profession has recognized your contribution and your acumen when it comes to identifying good research—you should realize that a journal's reviewers are the minor-league team from which the major-league team of editors recruits.

You have convinced me to review as much as I can. How can I be a good reviewer? Beyond responding to invitations in time, the key to being a good reviewer is to (i) write constructive reviews that are (ii) at the right level for the journal you are reviewing for and (iii) make comments at the right margin for the paper you have been asked to read.

Unpacking the foregoing, by writing constructive reviews, what I mean is this: when you point out a problem, do your best to offer the way in which the authors can address it, even if you do not think the authors can do so. For example, if the authors would require more data to truly establish the result they are after, the authors would much rather be told "I do not think the authors can establish their desired result with the data they currently have, but they should be able to do so with more data" than "I do not believe the empirical results."

By suggesting that you write reviews at the right level for the journal you are reviewing for, what I mean is that not every journal is at the level of the *American Economic Review*, and pointing out every possible flaw you can find about a paper you are reviewing for a field journal or a second-tier general journal to make yourself look smart in the eyes of the editor in charge is likely to have the opposite effect; the quality of a review is only weakly correlated with its length.

Finally, and on a related note, by suggesting that you make comments at the correct margin for the paper, what I mean is that if you know that a paper has a fundamental flaw that the authors will be unable to address, it is perfectly fine to write a short (i.e., between a half-page and one page) review pointing out that flaw, and explaining why you do not think the authors can realistically fix it. But if you see a path to publication for a paper and recommend that the authors be given a chance at revising and resubmitting, then by all means give the authors a full list of what you expect them to have done for the next version, as this will shorten the review process considerably, and it will maximize the chances you will only have to read the paper one more time instead of two, three, or more times. And for the love of God, when you do recommend a revise and resubmit, do not decline the editor's request to review the paper when a revision is submitted.

What follows are some guidelines about how to structure and write a review.

1. *When you receive a request to review a manuscript*: Read the title and the abstract of the paper, determine whether you are a good fit for the paper, and respond immediately. You would be surprised how frequently some reviewers simply do not respond to review requests. As I have alluded to above, you might sometimes think you are not a good fit for the paper. Ultimately, however, the editor has asked you to review the paper for a reason. Often, she simply wants your advice as a non-expert, to see if the paper makes sense to (and will thus be cited) by people who are not experts on the topic. If you have refereed the paper before, or if there is a conflict of interest (i.e., the paper was written by one of your colleagues, one of your coauthors, one of your students, or one of your advisors), you should let the editor know about it and give her a chance to reconsider her request.

2. *Once you have agreed to referee a paper*: Do not wait until it is too late to do the review. You can certainly wait until you get a first reminder from the journal that your review is due, but do not wait until the second such reminder. Really, the earlier you submit your review, the better for everyone involved—you do not know your (future) self as well as you think you do.[6]

---

6. One of the most useful things my advisor ever taught me had nothing to do with economics, and everything to do with being organized, and thus productive: "Never touch a piece of paper twice." What he meant was that once you get started on something relatively short and self-contained (e.g., a referee report, a letter of recommendation), you should finish it before moving on to something else.

3. Once you decide to get started on your review, read the title, the abstract, the introduction, and the conclusion of the paper. Do you have a good idea of what the authors are doing? Perhaps more importantly, are you convinced that it is a worthwhile topic? If it is an empirical paper, can you understand from the tables what relationships the authors are after? If you answer "No" to any of those questions, you should encourage the editor to reject the paper. This may sound harsh, but before submitting, authors should work hard on the "sell" of their paper, i.e., on convincing the reader that the paper is worth their time. And generally speaking, the profession could certainly benefit from better writing. It is true that a groundbreaking idea that suffers from a bad sell deserves a second chance. The two, however, are rarely orthogonal to one another.

4. Corollary to the previous rule, as a referee, you don't "accept," "give a revise and resubmit," or "reject" a paper, you merely give your advice as to what is to be done in a cover letter which the editor will not share with the authors. So as a reviewer, to claim that you have "rejected" this paper and "given a revise and resubmit" to that paper seriously overstates your role in the peer-review process.

5. If you believe the paper should be rejected after reading the abstract, the introduction, the conclusion and, if the paper contains any, the tables, write up your review. Make sure you explain clearly why the paper is a nonstarter. More importantly, offer some constructive ways in which the authors can make their paper ready for prime time. Do so in less than two single-spaced pages, and skip the tedium (e.g., typos, missing references, etc.)

6. If you believe the paper should be given a chance after reading the abstract, the introduction, the conclusion and, if the paper contains any, the tables, read the paper thoroughly, then write up your review. Do so in as much space as you need, and do not skip anything, even the tedium.

7. A good review should start by summarizing the paper in one or two short paragraphs. Do not paraphrase the abstract—this is your chance to give your point of view to the authors as to what the paper really does, and sometimes your interpretation of what matters in the paper differs from theirs.

8. Then, offer a numbered list of major comments—those are the potential deal breakers, i.e., the things the authors have to do to get you to recommend that the paper be published—and a numbered list of minor comments—the small things you would like the authors to do in order

to improve upon the paper. If you are going to recommend rejection, you can skip the specific comments. These two lists are a clear indication of what you view as negotiable or not, and numbered comments increase efficiency as the authors can refer to specific comments more easily when responding to your review.

9. Again, make sure you give the authors suggestions as to how to address your comments. At the very least do so for your general (i.e., nonnegotiable) comments. If you do not think the authors can reasonably address your comments, you should recommend rejection so as to not waste anyone's time.

10. What is a constructive comment? There is a general misunderstanding of what constructive means that interprets the word as "A comment that I like." That is not what constructive means; a constructive comment is one that can actually be addressed, and one that is not demeaning to the authors. When in doubt as to whether a comment will be seen as demeaning, err on the side of being nicer.

11. That being said, you are not a coauthor on the paper, so you should not push the authors to write the paper you would have written on the topic. Moreover, it is extremely bad form to push the authors to cite all of your papers on the topic. Encourage them to cite the ones that are truly germane to their work—no more, no less. And encourage the authors to polish their writing. More specifically, if you can think of more (or better) motivations for their work, do not hold back, as this will enhance the paper's citation potential, and the editor will be grateful for that since for her, citations are the coin of the realm.

12. Once your review is written up, it is time to write your cover letter to the editor. That letter will generally not be shared with the authors (though sometimes excerpts from cover letters are shared with authors if it useful to do so), so you can be as candid as you want. Specifically, you make your recommendation—"reject," "weak revise and resubmit" (same as "major revision"), "strong revise and resubmit" (same as "minor revision"), or "accept"—to the editor, and you give your arguments as to why you make this specific recommendation. Do not cut and paste from your review. Again, this is an occasion for you to be as candid as you want about the reasons behind your recommendation.

13. The cover letter is also your chance to flag potential ethical problems. For example, if you believe the authors are "double dipping" (i.e.,

publishing only slightly different versions of the same paper), if you believe the paper is simultaneously being reviewed somewhere else, or if you believe the authors have plagiarized part of their paper, the cover letter is the place to mention it.

14. Once your review and your cover letter are written up, submit them to the editor. There is no good reason to sit on them; as long as you write clearly and cogently, no one will care about your prose in a referee report or cover letter.

15. *Once you have submitted your referee report*: The more considerate editors will let you know the decision they have made on the basis of your review. Often, they will agree with you. This is especially likely when you recommend rejection, as several editors will typically require the majority or all of the referees to recommend a "revise and resubmit" before they ask the authors for a revised version. Sometimes, however, the editors will go against your review. Do not take those cases personally, but if this happens often, you should take some time to reflect upon why it does.

16. You will eventually meet many of the authors of papers you have refereed. Resist the temptation to out yourself as a reviewer, even if you think you were especially kind as a referee. If you have ever spent any time on social media, you know how easy it is to misconstrue the intention behind a written comment; you never know whether your well-intended constructive remark may have been interpreted as an insult by the authors.

17. Think carefully before breaking any of these rules. Many seem to believe that they can get away with not responding to editors, with taking an unduly long amount of time before submitting their reviews, with being insulting to the authors of the papers they referee, and so forth. You get the idea. Those people forget that editors will remember such bad behavior and keep track of who is a good citizen of the profession—and who is not.

18. The converse of the previous rule is that good refereeing is a very good way to build a solid reputation for good citizenship in the profession. This is something that is overlooked all too often in a profession supposedly full of smart people who have a deep understanding of incentives.

6.4 Other Types of Peer Review

There are miscellaneous other kinds of peer review you are likely to be asked to do, such as reviewing conference submissions, grant proposals, book proposals, and the manuscripts of friends and colleagues who solicit your advice.

Organizing a conference, however small, is a lot of work, with the organizing committee having to make decisions ranging from lofty academic ones (e.g., whom to invite as keynote speaker) to resolutely unacademic ones (e.g., what vegan option to offer for lunch on the second day). Because of that, organizing committees will often delegate the task of selecting papers to a group of reviewers, and so you are highly likely to get asked to review papers for a conference at some point in your career if you have not done so already. When reviewing papers for conferences, you will either get asked to review abstracts (often so-called structured abstracts, i.e., two-page summaries of the papers submitted) or full papers. The task of reviewing papers for a conference is substantially easier than that of reviewing manuscripts for journals, and I believe any submission can be assessed in 15 minutes or so by asking yourself a few questions. First off, is the paper asking a research question that is of interest to those who will attend the conference (for a field conference like, say, the Society of Labor Economists' annual meeting) or a research question that is likely to make attendees attend the particular session it is slotted in (for a general conference like, say, the Western Economic Association International's annual conference)? Second, does the paper seem competently done? In other words, if you were to present this paper instead of the authors, would you be embarrassed by the execution? Finally, and this is a distant third, are the findings likely to stimulate discussion? Most conferences will ask you for an "up-or-out," "accept-or-reject" decision, and even when a conference you may review for asks for specific reasons behind such a decision or comments to the authors, those should be kept short.

I had much more to say about getting grants in the previous chapter, but if you are someone who relies on external funding for your research, you should expect to do a certain amount of reviewing for funding agencies and donors. Typically, you will usually get asked to review a single proposal at a time.

Less typically, you might get paid for your review. The pesky thing about grant proposals is that in this interest of minimizing review heterogeneity, funding agencies and donors tend to give you a scoring sheet which you have to fill out, and they often ask you questions you might feel less than ideally qualified to answer (e.g., "Are the investigators realistically assessing the various costs of undertaking this research project?"). To make things worse, the documents you need to review are often spread out across several files. When reviewing grant proposals, my rule is to judge what I feel qualified to judge, to provide comments that will aim to improve the investigators' methodology (since this is all *ex ante* of them doing the research, you can afford to send them back to the drawing board), and to confess my lack of qualification when it comes to the things I cannot realistically assess. Ultimately, funding agencies and donors are interested in knowing whether you think the authors are going to spend money on something the funder deems worthwhile. More specifically: Are the authors asking an important research question? Are the proposed methods suitable to answer it? Is the requested amount of money likely to allow them to get there? This is thus not the occasion for you to focus on details like standard errors or your favorite semiparametric estimator.

Another form of review wherein you will usually be given a rubric to assess the work at hand is when you review book proposals. Academic books such as the one you are currently reading go through peer review, just as journal articles do. When I submitted this book to MIT Press, it was sent to two academics, who were then asked to assess whether the press should agree to enter into a contract with me for this book. After I did sign the publication contract with MIT Press for this book and submitted a full draft of it, that draft was once again sent out to two academics to solicit their comments on the full manuscript. Usually when you are asked to review a book by a press, you will be sent a proposal, a few sample chapters (chapter 2 was the sample chapter for this book), and a list of questions about the proposal. Book proposals tend to be more fun to review than manuscripts for journals or grant proposals, because they get you to think about different things than when you review journal articles. The things you will likely be asked to comment on are the proposed book's relevance to the field or the discipline, which other works do you see as competing with it, the author's qualification, whether you can foresee the book being adopted in university-level classes, whether you think the book would sell well, and so on. Because each press is its own entity, none of these things is set in stone. For instance, you will sometimes get paid for reviewing book proposals. More commonly if the author is a young academic with little to no track record, you may be sent the draft of a whole book instead of a few chapters. And of course, the exact questions you will need to answer will vary from press to press, and between academic and commercial presses.

The last kind of reviewing, which is something you will get asked to do starting from early on in your career is "friendly reviewing," when friends and colleagues solicit your comments on a working paper before submitting it. This is probably the most impactful kind of reviewing, if only because it usually has you review the work of someone whose career success you are invested in, and because it usually has you review an early version of a paper which, assuming increasing and concave returns to comments, means that your comments have a higher expected return at the margin. If you are reading this book at any time after the second year of your doctoral studies, you have almost surely been asked to provide friendly comments. Here, there is not really any set standard. When friends and colleagues send me their papers, unlike when I write a review for a journal, I usually write my comments in an email, in order of appearance in the paper first. Then before I click "send," I usually go back to the beginning of the email to add some general thoughts if I have any. When writing a friendly review, anything is fair game.

Ultimately, a lot of the reviewing you do will be thankless, because you will not get paid for it, and because the authors will never know who their reviewers were. At best, you will be thanked as an anonymous reviewer and get an automatic (and perfunctory) email from the journal's editorial system informing you of the editor's decision and thanking you for your service.[7]

Yet even a purely selfish individual should recognize the value of reviewing to their career. Over the years, I have found that besides learning by doing (i.e., writing your own papers), one of the best ways to improve as a researcher is to learn from others. Obviously, this means that you should read good papers—but not *only* good papers, as I discussed in chapter 2. Many economists see refereeing as an unfortunate tax they need to pay to get their own papers reviewed and published. Unlike a tax, however, there is almost always something to be learned from reviewing—and from reviewing widely.

6.5   Ethics of Peer Review

I mentioned ethical considerations for authors in chapter 4, but here are, in no particular order, a set of ethical prescriptions for peer reviewers:

1. *If you have a conflict of interest, declare it; if you have reviewed the paper before, let the editor know.* Academics tend to work in silos, i.e.,

---

7. And that is really *at best*. Many journals do not see fit to inform their reviewers of the editor's decision, which is somewhat excusable considering that this is heavily dependent on whether a journal's editorial system is set up to do that. What is less excusable are those authors who fail to thank the anonymous reviewers who commented on their manuscript.

narrow areas of research wherein there are few others. This means that you will inevitably run into the same researchers at conferences and meetings, and that you may end up working with them. Moreover, the more time you spend in the profession, the more advisees you will have had, who may be working on topics close to yours, if not on the very same topics. If you get asked to review a coauthor, an advisee, an advisor, or a colleague's paper,[8] the right thing to do is to recuse yourself and refuse to serve as a reviewer in order to avoid any conflict of interest. Likewise, if you have reviewed a paper once before for another journal, let the editor know about it, especially if you have recommended a rejection. The idea here is that the principle of double jeopardy—the legal principle whereby someone should not undergo trial a second time for the same charges he was acquitted of the first time—should apply. Now, it is possible that the editor will tell you that she does not mind that you have seen the paper before in order to see whether the authors have incorporated some feedback in between journals, but you will at least have done due diligence. Similarly, it may occur that you have had a personal conflict with an author or set of authors. If that is the case and you feel that you cannot remain objective about that author or group of authors' work, you should recuse yourself. Though it can be tempting to stick it to someone who has slighted you, remember the Golden Rule, and ask yourself whether you would want them to be your reviewers.

2. *If you are working on the exact same topic, say so.* You have almost surely heard the expression "an idea whose time has come," and so it should come as no surprise to you that sometimes different people concurrently have the same idea for a paper and start working on that idea separately and at the same time.[9] If you are asked to review a paper that

---

8. Or worse, if you get asked to review *your own paper.* I once caught an author who had agreed to review his own paper, which was handled by another editor. To no surprise, his review of his own paper was overwhelmingly positive, with some light comments wondering about whether the standard errors were clustered at the right level. When I alerted the editor in charge, the paper was immediately rejected, and the author's name was circulated among editors as someone who could not be trusted.

9. For example, compare Baron (1970) with Sandmo (1971), both of which look at the effect of output price risk on the behavior of competitive firms respectively in the *International Economic Review* and the *American Economic Review*.

does (almost) exactly what you do in your own paper, bring it up with the editor. Some well-known papers originally started out as two distinct papers, only to have both groups of coauthors merge into one group to produce a stronger paper. Cole et al.'s (2013) seminal article on index insurance in developing countries started out as two distinct papers. As Xavier Giné, one of the coauthors in Cole et al., put it to me in an email: "Cole et al. (2013) was originally two independent RCTs to understand the barriers to adoption of rainfall insurance, one in Gujarat (Cole, Topalova and Tobacman) and the other in [Andhra Pradesh] (Townsend, Vickery and [Giné]). We did not learn of each other projects during the review process, but during early stages of presenting preliminary results at a conference. Since we knew Shawn [Cole] well, and it was clear that the papers were quite similar, we decided that a merged paper would be better than two separate ones" (Xavier Giné, personal correspondence, September 22, 2020). The worst thing you can do here is to hide the fact you are working on the same topic and recommend a rejection so you can beat the authors of the paper you were asked to review to the punch.

3. *Do not steal the ideas of the papers you review.* This should really go without saying, but do not steal other people's ideas after recommending that their paper be rejected. Not only is this type of behavior extremely unethical, but you should aim to come up with your own ideas. In the limit, it is much better to do work that is derivative of someone else's work than to do work that is not truly your own. If you have to resort to stealing other people's ideas, research is not for you.

4. *Plan on submitting your review on time.* Once again keeping the Golden Rule in mind, plan on submitting your review on time. Obviously, sometimes life will get in the way, and you will have to submit a review later than expected, but do not wait for a journal's editorial system to send you automatic notifications that your review is late and reminders that it was due a while ago. Rather, plan on submitting your review on time. If you do not think you can submit a review on time, you can either decline to review the manuscript, making sure to let the editor know your reason for doing so, or you can ask for a later deadline. Here, it helps to know your type, so to speak. If you know you suffer from time-inconsistency and that you tend to procrastinate, tie yourself to your own mast by starting your reviews as soon as you agree to do them. That is

preferable to starting them the night before they are due, only to realize you will need more time.

5. *Review for the journal that solicited a review from you, not for your ideal journal.* The Golden Rule applies here as well. When you submit to a field journal, you almost surely are not expecting your reviewers to treat your manuscript like it has been submitted for publication in the *Quarterly Journal of Economics.* The same logic applies in reverse: if you are asked to review a manuscript by a field journal, do not hold the manuscript to the standards of the *American Economic Review.*

6. *Do not review for predatory journals.* This goes without saying, but since this is about peer-review ethics and those journals are clearly unethical, do not review for them. At best, doing so will be a waste of your time. At worst, you will be lending credence to them rather than the other way around, as it is unlikely they will be using your feedback for anything other than putting up the pretense of respectability.

6.6   Editing Journals

Another bit of service that you may be asked to perform if you do well enough in your field is editorial service—the service task whereby one gets to handle manuscripts by coordinating the review process for those manuscripts.

As I have alluded to earlier, various journals use different terms to refer to the same tasks, so for the sake of clarity, I will be talking of two different editorial tiers:

• *Editor:* Whether the journal has one or more of those, the editor is the person who is ultimately in charge of the scholarly aspects of the journal. Typically, editors handle manuscripts, and they decide on the journal's aims and scope as well as on who gets to serve as associate editor.

• *Associate Editor:* A journal will typically have a number of those. An associate editor may or may not handle manuscripts, and when they do handle manuscripts, they may simply be in charge of getting reviews, with the final decision left to the editor.

The type of service I am talking about here is the kind where you are assigned a manuscript to handle—that is, to solicit reviews on, and usually make a final decision about whether it should be desk rejected, or sent out for review and then rejected, given a chance at being revised and resubmitted, or accepted. Getting asked to perform that kind of service is one of the highest honors your field or the profession can bestow upon you, because it signals that your peers view you as being both competent enough and as having good taste and that as such, they trust you to shape the direction the field is taking over the next few years.

How do you get asked to do editorial work? Though who you know and who is in your social network is obviously important,[10] it is no less important to have published well (i.e., if you want to be editor of a given journal, it helps to have published consistently *at least* at the level of that journal), to have been a good reviewer (i.e., to submit reviews that are both on point and on time), and to have a reputation for being organized.

When you do get asked, should you take on editorial service? Although the answer will depend on a variety of circumstances and on your other commitments, here are a few things which really make a difference in how onerous editorial responsibilities will be for you:

1. *Do you enjoy refereeing?* Most principal–agent models assume that the agent's cost-of-effort function is increasing and convex (Bolton and Dewatripont 2005). Be that as it may, just *how* convex that function is differs across individuals. Some people find refereeing enjoyable and look forward to taking the time to read a paper and write up their comments on it. Others find refereeing to be more of a chore than anything else, or a tax they have to pay in order to remain in their field's good graces. If you fall in the latter category, I strongly encourage you not to undertake any editorial work. We all know people who wanted to do a PhD because they cared more about putting "Doctor" in front of or "PhD" after their name than they did about taking a deep dive into a given topic and generating new knowledge about that same topic; more often than not, those people ended up struggling to complete their PhD, if they completed it at all. So if the only reason you want to do editorial work is because of the prestige it brings, you will be entirely unhappy as an editor, you are unlikely to be good at it, and you should spend your time more productively.

2. *How much administrative support will you be getting?* Some journals have an editorial assistant, who takes care of making sure submissions are

---

10. Fortunately, many journals post open calls for applications when they are looking for new editors. This is especially true of association journals, or journals that are run by professional associations, but it is changing for some unaffiliated journals.

properly formatted and of dispatching submissions to handling editors. At other journals, there is no such support, and an editor or co-editor has to do that job. At yet other journals, the editor has to proofread all articles before sending them on to the publisher's production department. Given that heterogeneity of administrative costs associated with editing a journal, it is worth asking what kind of administrative support you will be getting if you say yes, both from the publisher and from your institution.

3. *How good is your social network?* Would-be reviewers are more likely to respond quickly and favorably to a refereeing request if it comes from someone they have heard of, and they are significantly more likely to do the same if it comes from someone they know personally. Likewise, you are a lot more likely to be able to exert the necessary social pressure to get a reviewer to submit their review in a timely manner if the two of you know each other—virtually all of my disaster stories when it comes to reviewers comes from cases where I had never met the reviewer in person or, at the very least, interacted with them over email or social media. I have seen how the quality of one's social network maps directly into how effective they are as an editor often enough. If you rarely go to conferences or are not at all involved in social media in a professional manner (more on this in the next section), you may have a hard time connecting with would-be reviewers, and a lack of engagement with your field or with the profession is likely to be a liability.

4. *Does it pay?* Most journals pay their editors for their time, but it is very rare that the pay comes close to being a significant fraction of one's overall annual income, or reflects accurately how much time one spends on editing. Still, some form of monetary compensation definitely helps, and it is worth knowing how much you will be compensated for your time.

5. *Are you organized?* The most efficient editors, those who are best-positioned to make decisions on manuscripts in a reasonable time (i.e., significantly less than four months, and in under three months if possible), are people who spend a lot of time at their computer doing work, and often people who always have a browser tab open for their journal's editorial system. If you are someone who has an uneasy relationship with email, or who insists on not looking at their computer in the evening, on weekends, or during the holidays, editing a journal may not be for you.

Make no mistake: there is nothing wrong with prioritizing leisure time or prioritizing work–life balance if that is what you care about, but the task of editing a journal necessarily involves prioritizing work over leisure—at least if you hope to maintain some research productivity while you serve as editor.

To close this section, here are a number of observations about serving as editor.

First off, it can be hard to find reviewers. For every article I want to send out for review, I need at least two reviewers, ideally three. When reviewers disagree, unless I am an expert on the topic of the paper, I often have to ask for the help of an additional reviewer or associate editor. To get two reviewers, I have to ask about three people on average.

Second, it can be hard to find competent reviewers. Once I have found my two or three reviewers, it is not unlikely that one of them will send me a review that is not very useful—a short review offering very little in the way of comments the authors can use to improve their manuscript.

Third, I have already mentioned the "never touch a piece of paper twice" rule in a footnote in section 6.3, and it applies here as well: once you start looking at a manuscript or writing a decision letter, finish the task before moving on. It is really when you look at something, do a bit of work on it, decide to go do something else and come back to it later that things begin festering in your inbox and on your to-do list.

Fourth, personalized emails work a lot better. Instead of sending a form email to the reviewers I think are likely to decline my request to referee, I often personalize the email a bit by inserting a personal note before the automatic email. This has improved my reviewer response rates significantly, presumably because people realize there is a human being on the other side (and one whom they know personally).

Similarly, personalized desk rejections work a lot better, too. For that reason, when I desk reject, I often personalize the email by telling the authors (i) why I chose to desk reject (often, it is simply a question of fit with the journal, and not of quality; when it is a matter of quality, I make a broad comment that may help improve the manuscript substantially) and, as much as possible, (ii) where to submit next.

Fifth, plagiarism of all kinds is a huge issue. One of the perks of working with a big publisher is that the publisher can afford nice things. One of those nice things is access to plagiarism-detecting software, which constantly scours the worldwide web to find similarities between a fresh new submission and other documents on the web. Often, those similarities are between the submission and one of its earlier versions. But in (too) many cases, the software will uncover instances of plagiarism, whether this means self-plagiarism (e.g., an author reusing an entire page of a paper he has previously published and whose copyright resides with another publisher, with that previous paper not cited), "light" plagiarism (e.g., an author lifting a few sentences or a paragraph from his employer's website or from a document published by his employers, on which he was not one of the authors), or "hard" plagiarism (e.g., an author submitting an article that is about 50 percent copied from papers written by others).

Sixth, editing a journal will bring one new source of anxiety to your life, namely impact factor anxiety, or the anxiety derived from the desire to maintain or improve the impact factor of the journal you edit. Editing a journal with a high or rising impact factor is a double-edged sword, because "Can we keep this up? Can we keep improving?" is the kind of thing that keeps editors awake at night.

That said, serving as journal editor can be incredibly fulfilling. Over and above the pay and the prestige that come with serving as associate editor or editor, it is very rewarding to see good manuscripts come in, go through the peer-review process, come out better than they came in, and finally be published in the journal. The whole thing is doubly rewarding when the submission comes from a young researcher for whom the publication really makes a difference at the margin.

6.7 Social Media as Professional Service

Although it may seem strange at first blush to equate the use of social media with professional service, there is a form of social media engagement which can enhance your professional life. To differentiate that form of social media engagement from the more common way in which social media is used (i.e., to keep in touch with friends and family, or to follow celebrities), I will refer to that form of social media engagement as "professional social media engagement."

Although there are horror stories of people allegedly being denied tenure or promotion because of their social media engagement, two distinct facts are worth noting about those stories. First and foremost, the most prominent such story (Johnson 2005) is now over 15 years old, and academia's view of social media has changed substantially over the last decade. To paraphrase some of the comments I have heard from senior colleagues—that is, those colleagues who tend to be the most skeptical when it comes to social media—over the years, those comments have gone from saying things like "Social media is a waste of time; that time could have been used to write more or better papers" to saying things like "I choose not engage with social media, but I can certainly see its usefulness to academia." Still, my own endorsement of professional social media engagement should not be misconstrued as "social media engagement will not harm your career at all." And indeed, when I talk of professional social media engagement, I mean an *intelligent* use of social media in addition to a professional use of it. How should you approach social media? By "professional social media engagement," what I mean is social media use that primarily aims at (i) engaging with other scholars in one's research area, field, discipline, and adjacent disciplines, and to some (hopefully lesser) extent (ii) improving the visibility of one's own research.

6.7.1 Blogging

Though there is no way for me to know what the counterfactual would look like, I am 99 percent confident you would not be reading this book if, in December 2010, I had not decided to buy the marcfbellemare.com domain name and install a blogging platform on it, and write my first post the next day. Over the years, blogging (interacted with my use of other social media platforms) has done wonders for me in many, many ways, but off the top of my head, I can think of three such ways.

First, blogging made me a better writer and researcher. Though it is obvious that writing blog posts would make one a better writer, it is much less obvious that doing so would make one a better researcher. But writing for a broader public than the one your research papers are intended to (i.e., writing for a public composed of colleagues in other disciplines with an interest in the topics you are working on—science reporters, policy makers, and other economists) really helps clarify your thinking about the things you are working on. I have lost count of the number of times I started writing a blog post believing I had a solid grasp on the topic I was about to write about, only to realize along the way that I did not, which ultimately made me work much harder at understanding that topic. Because economics is fairly open (i.e., we present early versions of papers at seminars and conferences and circulate working papers, and findings are not embargoed), the wonderful thing about blogging as a research economist is that it is perfectly fine to write blog posts about a paper (or even about specific parts of a paper) you are working on, as this is a good means of clarifying your thinking, and having a conversation with other scholars about it. This can lead to pretty clear improvements in a paper, if only because someone might suggest a few robustness checks or data sources you had not thought about.

Second, blogging helps maximize your impact as a scholar. When I release a new working paper, I post about it. When that paper gets accepted for publication, I post about it again. And when that paper gets published, I post about it once more. Although there is a great deal of overlap in terms of who originally sees those three posts, each post is also seen by new people, because it gets shared (and re-shared) by different people every time. Blogging about a working paper (and then about the accepted and published versions of the paper) allows generating buzz for the paper's findings, which leads to your work getting cited more by other scholars. Equally important, blogging about a paper also associates your name with the topics you are working on, which also leads to more citations, if only because people will be quick to suggest your name to others working on those topics.

Third, and more broadly, blogging allows you to define who you are as a scholar instead of letting others do so. One of the reasons that pushed me to start a blog in the first place was that at that time in my career, I was surrounded by colleagues who were at best indifferent to what I was doing, and those colleagues would be the ones voting on whether I would get tenure. So I first wanted to make sure to publicly define myself in my own words to prevent any mischaracterization of my research agenda, and second, I wanted to get my name out there so that people who were hiring the year I was up for tenure would have heard about me. As it turns out, when I was indeed denied tenure in 2012, the person who was most instrumental in getting me to the University of Minnesota was someone who had learned about my research because of my blog.

Consistent with the foregoing, McKenzie and Özler (2014) show that economics blogs play an important role in the dissemination of knowledge, they raise the profile of bloggers and their institution, and they improve the knowledge of the blog's subject matter for the average reader.

6.7.2 Other Social Media

The popularity of various social media platforms ebbs and flows too much for me to discuss any specific such platform. But beyond blogging, should you use social media? Again, it all depends on how you think of your career, and just as there does not seem to be any penalty associated with (smart) professional social media use, there is also no penalty associated with not using social media. So if you do not feel you have time for social media, that is fine.

Why use social media? Besides the obvious, you can use social media to keep informed in two ways. First and foremost, it can keep you informed about what other scholars, policy makers, and the media are saying about the issues you are currently doing research on. In that sense, social media can make you a better researcher.[11]

Second, it can keep you informed about developments relevant to policy or industry developments surrounding your research topics. This is a good way, for instance, to hear about new trends which are not necessarily relevant to your research, but which make for great examples of the concepts related to it. In that sense, social media can make you a better teacher or presenter.

Generally speaking, social media is also a helpful self-promotion tool for academics who want their research to be read outside of academia. This is especially relevant for those whose primary appointments are in business schools, at policy schools, or at think tanks.

Finally, using social media seems to be increasingly perceived in some quarters as a fourth responsibility besides research, teaching, and service. From an editorial titled "Online Image" in *Nature* (2011):

> Through responsible use of blogs and social media, researchers have the power to chip away at misperceptions. This . . . involves getting the right facts out there, and citing and linking to the best, most trustworthy sources of information.

> Such diligence can also benefit scientists as members of a professional community. Researchers who make sure that personal and institutional websites, blogs, and social-media pages are accurate and honest will enhance the usefulness of web searches by pushing the most relevant and trusted information to the top. This can make it easier for scientists to find one another for collaboration and reviewing papers, and to locate and fill jobs.

> Enhancing visibility and promoting a digital image may strike some as unsavoury, but it is not. Researchers are right to promote themselves and their work in a reasonable capacity.

---

11. I can think of at least two of my papers that came out of social media. My paper on food prices and food riots (Bellemare 2015) came from seeing many people on social media claiming that food price volatility led to social unrest, and from my asking myself: "Is it really food price volatility, or is it rising food price levels that cause social unrest?" My paper on the use of lagged endogenous variables for identification purposes (Bellemare et al. 2017) came from a conversation with Tom Pepinsky on social media where we both observed that, in the papers we reviewed, we saw too many instances of people lagging an explanatory variable in an effort to exogenize it.

There are a number of available guides for academics who wish to get involved in social media, and I encourage you to consult some of them if you are interested in using social media to promote your career, such as the lexicon by Miah (2019) or the book by Carrigan (2019). The principles promoted by most of those guides are roughly similar from one guide to the next, however. First and foremost, do not be a jerk. Remember that you are interacting with human beings, each endowed with agency and dignity, and whose interior life is as rich as your own. In that sense, it is always a good idea to check your ego at the door, and to try to interpret things as charitably as you possibly can. This is even more important on social media, where we lack the social cues and body language that can often help us infer meaning beyond the literal. Whatever you would not say to someone in person, do not say on social media. Likewise, whatever you do not wish to have on public record (i.e., search engines) as you saying, do not say on social media. And because people are seemingly becoming increasingly literal and unable to read between the lines or appreciate sarcasm, avoid sarcasm. There will certainly be times where people will seek to deliberately bait you into having a public argument with them, and your first inclination may be to come out swinging. Avoid doing so. Like political strategist Rick Wilson once said, on social media, the power to ignore is the power to destroy. If you realize that someone is not really interested in having an actual conversation, move on. A fine strategy for social media—one that works well for many academics—is to not engage in online discussions, but only share interesting things. In other words, to talk at—and not speak with—social media.

Second, make sure that your profile on whatever social media platform you choose to use is filled out and clearly identifies you as a researcher, ideally in your field of research. This will help others determine whether they should follow you or not, and an empty profile, without a picture or an accurate description, can easily be dismissed as a fake profile.

As a corollary to these first two points: avoid anonymous social media, meaning both "avoid remaining anonymous," as being on social media under your real name will force you to be on your best behavior, but also "avoid social media platforms where users are anonymous," as those tend to bring out the worst in people as well as the worst people. See Wu (2020) for quantitative evidence on how anonymous social media fosters misogyny in economics, among other kinds of prejudice.

Third, follow like-minded people. By this, I mean not just economists working in your field, but economists who work on topics adjacent to yours as well as people in other disciplines who work on (and people outside of academia with an interest in) your research topics. And avoid following only famous economists, as this is a recipe for frustration: by virtue of being famous, they are unlikely to have time to interact with or even take much notice of you.

Fourth, use your social media account regularly. Most people already have too many things to keep track of in their lives, and so they will be reticent to follow a social media account that never shares or posts anything new, or only rarely does so.

Finally, never lose sight of the fact that social media is a nice form of professional service, no more. I can think of a few examples of academics who are Very Online People, but whose CVs are woefully short on publications. Social media use will not be penalized by those who will judge your professional accomplishments if it is clear that you prioritize your research. But if it becomes clear that you should have spent your time more productively away from social media and your research has suffered for it, you are likely to be penalized. Social media is a complement to good research—not a substitute for it.

6.8   Guidance for Women and Minorities Doing Service

Before closing this chapter on doing service, I should discuss service for women and minorities. As a straight Caucasian male, I will never know what it is like to be a woman, a member of an underrepresented minority (URM), or both in academia, and my understanding of the specific issues women and URMs face is very much second-hand. Nevertheless, I would be remiss if I did not at least address the fact that the demands of service can be much more onerous for women and URMs, and if I did not address what people like me can do about it.

If you are a woman or an URM, you are much more likely to be asked to do service than someone like me.[12] That is because in most cases, the

---

12. A female colleague at a liberal arts college commented: "[W]omen and BIPOC faculty do a *lot* of invisible advising and mentoring. At [my institution], I think one of the main burnout factors, particularly for BIPOC faculty, is all of the informal advising they are asked (or sought out) to do. When I was on the college promotion and tenure committee, I was astounded at how intense it was. Further, I personally get female students in my office probably once a week who want to talk about what it is like to be a woman in our department, and to strategize about how to manage this. You don't get credit for this generally, and it comes at a steep opportunity cost, especially if you are junior."

institution you will be working with will value diversity and inclusion, and so it will want to have voices like yours represented everywhere possible. Obviously, the fact that there are fewer women than men and fewer URMs than straight white men in tenured positions means that if we are to have diversity and inclusion everywhere possible, one group will do more work than the other. So depending on *how* underrepresented the groups you belong to are at your institution, you may have to fight tooth and nail to protect your time. This starts with having a conversation with your immediate supervisor (usually a department chair, less commonly a dean) or a mentor to whom you explain that since they are invested in your success by virtue of having hired you, they will understand the foregoing, and so you may have to say "No" to service opportunities more often than some of your colleagues.

Though it can be especially daunting to say "No" to senior colleagues who will be the ones deciding on the fate of your career, you must develop an argument you can deploy when you are asked to do more than your fair share of service. This can be something as simple as "I would love to help, but as a member of an underrepresented minority, I tend to be solicited for service more than most, and so I have to respectfully decline this time. Once my place in the profession is secure, I will be more than happy to help, but I am sure you will understand that for the foreseeable future, I have to budget my time wisely." Additionally, a good supervisor or mentor can also advocate for you by in turn explaining to others that, as a woman or an URM, you have to protect your research time. For example, when you go up for tenure, your department chair should include a paragraph that clearly explains that you have done the right amount of service for someone in your position, and that as a woman or an URM, you may have had to decline some service opportunities.

In recent years, various professional organizations have been providing service and support resources for women, URMs, and LGBTQ+ economists. The AEA, for instance, has its Committee on the Status of Women in the Economics Profession, its Committee on the Status of Minority Groups in the Economics Profession, and its Committee on the Status of LGBTQ + Individuals in the Economics Profession. Some smaller professional associations (e.g., the Agricultural and Applied Economics Association) also offer such support networks. These are good resources to address the issues addressed in this section and provide mentorship.

If you are a straight Caucasian male, you are privileged by virtue of being in the majority, at least by historical standards if not in actual fact at your institution. The least you can do is to keep the previous paragraph in mind when interacting with your female and URM colleagues. More importantly, you should use your privilege to argue for diversity and inclusion in hiring, for forming conference panels that reflect diversity, and for inviting diverse sets of seminar speakers to speak at your institution. You should also strive to create opportunities to highlight the research done by women and URM scholars. Privilege is entirely wasted on the privileged if it is not deployed to lift up those without it.

7

Advising Students

I stated in the introduction that I would not be discussing teaching. Although advising and mentoring sometimes counts as teaching, and sometimes as service, I view it as a mixture of both. Because of the teaching-and-service nature of advising and mentoring, and because advising is not something that is taught in graduate school, the topic deserves its own chapter.

Before anything else, I should distinguish between advising and mentoring. In what follows, I use "advising" to refer to a formal relationship wherein a faculty member formally guides a student through their studies, and I use "mentoring" to refer to an informal relationship wherein a researcher occasionally offers their advice to a student or a (usually junior) colleague in the context of a less formal relationship. This is not a hard and fast rule; it is merely a convention I follow in this chapter.

Why advise and mentor? In the case of advising, you may get formal credit for it. In my first job, I would get credit for every master's student whose thesis I advised, and when I had enough credits I could buy out of teaching one class. In my current job, advising master's theses and PhD dissertations is expected of me, and doing so only counts insofar as annual merit raises go. In other words, the more students I help get through our graduate program, the more likely I am to see a greater salary increase. Another incentive to advise students is that you may see promise in a given student as a future collaborator or coauthor. Mentoring, for its part, is usually done because the mentor has an interest in seeing the person they mentor succeed. In either case, much like participating in volunteer organizations, you get out of advising and mentoring what you put into them.

The remainder of this chapter will first discuss some general principles. It will then discuss each of advising undergraduate and graduate students—master's and PhD—and mentoring students and colleagues.

7.1   General Principles

Before launching into general principles of advising and mentoring, I should note that the type of institution where you work matters. What you will need to do as an advisor to a student in a given category will vary dramatically depending on the type of institution you work for according to the Carnegie Classification of Institutions of Higher Education discussed in chapter 5.[1] For instance, undergraduate advising at a small liberal arts college (SLAC) tends to be considerably more hands-on than at a state flagship R1 university.

The first principle of advising and mentoring is that you should respect your advisees and mentees' life choices. Although it often seems as though the goal of professors is to reproduce (not *that* way, but by training the next generation of professors), not every undergraduate student wants to go to graduate school (some of them are more interested in making money than in doing research), not every graduate student wants an academic job (some of them have lexicographic preferences when it comes to the city or country they live and work in), and not every junior colleague wants to have a career that is identical to yours. In *The Making of an Economist, Redux*, Colander (2008) tells the discouraging story of a young woman at a top PhD program who had to lie to her advisors about the kind of job she wanted (assistant professor at a policy school) in order not to be neglected by her advisors (they wanted her to go for an assistant professor position in an economics department). So if you somehow intend to give any less than your best to students and mentees who do not share your vision of what is best for themselves, your time is probably better spent doing something other than advising and mentoring.

A close second principle of advising and mentoring is that honesty is the best policy. Although it may be tempting to hem and haw when, say, a middling student asks for a letter of recommendation for a top program you know they would never get into, the buck has to stop somewhere, and it may as well be with you. It is tempting to avoid being the bearer of bad news, but much like the interest on some financial products, unrealistic student or colleague expectations tend to compound—and thus become worse problems—over time.

---

1. See https://carnegieclassifications.iu.edu/lookup/standard.php.

Advising Undergraduate Students

At most institutions, faculty are called upon to advise undergraduate students. As discussed in the previous section, however, what this means will differ depending on the type of institution. For example, having just concluded my fifteenth year as a tenure-track academic, I have literally had scores of undergraduate major advisees (i.e., advisees assigned to me by virtue of having chosen one of the majors offered by my department), but I have had meetings with at most a quarter of those advisees. In part, this is because I have only worked at R1 universities, where the undergraduate advising expectation was minimal for tenure-track faculty, and where a lot of the advising undergraduate students seek tends to be specific to the institution (e.g., "Should I take HIST1471 or HIST1312 next fall for my humanities elective?") rather than general advising (e.g., "Should I major in economics or political science?," "Should I take a gap year before applying to grad school?," and so on).

At R1, R2, and D/PU universities, undergraduate advising will generally follow the pattern just described. In non-doctoral schools, however, and especially at institutions that focus primarily on undergraduate teaching (i.e., master's colleges and universities, baccalaureate colleges, and so on), undergraduate advising is a crucial aspect of the job. So while someone at a doctoral institution can get by with encouraging students to talk to their peers, to talk to college- or university-level professional advisors, to consult available reviews of the classes they are considering, and to go with what interests them, faculty at institutions that focus on undergraduate teaching will need to be intimately familiar with the requirements of the major or majors in which they teach, with the contents of the courses offered by their department, and so on.

One task that is likely common to all undergraduate advisors is helping students figure out answers to questions that go beyond the time they will be spending at your institution. Once again, the worst you can do is to try to force your own preferences on your students. Rather, it is your job to help students see the myriad of paths that are available to them. Even if you have not spent any time working between your undergraduate and graduate degrees or taken a gap year, you can draw from the experiences of your friends, family members, and acquaintances to help your undergraduates decide for themselves what they would like to do with their lives. Because a lot of students are undecided about what they want to spend the rest of their life doing, one of my go-to pieces of advice is for students to take a year off to travel or to work abroad (even if it means just tending bar somewhere) before committing to a career path, as my own experience working abroad after finishing my master's helped solidify my desire to do a PhD and become a researcher.[2]

A colleague who teaches at a liberal arts college further advises the following.

1. It helps to learn a few of your department's rules of thumb that consist of good advice about classes or the order in which classes should be taken—think of things that do not usually show up on the registrar's page. For example, that it may be better to take intermediate micro before taking intermediate macro, even though the former is not a prerequisite for the latter. Or that if you are interested in applied econometrics, it might be wise to take a labor economics class. As an advisor, you can usually learn these rules of thumb from your more senior colleagues.

2. You should know what things the professional advisors or the advising center (if your institution has either or both) can handle for you, and be sure to forward advising issues to them.[3] At some institutions, students have both a faculty advisor and a college-level advisor.

3. The benefit you can provide from simple check-ins can mean a lot to a student, making them feel like someone knows that they are actually a student and cares about their well-being. Even if you do not give any useful advice, a simple "How are your classes going?" in the hallway can go a long way toward making a student feel like they belong.

Another colleague at a SLAC notes that an important part of an advisor's job is to help facilitate student contact with the alumni network. To that effect, advisors generally have to know where their former students work, and they often connect current and former students. That colleague also notes that advising and mentoring at a SLAC can be an intensive

---

2. Alternatively, a colleague who teaches at a liberal arts college notes: "When students are in debt, I assuage some of these fears by telling students that the first job they get out of college with that fancy economics degree is likely not the one that will become their career, and is just a job that will help pay down their college debt."

3. Another liberal arts college colleague notes: "Advising and mentoring . . . is often emotional work. It is way more emotionally draining than one would expect. At [my institution], professors are a 'first line of defense' for all sorts of student issues, including mental health issues. If a student is not in class a few times in a row, we are told to contact the Dean of Students so they can check in on them."

task, as advisors are often expected to have students over for dinner at their house, or to attend their students' extracurricular events. In such cases, it is important to define and enforce healthy boundaries while still having a close mentoring and advising relationship with students.

7.2   Undergraduate Research

When it comes to advising undergraduate students as researchers, what and how much you can expect from your students will largely depend on the type of institution you find yourself working for. When I talk to colleagues at a SLAC, I am always amazed at what they can reasonably expect their undergraduate students to do in terms of research. In an interview for this book, a colleague who teaches at a SLAC and who also taught at a state flagship university before that admitted:

> Students at SLACs have a much better handle on economic theory and econometrics than students at other institutions. Students at my institution have taken really intense micro theory and econometrics. In my [field] class, I teach stuff from the same [field] class I took during my PhD program! We go over papers, and while we skip the really hard stuff, my students still read the landmark papers.

Another colleague who teaches at a SLAC adds:

> I assign the same papers I read for my own research to my students [because] our students take calculus before taking microeconomic and macroeconomic theory, so they learn optimization. They also take statistics before econometrics so they are ready to jump into . . . multivariate regression. Then, they can take [field courses] in which they use those coding skills to do more empirical research. [B]y the time they are a senior, they have coding skills and writing skills . . . so they are ready to write a good thesis.

Another SLAC colleague said:

> Students at SLACs are really creative in the questions they ask, and they are not yet bogged down by what is feasible or not. They come in having good questions that you only have to help them hone. They are also really good at coding, and they know how to critique each other's work.

What motivates undergraduates to do research? My coauthor Seth Gitter, who has written a formal guide to help both faculty and students navigate the undergraduate research process (Gitter 2021), told me:

> Fewer than half of students interested in undergraduate research are grad school-bound. Most think they *might* eventually go to grad school. Most students are thinking about doing a master's at some point, however. The best students are the ones who have outside interests; I advise a lot of dual

economics–political science majors. Those are the most interesting: people who want to do a deep dive into a given topic instead of a given discipline.

The right advising can be transformational, and cause undergraduates to develop a passion for the discipline and end up being superstars in their own right. In an interview for Bowmaker's (2012) book *The Art and Practice of Economics Research*, Susan Athey said

> When I discovered economics, it seemed like a wonderful opportunity to apply abstract ideas and mathematical techniques to something really important. And I was exposed early on to a policy problem through a summer job. My mentor . . . showed me how to take a real-world problem about procurement auctions . . . and translate it into a possibility to change policy in a way that would make procurement more efficient . . . [he] made a big effort to pick up promising undergraduates. He got me a full-time research assistant job with summer funding and a little office. He was really influential in getting me into economics, which I had never considered.

Whenever an undergraduate student shows up at your door wanting to do research, it is your job to establish early on in your relationship with them (i) what they know and what they do not know, (ii) how much time they have until they have to submit a thesis in order to graduate, in order to know (iii) what they need to learn and what you can reasonably expect from their research. Once again, the guide by Gitter (2021) provides a clear roadmap to navigating undergraduate-led research in economics, and should be required reading for faculty interested in advising undergraduate researchers as well as for undergraduate researchers themselves.

7.3   Advising Graduate Students

If you are at a research institution, odds are you will eventually have to advise graduate students, either master's or PhD students.[4] Even in cases where your department does not have a graduate program, there is still a good chance that graduate students in other departments whose research interests are close to yours will find their way to you, even if it is to just to serve on their committee as an external member. In all cases, it is worth having some idea of how to advise graduate students.

---

4. In the interest of brevity, I cannot discuss specific types of master's degrees, namely Master of Arts in Economics, Master of Science in Economics, Master of Public Policy, Master of Public Administration, Master of Business Administration, and so on.

For most of us, how to advise graduate students is not immediately obvious. Much like our experience of the parent–child relationship before having children of our own is our own relationship with our parents; our experience of the advisor–advisee relationship before having advisees of our own is our own experience with our advisor. So how do you go about doing a good job of advising graduate students?

By my count, I have so far served as advisor or co-advisor for 24 graduate students—19 PhD students, and five MS students. If there are any general lessons to be drawn, they are as follows.

It is their degree, not yours. I mentioned this earlier in this chapter, but your graduate students are there for themselves, and not for you to bask in their reflected glory. You may have grand plans for a student whom you see as exceptional, but they may not want to continue on to a PhD program, or they may want to get a job in government or in the private sector, and there is nothing wrong with that. Conversely, some students may not show much promise even after going through the necessary pre-dissertation milestones (e.g., qualifying exams, second-year paper). In all cases, unless they have repeatedly ignored your advice or been downright antagonistic, the students whom you agree to advise deserve that you give them your best.

Think carefully before you refuse to advise someone. Once, a number of years ago, I declined to advise a student. My reason was simple: they had told me they could not take my class because it was held at 8:30 in the morning, and there was no way they could get up that early. Given that, I concluded that I was unlikely to want to advise someone who let their preference for sleeping in overrun their preference for the subject I was supposed to be advising them on. But at an early-career mentoring workshop in 2017, a colleague who has won numerous graduate teaching awards for his advising changed my view when he said that he never saw it as his place to refuse to advise a graduate student, and that by virtue of getting admitted into your graduate program and satisfying all pre-research requirements, a student has clearly earned the right to an advisor. There are obviously some exceptions. If a student has a reputation for having a toxic personality, you may wish to steer clear of them. Likewise, if you are on the tenure track and you already have more than your fair share of advisees, you should be careful about taking on more of them, and carefully weigh the costs and the benefits involved.

Lay out your expectations clearly and early. One of the things my institution has been encouraging (but not requiring) faculty to do these past few years is to write an advising statement, i.e., a document that tells prospective graduate advisees what you expect of them, and how you approach the advisor–advisee relationship in general. When our then-director of graduate studies asked me to write such a statement given how many students I typically advise, I saw it more as a chore than anything else—as something to write to help a friend cover their administrative bases. But as with so many things in this line of work, just writing about something will help you clarify how you think about it, and my advising statement has grown to two and a half single-spaced pages. It starts with a preamble explaining what kind of department our department is, and how that should affect what students work on. My statement then lists ten principles that guide my advising, from how it is an advisee's responsibility to seek my advising and to schedule meetings with me to how I approach coauthoring with them, and from how and when they should think about asking for letters of recommendation to how I envision a good thesis or dissertation.

Help students keep things in perspective. By virtue of being more senior in the profession, you can help students keep things in perspective. Graduate students going through coursework tend to think their entire career is doomed if they do not do well in their courses or if they fail their qualifying exams. Your role is to help them see that some of the best-known scholars have also struggled through coursework, and that there is little to no correlation between the ability to take tests and the ability to come up with (and do a good job answering) interesting research questions. Likewise, students on the job market tend to think their time in graduate school was wasted if they do not get the offers they wanted. Your role is to help them see that even if they do not land their ideal position, the investment they have made in their education practically guarantees that they will always have a job that pays well, or in a location of their choice if they are flexible about the industry they choose to work in.

When is a PhD student's dissertation prospectus ready to be defended? In many departments, students have to present and defend their dissertation prospectus before they can have all of their requirements completed save their dissertation (i.e., ABD, for all but dissertation status). Given that three-paper (instead of monograph-type) dissertations are now the norm in economics, the broad standard I have witnessed over the years is that a student is ready for ABD status when they have (i) a first paper that is ready to be circulated as a working paper and presented at conferences, (ii) some rough results for a second paper that is usually missing only robustness checks and extensions, and (iii) a collection of bullet points outlining what they plan on doing in their third paper. This strikes me as a reasonable norm in that it allows students to use their second-year paper (if applicable) as that first paper, a term paper for a field class as their second paper, and an idea that may or may not come to fruition as their third paper. Equally importantly, this allows a student's advisor or committee to correct the student's course early on.

The best PhD dissertations consist of three essays on a coherent theme. By "best dissertations," I mean those that will best prepare a student to make a contribution in a given area of research as well as those that are most likely to win awards. Indeed, three essays on a coherent theme allows a student to demonstrate both the depth *and* breadth of their research. It allows a student to demonstrate depth by virtue of having them explore a given topic or theme in more detail. But it also allows them to demonstrate breadth by exploring that topic or theme from different angles. The best dissertation I supervised consisted of three essays on price volatility; two of those were experimental papers, and the third was observational and included a fair bit of theoretical modeling.

The essays in a dissertation will typically be of unequal quality. Many dissertations consist of an excellent first paper (usually the student's job market paper), a paper that shows promise, and a third paper that has been put together rapidly in order to graduate soon after the student has received a job offer. Even for students headed toward an academic career, that is fine, as it gives them three papers they can submit within their first two years on the tenure track. Even with the best students, expecting three papers of the same quality may be unrealistic.

When is a master's student's thesis ready to be defended? A few rules of thumb apply when comparing a PhD dissertation and a master's thesis. First, whereas a PhD dissertation tends to consist of three essays, a master's thesis tends to consist of one essay. Second, it is generally acceptable for a master's thesis to consist of an essay replicating someone else's work using a different data set, but one would likely have a hard time defending a dissertation that consists of three such essays. Third, the level of technique that can be expected from a master's student is strictly less than what can be expected of a PhD student. Broadly speaking, it helps to think of the goal of a master's degree to be to bring students to the research frontier, and to think of the goal of a PhD to have students push that research frontier further.

Different students respond differently to the same incentives. Some students thrive in a program where they are surrounded by people who are smarter than they are. Others thrive when they are top dog and are empowered by feeling like they are the smartest person in the room. Similarly, some students thrive when they only have limited time for research (say, because they have to teach in exchange for funding), whereas others do better when they have long periods of unencumbered time they can dedicate to research. Helping each student figure out their "type" can help them do better, and it will help tailor your advising to their needs.

Graduate students should avoid consulting. One exception to the previous rule is that graduate students should avoid (and advisors should avoid roping their graduate students into) consulting like the plague, both because of the immediate opportunity cost (time spent consulting is time not spent working on one's research), and because a little bit of consulting is a gateway drug to more consulting. Some graduate programs in the Washington, DC area are notorious for their low completion rates, and the reason that is often cited is proximity to US government agencies, multilateral institutions (e.g., World Bank, International Monetary Fund), and beltway bandits (i.e., consulting firms that derive most or all of their business from government contracts), which leads to graduate students realizing that they can make a lot more money by consulting than what their graduate student stipend brings in. This is not bad in and of itself when done in moderation, but the temptation to make even more money by consulting can lead to not finishing one's degree, or taking a long time to do so. The obvious (and rare) exception is when consulting activities directly align with one's research and can generate publications. Unfortunately, most graduate students are not yet known for being experts on anything, and so it is rare that they get consulting opportunities that can feed into their research, and cobbling a thesis or dissertation from consulting deliverables tends to make for a thesis or dissertation that lacks coherence, which limits the work's publication potential.

Grad school is a time for focusing. People who select into going to graduate school often have wide-ranging interests and, as a result, are often interested in a wide range of economic questions—if not of fields. To put it like Hamermesh (2011) did in his advice to junior faculty, a graduate student should "become an expert on 1.5 topics." Early on in his studies, one of my former PhD students would fall in love with the topic of every seminar, and he would start reading on a new topic virtually every week until I sat him down and explained to him that the market for dilettantes was rather thin. That student has since then become an expert on roughly one and a half topics.

You can lead a horse to water, but you cannot make it drink. Some students will see their time in grad school as a time to learn as much as possible, including from the feedback they receive from their advisor. Others will seem to pick and choose which pieces of feedback they incorporate. Yet others will be very reticent to incorporating any feedback they receive. In my experience, the students who approach graduate school with humility and treat it as an opportunity to learn as much as possible are the ones who end up being the most successful—in graduate school, on the job market, and in their career.

Be on the lookout for your advisees' mental well-being. A recent article in *Nature Biotechnology* (Evans et al. 2018) begins by noting that 6 percent of the general population rated as moderate to severe on the depression scale. Surveying over 2,200 graduate students (90 percent PhD students and 10 percent master's students), the authors found that the proportion of respondents who rated as moderate to severe on the depression scale attains 39 percent—a staggering six and a half times the proportion of people from the general population. Whether that is due to selection or treatment effects is irrelevant, but knowing how toxic the culture in the economics profession and in some programs can get, it is likely that things are even worse in economics. You are obviously not your advisees' therapist, but much like you would tell an advisee exhibiting signs of physical illness to go see a doctor, you should be on the lookout for signals of mental illness, and refer them to your institution's counseling and psychological services if you feel it is necessary. This is especially important for first-generation students (i.e., students whose parents may not have gone to college, let alone graduate school, and for whom graduate school is entirely uncharted territory) and for foreign students, who may hail from cultures where admitting to mental illness is seen as a moral failure.

Sometimes, tough love is necessary. I have served as graduate placement officer for our department for a number of years on and off. A few years ago when we were hiring, one of our recent alums who happened to be on sabbatical in our department that year decided to apply for the job we were hiring for, and we decided to give them a first-round interview. When they failed to make our short list, they wanted to meet with the members of the search committee (which included me) to figure out why they had not been invited to give a job talk. I had to tell them that we had received several applications from candidates who had publications (often more than one) in top field and top general journals, and that the candidate's lack of publications after being out three or four years did not compare well. Generally, there is no use sugarcoating. As I have mentioned above, people's mistaken perceptions tend to compound and become further and further removed from objective reality over time, and sometimes being a good advisor means having to be the bearer of bad news.

Perfect is the enemy of good. A good thesis or dissertation is a finished thesis or dissertation. Though most people who select into going to graduate school aim for excellence, one thing that too many graduate students fail to realize is that their thesis or dissertation is unlikely to be read by more than a dozen people: members of their committee will (hopefully) read it, as will the members of whatever awards committee it is sent to, and (maybe) other grad students writing literature reviews on the same topic. As a result, one should stop polishing one's thesis or dissertation when it is deemed good enough by one's committee, which means that one should develop a certain tolerance for imperfection. For PhD students, one has to know when a dissertation is "good enough," and defer polishing in view of submitting to journals to the summer (and maybe the first few semesters) after graduating. At any rate, dissertation papers often undergo radical transformations on the way to getting published.

When is a PhD dissertation ready to be defended? Barring a student needing to defend because your institution sets a specific time limit on doctoral programs, a student is ready to defend her dissertation when she has a job offer in hand. No economist worth his salt thinks he knows better than the market does.

Avoid the temptation to oversell students, but also avoid having to write letters of recommendation that are not positive. After spending three, four, five years advising a student, you likely want them to be successful or, at the very least, get them out of your hair. It can thus be very tempting when writing letters of recommendation to oversell them, and make it seem as though they are better than they really are. Overselling a student is likely to work once or twice, but once the jig is up and people know that your word is not to be trusted, your recommendations will not be worth much. As a result, it behooves you to be honest about a student's strengths and weaknesses, and to give the readers of your letters of recommendation an accurate read on where you see the student being successful. If, however, you do not feel as though you can write a good letter of recommendation for one of your advisees, let them know so that they can get the best possible letters for themselves.

When should you coauthor with students? In some graduate programs, faculty have a sink-or-swim attitude toward graduate students and avoid coauthoring with anyone but the most promising students. Yet if you see your role as advisor as helping students make the transition from students to scholars, then you should think about coauthoring with your students. By that, I do not mean that you should coauthor with your students no matter what, but you should certainly do so in those frequent cases where there is a double coincidence of research interests. That being said, you do not deserve to be a *de facto* coauthor on every one of your students' papers simply by virtue of having advised them.

The advisor–advisee relationship does not end at graduation. In my third year in grad school, I recall excitedly telling one of my econometrics instructors, whose advisor had been Bill Greene, about a new textbook by some guy named Wooldridge that seemed so much better to me than Greene's textbook. My instructor made me understand that advisor–advisee relationships die hard, and do not end at graduation. Much like your child will never stop being your child, no matter how old you both get, you will remain your student's advisor once they graduate, and they are likely to turn to you for advice when they come across situations they are uncertain about. Embrace the fact that, after you are done being their advisor, you are likely to become one of their mentors.

Warn your advisees against the often toxic culture of the discipline, and support them when they encounter it. Experimental evidence has shown that people tend to favor people in their group, and discriminate against people outside of their group (Abbink and Harris 2019). And on the basis of casual empiricism as an observer of US social and political life over the last few decades, I would speculate that when members of a group that has traditionally been at the top of a hierarchy see their hierarchical position threatened by members outside their group, in-group members react by discriminating (if not by retaliating) against members of the out-group, making life difficult for the latter. Worse: when in-group members' reflexive discrimination or retaliation is combined with the veil of anonymity provided by the Internet, the culture gets even more toxic, which can make life downright unbearable for members of the out-group. Media accounts of the discrimination experienced by women and minorities in economics certainly support that conjecture (Parramore 2020, Rosalsky 2020, Wolfers 2017). Given that, it is no surprise that economics has a pipeline problem (Buckles 2019, Corban and Ryssdal 2020, Hughes 2021), wherein women and underrepresented minorities either opt out of the profession after their studies or never elect to study economics to begin with. As advisor, your job is to make your students realize the toxic nature of the discipline, to support those who are vulnerable to it, and to educate those who are not as to the realities of their privilege and about what they can do to be a part of the solution.

7.4   Advising Foreign Students

Given the preponderance of economists in the policy apparatus of most if not all countries, graduate programs in economics and related disciplines tend to attract students from all over the world. Given that, it is useful to be aware of the specific issues that may arise when advising foreign students.

First and foremost, not everyone is a native speaker of English. Although most graduate programs tend to screen students on the basis of their score on the Test of English as a Foreign Language (TOEFL) or some similar exam, it is possible to prep enough to get an acceptable score on the TOEFL even with less-than-adequate English language skills, and I have heard rumors over the years of cheating on the TOEFL and other standardized tests being rampant in some countries. To make matters worse, although most graduate programs insist on a perfect or near perfect score on the quantitative portion of the Graduate Records Examinations (GRE), rarely do graduate programs treat the GRE verbal as anything more than an afterthought. In this job, however, the quality of one's written (and, to a somewhat lesser extent, spoken) English can be a major determinant of one's success.[5]

When advising foreign students who wish to have a career in the English-speaking world, the first thing to make sure of is that they understand the importance of being able to express themselves well in English, both when writing papers and presenting them in seminars. At the same time, it is not necessarily your job to teach them proper English grammar and vocabulary, and even if you wanted to do so, you may not have the requisite knowledge or the time to do so.

The good news is that most institutions of higher learning in the US have a writing center which foreign students are welcome to consult. Time and again, I have been surprised by how much the foreign students I have referred to my institution's writing center have benefited from it. If

---

5. This has nothing to do with whether one has an accent or not. Having grown up in Quebec speaking French, I retain a hint of a French Canadian accent even after 20 years in the US. But I did make a conscious investment in learning proper English grammar and vocabulary early on, which has served me well in this profession.

your institution has such a center, it is well worth sending your students to consult with it.

If a foreign student asks you for advice about how to improve their English, one thing that worked for me when I wanted to learn Italian when I moved to Rome was to make friends who spoke neither French (my native language) nor English (my second language) and to spend time with them. Though it was certainly comforting at the time to spend time with people who hailed from francophone or anglophone countries, nothing beat having to spend time speaking Italian over drinks or a meal, or at parties, which brought me to near-fluency in a matter of months.

To improve their written English, foreign students should make a point of reading in English. Whether that means reading *The Economist*, English translations of their favorite novels, or other printed materials, the important thing is to go beyond textbooks and the papers assigned in graduate classes, and the key is simply to read things that are competently written in English about things one is interested in.

Finally, as an advisor, you should be mindful of cultural differences. Even if you grew up in a community that lacked diversity and did not get to interact with foreigners until you went to graduate school, you can still be respectful of those differences, and you can still err on the side of cultural relativism. As much as our microeconomic theory training would have us believe that different individuals would (or should) behave the exact same way when facing the exact same situations, Fisman and Miguel (2007) have shown that cultural norms die hard, and that people's cultural upbringing often takes precedence over changing external incentives. In some cultures, the levels of shame and embarrassment one suffers when failing out graduate school can lead to serious depression. Likewise, the gender norms in some cultures may cause talented women to have to follow the lead of their significantly less-talented husbands. As in all things, even though you might be disappointed that cultural differences might lead one of your advisees to make a sub-optimal decision (from your point of view, that is), do try to be understanding and show empathy, and beyond providing advice, keep your opinions to yourself unless you are directly asked for them.

8
Conclusion

I wrote this book to demystify the unspoken rules of the economics profession. In so doing, I have tried to shine some light upon the so-called hidden curriculum—those things that are normally "learned but not openly intended" (Martin 1983)—guiding how research economists go about doing their job.

In *Wind, Sand, and Stars* (1939), Antoine de Saint-Exupéry writes:[1]

> When by mutation a new rose is born in a garden, all the gardeners rejoice. They isolate the rose, tend it, foster it. But there is no gardener for men. This little Mozart will be shaped like the rest by the common stamping machine. This little Mozart will love shoddy music in the stench of night dives. This little Mozart is condemned . . . I am not weeping over an eternally open wound. Those who carry the wound do not feel it. It is the human race and not the individual that is wounded here, is outraged here. I do not believe in pity. What torments me tonight is the gardener's point of view . . . What torments me is not the humps nor hollows nor the ugliness. It is the sight, a little bit in all these men, of Mozart murdered.

Over the years, I have realized that many research economists fail to be as successful as they could have been not because they are not smart enough, not because they are not good enough, but because they were never taught the rules of the game—because the hidden curriculum has remained hidden from their view, at least partially.

But just as there is a clear economic argument to be made against discrimination—a profit-maximizing employer would be foolish to willingly refuse to hire people whose skin happens to be of a certain color, because their likelihood of hiring the best person for the job would at best remain constant and at worst decrease as a result of that employer's

---

1. Readers who are put off by Saint-Exupéry's gendered writing should bear in mind that he wrote in the 1930s, at a time when the masculine referred to both genders.

attitude—there is a clear economic argument to be made against the hidden curriculum. Just imagine *how much better* economic research (and the discipline) would be if every graduate student in economics and adjacent fields in the world had access to the social norms and cultural mores of the profession—if the veil were lifted that covers the hidden curriculum!

Before closing both this chapter and this book, I would be remiss if I did not address an important, no-less-hidden—at least from the point of view of an early-career researcher—part of a research economist's curriculum, which relates to how we define success.

From one's very first few weeks in graduate school, the idea that one's success is a function of the number of top-five journal publications in one's CV is ingrained into one's mind. And to be sure, there is no denying that publishing articles in top-five journals implies success.

What many seem to forget, however, is a fundamental rule of logic also covered during those first few weeks in graduate school as part of most math review courses, namely the fact that $P \Rightarrow Q$ tells us nothing about whether $Q \Rightarrow P$. Although publishing in the top five journals certainly implies success in the economics profession, being successful in the economics profession does not necessarily imply publishing in the top five. Over the course of my career, I have met a number of people who did not have a top-five journal publication to their name but who were very successful as economists and were genuinely happy. Similarly, I have met a number of people who had an impressive number of top-five publications, but whose bitterness and pettiness betrayed a profound sense of insecurity and revealed a complete lack of self-esteem. For all I know, there is no correlation between one's sense of whether one has been successful and whether one is happy on the one hand and, on the other hand, the number of top-five journal articles to one's name.

Understand: no amount of top-five publications is liable to make you feel like you are successful or to make you happy if you constantly compare yourself to other, more successful economists. If you are going to compare yourself to someone, the key to happiness is to compare your present self with your past self.

There is also another tyranny of the top five, namely the tyranny of the top five departments.[2] At the beginning of their career, most if not all research economists are under the impression that since we are all

---

2. By "top five" departments, I am referring to the eight to ten or so departments that either are or like to think of themselves of as being in the top five.

competing in the marketplace of ideas, the best ideas and the most important topics rise to the top. More often than not, however, that impression is mistaken, because the economics profession can be eerily similar to the fashion or music industries, wherein what a handful of tastemakers say is what goes. The sooner an early-career research economist realizes that, the better.

The good news is that there are many ways to be successful in this profession. Besides publishing in top-five journals and getting a job in a top-five department, one obvious way is the pursuit of money. There are plenty of opportunities to make a very good living with a PhD in economics and related fields. Even as an academic whose salary is nowhere near what it could be in the private sector, consulting opportunities arise that allow one to pad one's income and afford nice things. Another way is the pursuit of knowledge for knowledge's sake, wherein you set out to answer research questions that are of genuine interest to you. Yet another way is in helping smart young people make the transition from student to scholar. And yet another way is by doing public service by working in government or influencing policy by working at a think tank.

During my first semester in graduate school, I remember being struck by the elegance of a metaphor used by Mas-Colell et al. (1995) to explain why the Slutsky matrix was symmetric under the usual assumptions of microeconomic theory—a result that is not intuitively obvious. The metaphor they use to describe why a change in the price of good i changes the quantity demanded of good j in the same way a change in the price of good j changes the quantity demanded of good i was as follows: no matter what path you choose to climb a mountain, you will have covered the same height once you attain the summit. A PhD in economics and related fields offers many paths to scaling the heights of success. It is up to you to find which of these many paths will work for you.

References

Abadie, A., S. Athey, G. Imbens, and J. Wooldridge. 2017. "When Should You Adjust Standard Errors for Clustering?" NBER Working Paper 24003, National Bureau of Economic Research, Cambridge, MA.

Abbink, K., and D. Harris. 2019. "In-Group Favouritism and Out-Group Discrimination in Naturally Occurring Groups." *PLoS ONE* 14(9): e0221616.

Adler, M. J., and C. Van Doren. 2014. *How to Read a Book.* New York: Simon and Schuster.

Altonji, J., T. E. Elder, and C. R. Taber. 2005. "Selection on Observed and Unobserved Variables: Assessing the Effectiveness of Catholic Schools." *Journal of Political Economy* 113(1): 151–184.

American Economic Association. 2020. "Data and Code Availability Policy." Accessed August 26, 2020. https://www.aeaweb.org/journals/policies/data-code.

Angrist, J. D., and J. S. Pischke. 2010. "The Credibility Revolution in Empirical Economics: How Better Research Design Is Taking the Con Out of Econometrics." *Journal of Economic Perspectives* 24(2): 3–30.

Backhouse, R., and B. Cherrier. 2017a. "The Age of the Applied Economist: The Transformation of Economics since the 1970s." *History of Political Economy* 49 (Supplement): 1–33.

Backhouse, R. and B. Cherrier. 2017b. "'It's Computers, Stupid!' The Spread of Computers and the Changing Roles of Theoretical and Applied Economics." *History of Political Economy* 49 (Supplement): 103–126.

Baron, David P. 1970. "Price Uncertainty, Utility, and Industry Equilibrium in Pure Competition." *International Economic Review.* 1970: 463–480.

Bellemare, M. F. 2012. "Insecure Land Rights and Share Tenancy: Evidence from Madagascar." *Land Economics* 88(1): 155–180.

Bellemare, M. F. 2015. "Rising Food Prices, Food Price Volatility, and Social Unrest." *American Journal of Agricultural Economics* 97(1): 1–21.

Bellemare, M. F., Y. N. Lee, and D. R. Just. 2020. "Producer Attitudes toward Output Price Risk: Experimental Evidence from the Lab and from the Field." *American Journal of Agricultural Economics* 102(3): 806–825.

Bellemare, M. F., T. Masaki, and T. B. Pepinsky. 2017. "Lagged Explanatory Variables and the Estimation of Causal Effects." *Journal of Politics* 79(3): 949–963.

Bera, A. K., A. Ghosh, and Z. Xiao. 2013. "A Smooth Test for the Equality of Distributions." *Econometric Theory* 29(2): 419–446.

Berrett, D. 2012. "Economists Adopt New Disclosure Rules for Authors of Published Research." *Chronicle of Higher Education*. Last accessed August 25, 2020. https://www.chronicle.com/article/economists-adopt-new-disclosure-rules-for-authors-of-published-research/.

Blattman, C. 2010. "The Discussant's Art." Last accessed August 20, 2020. https://chrisblattman.com/2010/02/22/the-discussants-art.

Bolton, P., and M. Dewatripont. 2005. *Contract Theory*. Cambridge, MA: MIT Press.

Bowmaker, S. 2012. *The Art and Practice of Economics Research: Lessons from Leading Minds*. Cheltenham: Edward Elgar Publishing.

Buckles, K. 2019. "Fixing the Leaky Pipeline: Strategies for Making Economics Work for Women at Every Stage." *Journal of Economic Perspectives* 33(1): 43–60.

Burke, M., L. Falcao Bergquist, and E. Miguel. 2019. "Sell Low and Buy High: Arbitrage and Local Price Effects in Kenyan Markets." *Quarterly Journal of Economics* 134(2): 785–842.

Card, D., and S. Della Vigna. 2018. "Update to 'Nine Facts about Top Journals in Economics." Working Paper, UC Berkeley.

Carrigan, M. 2019. *Social Media for Academics*, 2nd ed. Newbury Park, CA: Sage Publishing.

Cawley, J. 2018. "A Guide and Advice for Economists on the US Junior Academic Job Market." Working Paper, Cornell University.

Christensen, G., and E. Miguel. 2018. "Transparency, Reproducibility, and the Credibility of Economics Research." *Journal of Economic Literature* 56(3): 920–980.

Colander, D. 2008. *The Making of an Economist, Redux*. Princeton, NJ: Princeton University Press.

Cole, S., X. Giné, J. Tobacman, P. Topalova, R. Townsend, and J. Vickery. 2013. "Barriers to Household Risk Management: Evidence from India." *American Economic Journal: Applied Economics* 5(1), 104–135.

Conley, T. G., C. B. Hansen, and P. E. Rossi. 2012. "Plausibly Exogenous." *Review of Economics and Statistics* 94(1): 260–272.

Corban, A., and K. Ryssdal. 2020. "The Pipeline Problem for Black Women in Economics." Marketplace. Accessed May 18, 2021. https://www.marketplace.org/2020/07/01/the-pipeline-problem-for-black-women.

Datahound. 2014. "Indirect Cost Rate Survey." Last accessed September 29, 2020. https://datahound.scientopia.org/2014/05/10/indirect-cost-rate-survey/.

Deaton, A. 1997. *The Analysis of Household Surveys*. Washington, DC: World Bank Group.

Dionne, K. Y. 2011. "Why Not to Post Your Working Paper Online." Last accessed December 12, 2020. https://habanahaba.wordpress.com/2011/07/01/why-not-to-post-your-working-paper-online/.

Evans, D. 2020. "How to Write the Introduction of Your Development Economics Paper." Last accessed September 28, 2020. https://www.cgdev.org/blog/how-write-introduction-your-development-economics-paper.

Evans, T. M., L. Bira, J. B. Gastelum, L. T. Weiss, and N. L. Vanderford. 2018. "Evidence for a Mental Health Crisis in Graduate Education." *Nature Biotechnology* 36(3): 282–284.

Fisman, R., and E. Miguel. 2007. "Corruption, Norms, and Legal Enforcement: Evidence from Diplomatic Parking Tickets." *Journal of Political Economy* 115(6): 1020–1048.

Foster, A. D., and M. R. Rosenzweig. 1995. "Learning by Doing and Learning from Others: Human Capital and Technical Change in Agriculture." *Journal of Political Economy* 103(6): 1176–1209.

Gerber, A. S., and D. P. Green. 2012. *Field Experiments*. New York: W. W. Norton & Co.

Gitter, S. R. 2021. "A Guide for Student-Led Undergraduate Research in Empirical Micro-Economics." *Journal of Economics Teaching* 5(3): 83–115.

Glennerster, R., and K. Takavarasha. 2013. *Running Randomized Evaluations*. Princeton, NJ: Princeton University Press.

Glewwe, P. W., and M. Grosh. 2000. *Designing Household Survey Questionnaires for Developing Countries*. Washington, DC: World Bank Group.

Hamermesh, D. 2011. "10 Tips for Junior Faculty." *Inside Higher Ed*. Last accessed October 29, 2020. https://www.insidehighered.com/advice/2011/05/25/10-tips-junior-faculty.

Head, K. 2020. "The Introduction Formula." Last accessed January 2, 2020. http://blogs.ubc.ca/khead/research/research-advice/formula

Holiday, R. 2014. *The Obstacle Is the Way*. New York: Portfolio.

Holton, G. 2001. "Henri Poincaré, Marcel Duchamp and Innovation in Science and Art." *Leonardo* 34(2): 127–134.

Hughes, C. 2021. "Solving Economics' Diversity Problem." *Bloomberg*. Accessed May 18, 2021. https://www.bloomberg.com/opinion/articles/2021-05-18/women-economists-wanted-bank-of-england-ecb-and-fed-test-the-pipeline.

International Initiative for Impact Evaluation. 2020. "Replication." Last accessed August 26, 2020. https://www.3ieimpact.org/our-expertise/replication.

Jacobellis v. Ohio. 1964. 378 US 184.

Johnson, S. 2005. "Did Blogging Doom Prof's Shot at Tenure?" *Chicago Tribune*, October 14, 2005.

King, G. 1995. "Replication, Replication." *PS: Political Science and Politics* 28(3): 443–499.

Kleemans, M., and R. L. Thornton. 2021. "Who Belongs? The Determinants of Selective Membership into the National Bureau of Economic Research." *AEA Papers and Proceedings* 111: 117–122.

Lamott, A. 1995. *Bird by Bird: Some Instructions on Writing and Life.* New York: Anchor Books.

Lee, Y. N. 2021. "Does Aversion to Price Risk Drive Migration? Evidence from Rural Ethiopia." *American Journal of Agricultural Economics* 103(4): 1268–1293.

Leijonhufvud, A. 1973. "Life among the Econ." *Economic Inquiry* 11(3): 327–337.

Letchford, A., H.S. Moat, and T. Preis. 2015. "The Advantage of Short Paper Titles." *Royal Society Open Science* 2(8): 150266.

Lewbel, A. 2019. "The Identification Zoo: Meanings of Identification in Econometrics." *Journal of Economics Literature* 57(4): 835–903.

Manski, C. F. 1993. "Identification of Endogenous Social Effects: The Reflection Problem." *Review of Economic Studies* 60(3): 531–542.

Martin, J. 1983. "What Should We Do with a Hidden Curriculum When We Find One?" *The Hidden Curriculum and Moral Education*, edited by H. Giroux, and D. Purpel, 122–139. Berkeley: McCutchan.

Mas-Colell, A., M. D. Whinston, and J. R. Green. 1995. *Microeconomic Theory.* Oxford: Oxford University Press.

McCannon, B. C. 2019. "Readability and Research Impact." *Economics Letters* 180: 76–79.

McKenzie, D. 2012. "Beyond Baseline and Follow-Up: The Case for More T in Experiments." *Journal of Development Economics* 99(2): 210–221.

McKenzie, D., and B. Özler. 2014. "Quantifying Some of the Impacts of Economics Blogs." *Economic Development and Cultural Change* 62(3): 567–597.

Miah, A. 2019. "The A to Z of Social Media for Academia." *Times Higher Education.* Last accessed May 16, 2021. https://www.timeshighereducation .com/a-z-social-media.

Morgan, S. L., and C. Winship. 2015. *Counterfactuals and Causal Inference.* Cambridge: Cambridge University Press.

Ogden, T. 2017. *Experimental Conversations: Perspectives on Randomized Trials in Development Economics.* Cambridge, MA: MIT Press.

"Online Image." *Nature* (473): May 12, 2011, p. 124. Editorial.

Oster, E. 2019. "Unobservable Selection and Coefficient Stability: Theory and Evidence." *Journal of Business & Economics Statistics* 37(2): 187–204.

Pain, E. 2017. "How to Budget Your Grant Proposal." *Science.* Last accessed May 17, 2021. https://www.sciencemag.org/careers/2017/09/how-budget-your -grant-proposal.

Parramore, L. 2020. "What Happens When a Noted Female Economist Fights Toxic Culture in the Field?" Last accessed May 18, 2021. https://www.ineteconomics .org/perspectives/blog/what-happens-when-a-noted-female-economist-fights -toxic-culture-in-the-field.

Pearl, J. 2009. *Causality*, 2nd ed. Cambridge: Cambridge University Press.

Rosalsky, G. 2020. "Economics Still Has A Diversity Problem." *Planet Money*. Last accessed May 18, 2021. https://www.npr.org/sections/money/2020/01/07/793855832/economics-still-has.

Sahm, C. 2019. "we need to talk MORE . . . ." Last accessed September 28, 2020. http://macromomblog.com/2019/09/29/we-need-to-talk-more/

Sánchez de la Sierra, R. 2020. "On the Origins of the State: Stationary Bandits and Taxation in Eastern Congo." *Journal of Political Economy* 128(1): 32–74.

Sandmo, A. 1971. "On the theory of the competitive firm under price uncertainty." *American Economic Review* 61(1): 65–73.

Shea, A. 2007. "Jack Kerouac's Famous Scroll, *On the Road* Again." Last accessed November 19, 2020. https://www.npr.org/templates/story/story.php?storyId=11709924.

Shea, C. 2011. "Economist Slammed for Concurrent Publications." *Wall Street Journal*, July 13, 2011.

Sokal, Alan, and Jean Bricmont. 1999. *Fashionable Nonsense: Postmodern Intellectuals' Abuse of Science*, Macmillan.

Solon, G., S. J. Haider, and J. M. Wooldridge. 2015. "What Are We Weighting For?" *Journal of Human Resources* 50(2): 301–316.

Staudt, J. 2020. "The Impacts of Open Access on Scientists, Inventors, and the Public." Working Paper.

Stromberg, J. 2014. "'Get Me Off Your Fucking Mailing List' Is An Actual Science Paper Accepted by a Journal." Last accessed August 22, 2020. https://www.vox.com/2014/11/21/7259207/scientific-paper-scam.

Suri, T. 2011. "Selection and Comparative Advantage in Technology Adoption." *Econometrica* 79(1): 159–209.

Texas Beef Group v. Winfrey. 1998. 201 F.3d 680, 688.

Thomson, W. 2011. *A Guide for the Young Economist*, 2nd ed. Cambridge, MA: MIT Press.

Tomkins, A., M. Zhang, and W.D. Heavlin. (2017). "Reviewer Bias in Single-versus Double-Blind Peer Review." *Proceedings of the National Academy of Sciences* 114(48): 12708–12713.

Treisman, R. 2020. "Whistleblower Alleges 'Medical Neglect,' Questionable Hysterectomies Of ICE Detainees." National Public Radio News. Last accessed October 3, 2020. https://www.npr.org/2020/09/16/913398383/whistleblower-alleges-medical-neglect-ques.

Williamson O. E. 1975. *Markets and Hierarchies*. London: Collier McMillan.

Wolfers, J. 2017. "Evidence of a Toxic Environment for Women in Economics." *New York Times*, August 18, 2017.

Wu, A. H. 2020. "Gender Bias in Rumors Among Professionals: An Identity-based Interpretation." *Review of Economics and Statistics* 102(5): 867–880.

Zinsser, W. K. 2006. *On Writing Well*. New York: Collins.

Index

Abadie, A., 16, 93
Abbink, K., 163
Abstracts, 7, 19, 25, 26, 30, 73–74, 97, 98, 131, 134
  graphical, 76
  relation to the introduction, 27
  reviewer's reading of, 130, 131, 134
  structured, 134
  writing guidelines, 29–30, 31–32, 97, 98
Academic departments, top-five, 69–71, 168–169, 168n2
Academic integrity, 100
Academic year, journal article submissions during, 64
Acknowledgments, 73–74, 74n10
  of research funders, 73–74, 103, 112
Advising, 151–165, 169
  check-ins on students, 154, 154n3
  distinguished from mentoring, 151
  feedback in, 160–161
  of foreign students, 164–165
  general principles, 152
  for graduate students, 3–4, 156–164
  incentives for, 151
  refusal to, 157
  teaching-and-service nature of, 151
  for undergraduate students, 3–4, 153–156
Advising centers, 154
Advising statements, 157–158
Advisor-advisee relationship, 157–158, 163

Agricultural economics, 102
  output price volatility research, 106
Altonji, J., 19–20
American Economic Association (AEA), 48
  journals, 75
  support for women and underrepresented minorities, 149
American Economic Review, 31, 35n15, 67, 70, 129, 137n9, 139
American Journal of Agricultural Economics, 70
Angrist, J. D., 20, 22, 75, 101
Appendices, 7
  to conference presentations, 50
  to invited seminar presentations, 44, 45
  to journal articles, 73–74, 74–75
  to slide desk, 42
  theoretical models presented in, 10
Applied economics, 1–2
Art and Practice of Economics Research, The (Bowmaker), 156
Assistant professors
  job talks, 46
  publications, 86, 87
  service activities, 123
  tenure, 121n1
Associate professors
  service activities, 123
  tenure, 121n1
Assumptions, 9, 26, 42, 49, 169
Athey, Susan, 16, 93, 156

Attrition rate, 10
Audience
    for conference presentations, 48,
        50, 53
    for invited seminar presentations,
        40–41, 44, 45
    for job talks, 47
    for journal articles and research
        papers, 33, 67, 97, 144
    lay audiences, 54–57
    for practice talks, 58
    question asking by, 40, 59–60
Authorship, ethics of, 100, 132–133
Awards committees, 162

Baccalaureate/Associate's Colleges,
    102
Background sections, 7, 32–33
Backhouse, R., 1, 101
Balance tests, 11, 13, 17, 43, 49
Baron, David, 137n9
Behavioral economics, grant sources,
    103
Bellemare, Lee, and Just, 117, 118
Bellemare, M. F., 12, 91n21, 117, 118,
    144, 146n11
Bera, A. K., 13n4
Berrett, D., 75
Bhagwati, Jagdish, 34
Bias
    of reviewers, 79, 80
    statistical, 17, 18, 24n11
Bira, L., 161
Bird by Bird (Lamott), 36
Blattman, C., 52
Blogging, 144–145, 146
Bolton, P., 140
Book proposals, reviews of, 133–134,
    135
Bowmaker, S., 156
Bricmont, Jean, 31
Buckles, K., 163
Budget, as grant proposal item, 109,
    116–117, 116n12, 118
Bullet points
    in conference presentations, 49–50
    in dissertations, 158

    in invited seminar presentations,
        40–41, 42–43
    in job talks, 46
    in journal articles, 75–76
Burke, M., 18
Business insurance, 56–57
Business talks, 55

Card, D., 70
Career path, of undergraduate
    students, 153–154
Carnegie Classification of Institutions
    of Higher Education, 67n5, 101–
    102, 152
Carrigan, M., 147
Causal effects, 43–44, 113–114
Causal identification, 16–17, 18–19,
    20, 26, 55
Causal inference, 94
Causal relationship, colliders in, 24,
    24n11
Causal statements, 14–15, 22–23
Cawley, J., 2
CfP (call for papers), for grants, 108,
    109, 111, 113, 115
Cherrier, B., 1, 101
Christensen, G., 75
Churchill, Winston, 62
Citation counts, 34–35, 68, 68n6, 97,
    97n25, 98, 99, 145
    abstracts and, 31–32
    readability score and, 31
    reviewers' comments and, 132
Citations, for field journal articles,
    33–34
CITI program, 119
Clooney, George, 46
Coauthors, 9–10, 73, 80, 81n13, 88,
    104, 110–111, 130, 137, 138
    students as, 162–163
Coefficient estimates, 23
Colander, D., 152
Cole, Shawn, 138
Colliders, 24n11
Coltrane, John, 8
Conclusion. See Summary and
    concluding remarks

Conference presentations, 48–52, 71–72
 appendix, 50
 data and descriptive statistics, 49
 discussion of, 50–52
 distinguished from invited seminars, 48, 50
 empirical framework, 49
 introduction, 49
 length, 48, 50
 as lightning talks, 53
 online and hybrid, 52–53
 optimization problem in, 49
 results and discussion, 49–50
 serving as discussant at, 50–52
 summary and concluding remarks, 50
 theoretical framework, 49
 title, 49
Conferences, 3
 predatory, 66
 review of research paper submissions, 133–134
 as service activity, 124, 124n3
Conflicts of interest, 75, 80–81, 81n13, 128, 130, 136–137
Conley, T. G., 17
Consulting, 169
 by graduate students, 160
 legal liability issue, 56–57
Contracts, grants as, 104–105
Control groups, pairwise comparisons, 11, 13
Control variables
 consistency in empirical and theoretical frameworks, 43
 estimation strategy, 15
 listed on tables, 23–24
 in presentations, 43, 44
 relation to sample size, 24–25
 robustness checks, 19
Corban, A., 163
Cornell University, Department of Economics, 1
COVID-19 pandemic, 52
Creative work, 86–87

Credibility Revolution, 20, 22, 75, 101
Cross-sectional data, 83
Cross-tabulations, 13
Cultural norms and mores, 165, 168
Cultural relativism, 165
Curriculum, "hidden," 167–168
Curriculum vitae (CV), 46n5
 conference presentations and seminars noted on, 50, 59
 on grant proposals, 109
 publications noted on, 66, 85, 86, 88, 148, 168
 reviewer experience on, 126
 updating for manuscript revisions, 85

Data
 availability, 1
 balance tests, 11, 13
 in conference presentations, 49
 in invited seminar presentations, 42–43
 missing, 10
 revisions, 92
Data and descriptive statistics section, 7, 10–14, 42, 43, 49, 92
 contents, 11–13, 12t
 tables of variable descriptions, 11, 12
 use of tenses, 13–14
 writing guidelines, 13–14
Data collection and analysis, 10
 funding for, 3, 101
 in sponsored projects, 115
 survey questionnaires, 11
Davies, Robertson, 35
Davis, Miles, 8
Deadlines
 for grant proposals, 108, 110, 111
 for journal article reviews, 125, 138–139
 for journal article revisions, 84
 for special issue journal articles, 125
Decimals, 14, 23
Della Vigna, S., 70
Depression, 161

de Saint-Exupéry, Antoine, 167
Descriptive statistics, 55, 56, 73, 92
    See also Data and descriptive
        statistics section
Desk rejections, 34, 69–70, 82, 83,
    139–140
    personalized, 142
Dewatripont, M., 140
Dionne, Kim Yi, 11, 98n26
Disclosure forms, 75
Disclosure rules, for funding sources,
    103, 112
Discrimination, 163–164, 167–168
Discussion section. *See* Results and
    discussion section
Dissertation prospectus, defense of,
    158
Dissertations
    "best," 159
    completion, 148–149, 162
    defense of, 162
    essays in, 159
    readership for, 162
    three-paper, 158–159
Diversity, 148–149, 148–150, 165
Doctoral degree, goal of, 159
Doctoral programs, time limits on,
    162
Doctoral students, second- or third-
    year qualifying research paper, 64
"Double-dipping" practice, 132–133
Double jeopardy, 137
D/PU (doctoral/professional)
    universities, 67n5, 102
    advising at, 153
    grant sources at, 102
Due diligence, 137

Early-career researchers, 57–58
    as advisors or mentors, 157
    conference presentations, 50
    criteria for success, 168–169
    invited seminar presentations of, 42
    professional service by, 3, 124–125,
        129
    publications, 71, 78–79, 87, 87n18
EconLit bibliographic database, 65n3

Econometrica, 35n15, 67
Econometrics Journal, 77
*Economic Development and Cultural
    Change,* 33–34
Economic Inquiry, 64–65
Economics-adjacent disciplines, 1–2
Economics journals
    *See also titles of individual
        economics journals*
    submissions to, 67–70
Economic & Social Research Council
    (UK), 108
Economics profession, toxic culture
    of, 76, 84n16, 161, 163–164
Economists, as journal reviewers,
    76–77
Editorial service, 139–143
Editors
    See also Submission, of journal
        articles
    administrative support for, 140–141
    appeals of editorial decisions, 88–90
    associate, 139
    contact with, 81–82
    cover letters to, from authors, 72,
        80, 92, 95
    cover letters to, from reviewers,
        132–133
    decision-making process of, 82–90,
        141
    of field journals, 33
    of general-science journals, 72–73
    location and selection of reviewers
        by, 34, 72–73, 77–79, 127–128,
        141, 142
    monetary compensation, 141
    roles and responsibilities, 139
Elder, T. E., 19–20
Elements of Style, The (Strunk and
    White), 36k
Elsevier journals, 75n11
email, 37, 60
    from editors, 126, 128, 136
    to editors, 72, 82, 128, 141–142
    for publicizing research papers, 99
    from reviewers, 136, 141, 142
    to reviewers, 128, 142

Empirical economics, research paper
structure in, 8, 9, 21, 27, 30–31,
101
Empirical framework, 7, 14–19
for conference presentations, 49
definition, 14
estimation strategy subsection,
14–16, 22, 29, 43, 93
identification strategy subsection,
14–15, 16–19, 29, 43–44, 49, 51,
55, 79, 88–89
for invited seminar presentations,
43–44
revisions, 91n21, 92
Empirical relationships, 8, 9
Empiricism, 1–2
English-language skills, 35–36, 58, 89,
96, 164–165, 164n5
Environmental economics, 102
Ernest Hemingway on Writing
(Phillips), 36
Estimable equations, 15–16, 43–44,
49
Estimation samples, 24–25
Estimation strategy subsection, 14–16,
22, 29, 43, 93
Ethics
of authorship, 100, 132–133
of human subject research, 117,
119–120
of reviewers, 136–139
European Commission, 108
European Research Council, 108
Evans, David, 30–31
Evans, T. M., 161
Evidence, standards of, 20
Experimental Conversations (Yang),
106, 107
Experimental economics, grant
sources, 103
Expertise
of graduate students, 160
sharing of, 55–56
External review letters, 69, 123, 124
External validity, 10, 17n6, 23, 26, 29,
35, 43, 51, 54–55
limitations, 23

Faculty
Black, indigenous, or people of
color, 148n12
governance role, 121–122
Falcao Bergquist, L., 18
Falsification tests, for robustness,
20–21
Feedback
from advisors, 160–161
from editors, 83
in invited seminars, 45
from reviewers, 137, 139
Field experiments, 44
Field journals, 65
definition, 33n14
reviewers for, 129
reviews in, 139
submissions to, 33–34, 33n14,
70–72, 76
First drafts, 36
Fisman, R., 165
Flowcharts, 54
Follow-up papers, 26
Food libel laws, 56
Food price volatility, 146n11
Food systems economics, 61
Foreign students
advising of, 164–165
English language skills, 35–36, 58,
89, 96, 164–165, 164n5
mental well-being, 161
Foster, A. D., 5
Foundations, as grant source,
102–103
F-tests, 13n4
Full professors, 69
service activities of, 121n1, 123
Funding, 101–120
See also Grant proposals; Grants
disclosure rules, 103, 112
estimation of amount required,
104–107
internal *versus* external, 103–104,
103n3, 109–110
location of sources of, 107–108
open access publication and, 99
Future tense, 14

Gap year, 153–154
Gastelum, J. B., 161
Gender norms, 165
Gender variables, 13
General journals
    definition, 33n14
    reviewers for, 129
    submissions to, 34–35, 70–72, 76
General-science journals
    article structure for, 37, 113
    submissions to, 37, 58, 65, 67, 69,
        72–73
    titles of articles for, 27
Gerber, A. S., 10
Ghosh, A., 13n4
Gibson, William, 2
Giné, Xavier, 138
Gitter, Seth, 155–156
Gitter, Seth R., 11–12, 155–156
Giving talks
    conference presentations, 48–53
    invited seminars, 39–45
    job talks, 46–47
    keynote addresses, 57
    for lay audiences, 54–57
    lightning talks, 53
    outreach talks, 55–57
    policy or business talks, 55
    poster presentations, 54
    practice for, 57–59
Glass, Ira, 86–87
Glennerster, R., 10
Glewwe, Paul W., 10
Global Environmental Change, 67
Governance, as faculty's role, 121–122
Government agencies, as grant source,
    103, 108
Graduate admissions committees, 124
Graduate placement directors/officers,
    124, 161
Graduate programs, completion rate,
    160
Graduate Records Examinations
    (GREs), 164
Graduate students
    ABD (all but dissertation) status,
        158–159

advising, 156–164
    as coauthors, 162–163
    consulting by, 160
    mental well-being, 161
Grant proposals, 107, 108–117
    budget, 109, 116–117, 116n12,
        118, 118f
    CfP (call for papers), 108, 109, 111,
        113, 115
    deadlines, 108, 110, 111
    decision on, 110–111
    documentation for, 109–110
    institutional review board approval,
        117, 119–120
    introduction and motivations,
        113–114
    pre-proposal stages, 108–109
    project anticipated outputs, 115
    project timeline, 115
    review of, 112–114, 133–135
    RfA (request for applications), 108
    RfP (request for proposals), 108,
        109, 111, 113, 114
    rough sketch of, 113–115
    successful, preparation of, 113–117
Grants, 3, 101
    alternatives, 106
    application for, 102
    based on institutional
        categorization, 101–102
    as contracts, 104–105
    costs *versus* benefits, 105
    estimation of required amount,
        104–107
    final report and deliverables, 112
    indirect cost recovery (ICR) on,
        103–104, 104n4
    as inputs *versus* outputs, 103–104,
        105
    management of, 105, 105n5,
        106–107
    periodic progress reports on,
        111–112
    sources, 102–103
    sponsored project life cycle,
        108–113
Grantsmanship, 103–104

Great Recession, 75
Green, D. P., 10
Green, J. R., 169
Greene, Bill, 163
Grosh, M., 10

Haider, S. J., 16
Hamermesh, D., 160
Hansen, C. B., 17
Harris, D., 163
Head, Keith, 27–30, 31, 32, 41
Health economics, grant sources,
    102–103
Health Services Research, 67
Heavlin, W. D., 73n9
Heteroskedasticity, 16
Histograms, 13
Holiday, Ryan, 46
Holton, G., 90n20
How to Read a Book (Adler), 6
Huber-Sandwich-White correction, 15
Hughes, C., 163
Human resource management skills,
    106–107
Human subjects research, 117, 119–
    120, 119n16
Hybrid format, of seminars and
    conference presentations, 52–53
Hypothesis, 8–9
    tests of, 9, 16, 80

Identification
    causal, 16–17, 18–19, 20, 26, 55
    definition, 16, 94
    variables for, 13, 146n11
Identification strategy subsection,
    14–15, 16–19, 29, 43–44, 49, 51,
    55, 79, 88–89
Imbens, G., 16, 93
Impact factors, 65, 65n3, 68, 68n6,
    143
    See also Citation counts
Inclusion, 148–150
Index insurance, 138
Industrial organization economics,
    33, 102
Inference, 15, 16, 20, 24, 94

Institutional review boards (IRBs),
    117–120, 117n14
Interdisciplinary journals, 67, 68, 69
Interdisciplinary research, 55
Internal validity, 10, 26, 29, 35,
    54–55, 68, 75
    limitations, 22–23
    SUTVA violations and, 18
International Economic Review, 137n9
International Initiative for Impact
    Evaluations, 75
International organizations, as
    funding source, 103
Introduction, 6, 7, 92, 98
    antecedents section, 28
    as bait-and-switch, 30
    for conference presentations, 49
    for general-science journal articles,
        37
    to grant proposals, 113–114
    Head's formula for, 27–30, 31, 32,
        41
    the "hook," 28
    for invited seminars, 41, 43
    research question statement, 28
    revisions, 92
    roadmap section, 29, 31, 41
    structure, 27–31
    value-added section, 29, 30, 31
Invited seminars, 39–45
    appendices, 42, 44, 45
    concluding remarks, 44–45
    dialogue during, 39, 40, 45
    distinguished from conference
        presentations, 48, 50
    duration, 40
    introduction, 41, 43
    invitations to present, 45
    results and discussion, 44
    structure, 41–45
    summary, 44–45
    title, 41

Jabobellis v. Ohio, 26–27
Job interviews, 69, 114, 161
    job talks and, 46–47
    for senior positions, 47

Job market, 158, 161
  changing nature of, 2, 46
  research publications and, 10,
    63–64
Job talks, 46–47, 161
John Bates Clark Medal, 1
Johnson, S., 28, 143
Joint tests, 13n4
Journal(s)
  See also titles of individual journals
  acceptance rate, 70
  author processing charges (APCs),
    65n3
  bibliographic databases, 65n3
  edited volumes, 125, 125n4
  Elsevier, 75n11
  funding disclosure rules, 103
  impact factors, 65, 65n3, 68, 68n6,
    143
  open access, 99
  predatory, 65–66, 65n3, 66n4,
    86n17, 139
  quality ranking, 66–67
  requests or inquiries from, 66
  special issue, 125
  title page, 73–74
  top-five, 34–35, 35n15, 64, 70–71,
    78, 97n25, 168, 169
  writing for specific journals, 33–35
Journal articles
  See also Editors; Peer-review
    process; Reviewers; Submission,
    of journal articles
  acceptance rate, 70
  author ethics for, 100
  as basis for professional reputation,
    61
  citation counts, 31–32, 34–35, 68,
    68n6, 97, 97n25, 98, 99, 132,
    145
  citations in, 78–80, 94–95
  coauthors, 9–10, 73, 80, 81n13, 88,
    104, 110–111, 130, 138
  code and data for, 75
  credibility, 75
  disclosures, 75
  "double-dipping" practice, 132–133

  formatting, 69–70, 72
  galley proofs, 96
  general interest criterion, 71
  highlights, 75–76, 75n11
  manuscript, 74
  online publication, 86
  preprints, 98, 98n26
  publicizing after publication,
    96–100
  search engine optimization (SEO),
    98
  self-plagiarism, 100, 111, 132–133
  title page, 73–74, 98, 131
  transparency and replicability, 75
*Journal of Business & Economics
  Statistics*, 77
Journal of Development Economics,
  33–34, 68, 70
Journal of Econometrics, 77
*Journal of Economic Behavior and
  Organization*, 80n12
Journal of Economic Growth, 80n12
Journal of Economic Literature (JEL)
  codes, 78
Journal of Health Economics, 70
Journal of Human Resources, 80n12
Journal of Labor Economics, 33–34
Journal of Monetary Economics, 68
*Journal of Money, Credit and
  Banking*, 68
Journal of Political Economy, 35n15
Journal of Public Economics, 67
Just, D. R., 117

Kernel density estimates, 13
Keynote addresses, 57
King, G., 75
Kleemans, M., 72n8
Krugman, Paul, 34

Lab-in-the-field experiments, 23,
  23n10
Laboratory experiments, 44
Labour Economics, 33–34
Lagged endogenous variables,
  146n11
Lamott, Anne, 36

Lay audiences, giving talks for, 54–57
    multidisciplinary research talks,
        54–55
Lee, Y. N., 106, 117, 118
Legal liability, for outreach or
    consulting, 56–57
Leijonhufvud, A., 1
Letchford, A., 27, 97
Letters of recommendation, 158,
    162
Lewbel, A., 16
LGBTQ+ community, 149
Lightning talks, 53
Literature reviews, 28, 32, 162
    mini, 32, 49
    revisions, 92

Macroeconomics, research paper
    structure, 30–31
Making of an Economist, Redux, The
    Colander), 152
Mallory, George, 107
Manski, C. F., 76
Marie Curie Fellowships, 108
Martin, J., 167
Marx, Groucho, 66
Masaki, T., 146n11
Mas-Colell, A., 169
Massachusetts Institute of Technology
    (MIT) Press, book proposal review
    process, 135
Master's colleges or universities,
    102
Master's degree, goal of, 159
McCannon, B. C., 31
McKenzie, D., 19n8, 145
McKenzie and Özler, 145
Means
    across treatment and control
        groups, 13n4
    tables of, 11
Media appearances, 55–57
Media-relations offices, of universities,
    99–100
Mediation analysis, 22, 29
Mediocrity, 36
Melitz. Marc, 34

Mentoring
    definition, 151
    distinguished from advising, 151
    general principles, 152
    incentives for, 151
    post-graduation, 163
    for underrepresented minorities, 149
    for women, 149
Merit raises, 121
Methods section, 6
Miah, A., 147
Microeconomic theory, 165, 169
Microeconomists, 68
Miguel, E., 18, 75, 165
Misogyny, 147
Moat, H. S., 27, 97
Monetary economics, grant sources
    in, 103
Morgan, S. L., 12–13, 24n11
Motivation section, of research
    papers, 30, 31, 37, 51–52, 53, 92,
    113, 132
Multidisciplinary research talks,
    54–55

National Bureau of Economics
    Research (NBER), 71–72
National Institutes of Health (NIH)
    as grant source, 102, 103
    Public Access Policy (PAP), 99
National Science Foundation (NSF),
    as grant source, 102, 103, 116
Nature, 37, 64, 67, 146
Nature Biotechnology, 161
Networking/networks, 89
    of alumni, 154–155
    for editorial services, 140, 141
    for grant proposals, 113
    through invited seminars, 45
"Never touch a piece of paper twice"
    rule, 130n6, 142
New Institutional Economics, 81
New York Times, 56
Nobel Prize, in Economic Sciences, 1
Null findings, 21–22
Null hypothesis, 16
Nuremberg Code, 117, 119

Observational data
  balance tests for, 11, 13
  number of (R2), 24
  treatment variables, 20
Obstacle Is the Way, The (Holiday), 46
Ogden, T., 106, 107
Online format
  journals, 86
  seminars and conference
    presentations, 52–53
On the Road (Kerouac), 36n16
On Writing (King), 36
On Writing Well (Zinsser), 14n5, 36
Open access, 99
Oster, E., 19
Output price risk, 137n9
Outreach talks, 55–57
Özler, B., 145

Pain, E., 109
Pairwise comparisons, 11, 13, 13n4
Parametric regression, 21
Parramore, L., 163
Past tense, 13–14
Pearl, J., 17
Peer-review process, 3, 61–100
  See also Reviewers; Reviewing/
    refereeing; Submission, of journal
    articles
  anonymity of, 62, 73n9, 76
  appeals of rejection, 82, 88–90
  "double-blind," 73–74, 73n9
  duration, 64, 81–82, 128
  editorial decisions in, 82–86
  gatekeeping function, 62–63
  of general journals, 71
  grant proposals as, 103–104
  how to get good reviews, 76–80
  rationale for, 61–63
  "single-blind," 73n9, 79
Pepinsky, Tom, 146n11
Pischke, J. S., 20, 22, 75, 101
Placebo tests, for robustness, 20–21
Plagiarism, 100, 142–143
  "hard," 143
  self-plagiarism, 100, 143
  "soft," 143

Plagiarism-detecting software,
  142–143
*PNAS. See Proceedings of the
  National Academy of Science*
Poincaré, Henri, 90n20
Policy talks, 55
Population sample, 10
Poster presentations, 54
Predictions
  out-of-sample, 10
  testable, 9, 10, 49, 107
Preis, T., 27, 97
Present tense, 13–14, 14n5
Primitives
  in conference presentations, 49
  in invited seminar presentations, 42
Principal-agent models, 140
*Proceedings of the National Academy
  of Science (PNAS)*, 27, 37, 64,
  65n3, 67, 80n12
Professional associations, service
  activities for, 125–126
Program directors, 123
Promotion
  external review letters for, 68–69
  grantsmanship and, 103, 105
  journal publications and, 66–67,
    70–71
  teaching, research, and service
    requirements, 121, 121n1
Public goods, 127
Public policy, effect of economics
  research on, 25–26, 62–63, 75
p-values, 11, 24

Quantitative Economics, 77
Quarterly Journal of Economics,
  35n15, 139
Question asking, by audiences, 40,
  59–60

Randomized controlled trials (RCTs),
  138
  average treatment effect (ATE),
    88–89
  intention to treat (ITT), 88–89
  treatment variables, 20

Readability score, 31
Reading
  inspectional, 6, 6n1, 98
  relation to writing skills, 35–36
  of research papers, 5–6, 28, 30
Refereeing. *See* Reviewing/refereeing
References, 7, 34, 35, 71
  for grant proposals, 114, 115
  missing, 131
  revision, 92
Research
  agenda, 47
  blogging-enhanced, 144
  design, causal identification and, 17
  graduate, 160
  indirect cost recovery (ICR) on,
    104
  periodic progress reports on,
    111–112
  undergraduate, 155–156
  by underrepresented minorities,
    149, 150
  by women, 149, 150
Research economists, 2
Research funders, acknowledgments
  of, 73–74, 103, 112
Research papers
  See also Journal articles
  blogs about, 144–145
  contributions of, 29
  "determinants" of, 83
  "double-dipping" practice, 132–133
  first-year-qualifying, 64, 158–159
  inspectional reading of, 6, 6n1, 98
  preliminary work on, 111
  quality, 5–6
  readability score, 31
  real-world implications, 25–26
  review of, 39
  second- or third-year-qualifying, 64,
    158–159
Research questions, 169
  of conference paper submissions,
    134
  frequently asked, 7, 8
  reviewers' evaluation of, 135
  single, 8, 8n2

stated in grant proposals, 113–114
stated in the introduction, 28, 31
Reservation wages, 66
Results
  ancillary, 44
  presented in research paper title,
    27
  stated in research paper
    introduction, 31
Results and discussion section, 6, 7,
    19–25
  of conference presentations, 49–50
  for general-science journal articles,
    37
  of invited seminar presentations,
    42, 44
  limitations, 22–23, 25
  mechanisms, 22, 22n9
  order of results, 19–20
  robustness checks, 19–20, 29
  tables, 23, 25
Résumé. *See* Curriculum vitae (CV)
Reviewers
  acknowledgment or compensation,
    126–127, 127n5, 136, 136n7
  anonymity, 62, 76, 126–127, 136,
    136n7
  author's preferences/suggestions
    regarding, 80–81, 80n12
  bias of, 79–80
  of book proposals, 133–134, 135
  comments of, 90–94, 129–130,
    131–132, 134–135
  of conference proposals, 133–134
  cover letters from, 132–133
  dialogue with, 39
  ethics of, 136–139
  of friends'/colleagues' manuscripts,
    133–134, 135–136, 137
  of grant proposals, 112–113,
    116n12, 133–135
  rejection appeals and, 88–90
  rejection recommendations, 83,
    132, 133, 137, 138, 139–140
  relationship with authors, 133,
    136–137
  relationship with editors, 141, 142

Reviewers (cont.)
  selection of, 34, 72–73, 77–81,
    127–128, 130, 141, 142
  tone of, 76–77
  "up-or-out"/"accept-or-reject"
    decisions, 134
Reviewing/refereeing
  how to decline, 128–129, 138
  how to structure and write reviews,
    130–133
  as service activity, 126–139, 142
Review of Economic Studies, 35n15
Rewriting, 36, 68
Roadmap section, 29, 30, 41
Robert Wood Johnson Foundation,
    102–103
Robustness checks
  in appendices, 45
  in introduction, 29, 30, 31
  in journal articles, 51, 111, 144–
    145, 158
  in results and discussion section,
    19–20, 29, 30, 37, 44, 49–50
R1 universities, 67, 67n5, 101
  advising at, 152, 153
Rosalsky, G., 163
Rosenzweig, M. R., 5
Rossi, P. E., 17
R2 universities, 67n5, 102
  advising at, 153
Russell Sage Foundation, 103
Ryssdal, K., 163

Sahm, Claudia, 30, 31
Salary
  consulting as adjunct to, 169
  grant-funded, 108, 109, 109n10,
    114, 116, 118
  merit raises, 151
Sample size, 10
  relation to control variables,
    24–25
Sánchez da la Sierra, R., 9n3
Sandmo, A., 137n9
Science, 27, 64, 67, 68, 80n12
Search engine optimization (SEO), 98

Self-plagiarism, 100, 143
Self-promotion, social media use for,
    145, 146, 147
Seminars, 3
  See also Invited seminars
  departmental brown-bag, 39–40, 58
  online and hybrid formats, 52–53
Service, 3, 121–150, 169
  definition, 121
  departmental-level, 123
  editorship of journals as, 139–143
  external review letter
    considerations, 123, 124
  institutional *versus* professional,
    125–126
  by junior faculty, 121, 122–124
  reviewing/refereeing as, 126–139,
    142
  social media as, 143–148
  time required for, 123–124
  by women or underrepresented
    minorities, 148–150, 148n12
Shea, A., 36n16
Shea, C., 100
Silos, academic, 136–137
Slides
  for conference presentations, 48–52
  introduction formula for, 41
  in invited seminar presentations,
    41–42
  for invited seminars, 40–42
  for job talks, 46–47
  for lightning talks, 53
  one-slide-per-minute rule, 40, 48
Slutsky matrix, 169
Small liberal arts colleges (SLACs)
  advising and mentoring at, 152,
    154–155
  undergraduate research at, 155
Social media, 3, 99, 133
  anonymous platforms, 147
  guides to use, 147
  online discussions on, 147
  as professional service media
    engagement, 143–148
  profile on, 147

Sokal, Alan, 31
Solon, G., 16
Stable unit treatment value
    assumption (SUTVA) violations, 18
Standard deviation, tables of, 11, 13
Standard errors, 23
Statistical endogeneity, 18, 18n7
Statistical significance
    pairwise comparison, 13
    symbols on tables, 24, 24n12
Staudt, J., 99
Stewart, Potter, 26–27
Stromberg, J., 65n2
Structure, of economics papers, 2–3,
    5–37
    abstract, 31–32
    background review, 32–33
    data and descriptive statistics
        section, 10–14
    empirical framework, 14–19
    introduction, 27–31
    literature review, 32
    results and discussion section,
        19–25
    for specific journals, 33–35
    structure of papers, 7–8
    summary and concluding remarks,
        25–26
    theoretical framework, 8–10
    titles, 26–27
    writing for the right journal, 33–35
Submission, of journal articles, 63–76,
    77–78
    acceptance, 82, 85–86, 96
    acceptance with minor revisions
        decisions, 85
    appeals of editorial decisions,
        88–90
    conditional acceptance, 85
    cover letters for, 72, 73, 80
    to economics journals *vs.* other
        journals, 67–70
    editorial decisions about, 81–86
    electronic, 81
    to general-science journals, 72–73
    to general *vs.* field journals, 70–72

reject-and-resubmit decisions, 73,
    85
rejection, 73, 74, 77, 81–82, 83,
    86–90, 131
revise-and-resubmit decisions,
    84–85, 84n16, 90–95, 91n21,
    93n22, 95n23, 130, 131, 133,
    139–140
revisions, 90–95
time to acceptance/rejection, 64,
    81–82
timing of, 63–65
transaction costs, 81
"up and out system," 64–65
where to submit, 65–76
Success, criteria for, 167–169
Summary and concluding remarks, 6,
    6n1, 7, 25–26
    for conference presentations, 50
    for invited seminars, 44–45
    in reviews, 131
    revisions, 92
Suri, T., 1, 5
Surveys, 104n4, 106, 161
    data, 10
    grant funding for, 101, 114, 116
    human subjects in, 117, 119–120
    methodology, 10
Syllabi, 5–6

Taber, C. R., 19–20
Tables, 23–25, 131
    in conference presentations, 49–50
    in invited seminar presentations,
        43
    statistical significance symbols on,
        24
    two-by-two, 13
Takavarasha, K., 10
Technical skills, 2
Tenses, 13–14, 14n5
Tenure
    blogging and, 145
    external review letters and, 68–69
    grantsmanship and, 103, 105
    publications and, 66–67, 70–71

Tenure (cont.)
service activities and, 121n1,
122–123
Tenured faculty, women and
underrepresented minorities, 149
Test of English as a Foreign Language
(TOEFL), 164
Texas Beef Group v. Winfrey, 56,
56n8
The Economist, 35
Theoretical framework, 7, 8–10
of conference presentations, 49
of grant proposals, 114
of invited seminar presentations,
42
revisions, 91–92, 91n21
verbal *versus* mathematical, 9
Theoretical models, 9–10, 91n21
Theory of change, 9, 10, 54
Thesis
completion, 162
defense of, 159
readership, 162
Think tanks, 103, 169
This American Life (radio show), 87
Thomson, W., 1, 2, 49
Thomson, William, *A Guide for the
Young Economist,* 1, 2, 9, 49
Thornton, R. L., 72n8
Title, 7, 26–27, 29–30
of applied economics papers, 26–27
citation counts and, 97
of conference presentations, 49
of empirical economics papers, 27
of invited seminar papers, 41
of tables, 23
Tobacman, J., 138
Tomkins, A., 73n9
Topalova, P., 138
Toxic culture, of the economics
profession, 76, 84n16, 161,
163–164
Transaction costs, 25
Treatment effect, controls and, 19,
19n8
Treatment groups, pairwise
comparisons, 11, 13

Treatment heterogeneity, 21 22, 26
Treisman, R., 119n16

Undergraduate students
advising for, 153–156
research by, 155–156
Underrepresented minorities
discrimination toward, 163
service activities, 148–150, 148n12
Universities
Carnegie Classification, 67n5,
101–102
governance, 121–122
media-relations offices, 99–100
sponsored programs offices, 110,
113
University of Minnesota, 145

Van Doren, C., 6
Variables
categorical, 13
in conference presentations, 49
gender, 13
in invited seminar presentations,
43
kernel density estimates, 13
as proxies, 23
subscripts, 15
treatment, 11, 17, 20

Whinston, M. D., 169
Williamson, O. E., 81, 121
Wilson, Rick, 147
Wind, Sand, and Stars (de Saint-
Exupéry), 167
Winfrey, Oprah, 56
Winship, C., 12–13, 24n11
Wolfers, J., 163
Women
discrimination toward, 148–149,
163
gender norms' effects on, 165
Wooldridge, J. M., 16, 93, 163
Working papers, 69, 70, 98n26, 99,
158
"friendly reviews" of, 135–136
posted on blogs, 145

theoretical models, 10
typos in, 51
Workshops, 3
World Development, 67, 68
Writing, of economics papers. *See*
Structure, of economics papers
Writing centers, 164–165
Writing skills, 35–37
blogging-enhanced, 144
Wu, A. H., 147

Xiao, Z., 13n4

Yang, Dean, 106, 107

Zhang, M., 73n9
Zinsser, W. K., 14n5, 36